# Financial Development and Economic Growth in Malaysia

This book is concerned with the role of financial intermediation in economic development and growth in the context of Malaysia. Using an analytical framework, the author investigates the Malaysian economy from 1960 onwards to examine how far financial development has progressed in the course of economic development, and whether it has been instrumental in promoting economic growth.

A significant improvement in the Malaysian financial system, coupled with rapid economic growth and a rich history of financial sector reforms, makes Malaysia an interesting case study for this subject. The author shows that some government interventions seem to have impacted negatively on economic growth, whereas repressionist financial policies such as interest rate controls, high reserve requirements and directed credit programmes seem to have contributed positively to financial development. The analysis concludes that financial development leads to higher output growth via promoting private saving and private investment.

Shedding light on the evolutionary role of financial system and the interacting mechanisms between financial development and economic growth, this book will be of interest to those interested in economic and financial development, financial liberalization, saving behaviour and investment analysis and Asian Studies.

**James B. Ang** is Senior Lecturer in the Department of Economics, Monash University, Australia. His research interests are Finance and Development, Financial Liberalization, Macroeconomics and the Southeast Asian Economies.

# Routledge Studies in the Growth Economies of Asia

1 **The Changing Capital Markets of East Asia**
*Edited by Ky Cao*

2 **Financial Reform in China**
*Edited by On Kit Tam*

3 **Women and Industrialization in Asia**
*Edited by Susan Horton*

4 **Japan's Trade Policy**
Action or reaction?
*Yumiko Mikanagi*

5 **The Japanese Election System**
Three analytical perspectives
*Junichiro Wada*

6 **The Economics of the Latecomers**
Catching-up, technology transfer and institutions in Germany, Japan and South Korea
*Jang-Sup Shin*

7 **Industrialization in Malaysia**
Import substitution and infant industry performance
*Rokiah Alavi*

8 **Economic Development in Twentieth Century East Asia**
The international context
*Edited by Aiko Ikeo*

9 **The Politics of Economic Development in Indonesia**
Contending perspectives
*Edited by Ian Chalmers and Vedi R. Hadiz*

10 **Studies in the Economic History of the Pacific Rim**
*Edited by Sally M. Miller, A. J. H. Latham and Dennis O. Flynn*

11 **Workers and the State in New Order Indonesia**
*Vedi R. Hadiz*

12 **The Japanese Foreign Exchange Market**
*Beate Reszat*

13 **Exchange Rate Policies in Emerging Asian Countries**
*Edited by Stefan Collignon, Jean Pisani-Ferry and Yung Chul Park*

14 **Chinese Firms and Technology in the Reform Era**
*Yizheng Shi*

15 **Japanese Views on Economic Development**
Diverse paths to the market
*Kenichi Ohno and Izumi Ohno*

16 **Technological Capabilities and Export**
Success in Asia
*Edited by Dieter Ernst, Tom Ganiatsos and Lynn Mytelka*

17 **Trade and Investment in China**
The European experience
*Edited by Roger Strange, Jim Slater and Limin Wang*

18 **Technology and Innovation in Japan**
Policy and management for the 21st century
*Edited by Martin Hemmert and Christian Oberländer*

19 **Trade Policy Issues in Asian Development**
*Prema-chandra Athukorala*

20 **Economic Integration in the Asia Pacific Region**
*Ippei Yamazawa*

21 **Japan's War Economy**
*Edited by Erich Pauer*

22 **Industrial Technology Development in Malaysia**
Industry and firm studies
*Edited by Jomo K. S., Greg Felker and Rajah Rasiah*

23 **Technology, Competitiveness and the State**
Malaysia's industrial technology policies
*Edited by Jomo K. S. and Greg Felker*

24 **Corporatism and Korean Capitalism**
*Edited by Dennis L. McNamara*

25 **Japanese Science**
*Samuel Coleman*

26 **Capital and Labour in Japan**
The functions of two factor markets
*Toshiaki Tachibanaki and Atsuhiro Taki*

27 **Asia Pacific Dynamism 1550–2000**
*Edited by A. J. H. Latham and Heita Kawakatsu*

28 **The Political Economy of Development and Environment in Korea**
*Jae-Yong Chung and Richard J. Kirkby*

29 **Japanese Economics and Economists since 1945**
*Edited by Aiko Ikeo*

30 **China's Entry into the World Trade Organisation**
*Edited by Peter Drysdale and Ligang Song*

31 **Hong Kong as an International Financial Centre**
Emergence and development 1945–1965
*Catherine R. Schenk*

32 **Impediments to Trade in Services**
Measurement and policy implication
*Edited by Christoper Findlay and Tony Warren*

33 **The Japanese Industrial Economy**
Late development and cultural causation
*Ian Inkster*

34 **China and the Long March to Global Trade**
The accession of China to the World Trade Organization
*Edited by Alan S. Alexandroff, Sylvia Ostry and Rafael Gomez*

35 **Capitalist Development and Economism in East Asia**
The rise of Hong Kong, Singapore, Taiwan, and South Korea
*Kui-Wai Li*

36 **Women and Work in Globalizing Asia**
*Edited by Dong-Sook S. Gills and Nicola Piper*

37 **Financial Markets and Policies in East Asia**
*Gordon de Brouwer*

38 **Developmentalism and Dependency in Southeast Asia**
The case of the automotive industry
*Jason P. Abbott*

39 **Law and Labour Market Regulation in East Asia**
*Edited by Sean Cooney, Tim Lindsey, Richard Mitchell and Ying Zhu*

40 **The Economy of the Philippines**
Elites, inequalities and economic restructuring
*Peter Krinks*

**41 China's Third Economic Transformation**
The rise of the private economy
*Edited by Ross Garnaut and Ligang Song*

**42 The Vietnamese Economy**
Awakening the dormant dragon
*Edited by Binh Tran-Nam and Chi Do Pham*

**43 Restructuring Korea Inc.**
*Jang-Sup Shin and Ha-Joon Chang*

**44 Development and Structural Change in the Asia-Pacific**
Globalising miracles or end of a model?
*Edited by Martin Andersson and Christer Gunnarsson*

**45 State Collaboration and Development Strategies in China**
The case of the China-Singapore Suzhou Industrial Park (1992–2002)
*Alexius Pereira*

**46 Capital and Knowledge in Asia**
Changing power relations
*Edited by Heidi Dahles and Otto van den Muijzenberg*

**47 Southeast Asian Paper Tigers?**
From miracle to debacle and beyond
*Edited by Jomo K. S.*

**48 Manufacturing Competitiveness in Asia**
How internationally competitive national firms and industries developed in East Asia
*Edited by Jomo K. S.*

**49 The Korean Economy at the Crossroads**
*Edited by MoonJoong Tcha and Chung-Sok Suh*

**50 Ethnic Business**
Chinese capitalism in Southeast Asia
*Edited by Jomo K. S. and Brian C. Folk*

**51 Exchange Rate Regimes in East Asia**
*Edited by Gordon de Brouwer and Masahiro Kawai*

**52 Financial Governance in East Asia**
Policy dialogue, surveillance and cooperation
*Edited by Gordon de Brouwer and Yunjong Wang*

**53 Designing Financial Systems in East Asia and Japan**
*Edited by Joseph P. H. Fan, Masaharu Hanazaki and Juro Teranishi*

**54 State Competence and Economic Growth in Japan**
*Yoshiro Miwa*

**55 Understanding Japanese Saving**
Does population aging matter?
*Robert Dekle*

**56 The Rise and Fall of the East Asian Growth System, 1951–2000**
International competitiveness and rapid economic growth
*Xiaoming Huang*

**57 Service Industries and Asia-Pacific Cities**
New development trajectories
*Edited by P. W. Daniels, K. C. Ho and T. A. Hutton*

**58 Unemployment in Asia**
*Edited by John Benson and Ying Zhu*

**59 Risk Management and Innovation in Japan, Britain and the USA**
*Edited by Ruth Taplin*

**60 Japan's Development Aid to China**
The long-running foreign policy of engagement
*Tsukasa Takamine*

**61 Chinese Capitalism and the Modernist Vision**
*Satyananda J. Gabriel*

**62 Japanese Telecommunications**
*Edited by Ruth Taplin and Masako Wakui*

63 **East Asia, Globalization and the New Economy**
*F. Gerard Adams*

64 **China as a World Factory**
*Edited by Kevin Honglin Zhang*

65 **China's State Owned Enterprise Reforms**
An industrial and CEO approach
*Juan Antonio Fernandez and Leila Fernandez-Stembridge*

66 **China and India**
A tale of two economies
*Dilip K. Das*

67 **Innovation and Business Partnering in Japan, Europe and the United States**
*Edited by Ruth Taplin*

68 **Asian Informal Workers**
Global risks local protection
*Santosh Mehrotra and Mario Biggeri*

69 **The Rise of the Corporate Economy in Southeast Asia**
*Rajeswary Ampalavanar Brown*

70 **The Singapore Economy**
An econometric perspective
*Tilak Abeyshinge and Keen Meng Choy*

71 **A Basket Currency for Asia**
*Edited by Takatoshi Ito*

72 **Private Enterprises and China's Economic Development**
*Edited by Shuanglin Lin and Xiaodong Zhu*

73 **The Korean Developmental State**
From dirigisme to neo-liberalism
*Iain Pirie*

74 **Accelerating Japan's Economic Growth**
Resolving Japan's growth controversy
*Edited by F. Gerard Adams, Lawrence R. Klein, Yuzo Kumasaka and Akihiko Shinozaki*

75 **China's Emergent Political Economy**
Capitalism in the dragon's lair
*Edited by Christopher A. McNally*

76 **The Political Economy of the SARS Epidemic**
The impact on human resources in East Asia
*Grace O. M. Lee and Malcolm Warner*

77 **India's Emerging Financial Market**
A flow of funds model
*Tomoe Moore*

78 **Outsourcing and Human Resource Management**
An international survey
*Edited by Ruth Taplin*

79 **Globalization, Labor Markets and Inequality in India**
*Dipak Mazumdar and Sandip Sarkar*

80 **Globalization and the Indian Economy**
Roadmap to a convertible rupee
*Satyendra S. Nayak*

81 **Economic Cooperation between Singapore and India**
An alliance in the making
*Faizal Yahya*

82 **The United States and the Malaysian Economy**
*Shakila Yacob*

83 **Banking Reform in Southeast Asia**
The region's decisive decade
*Malcolm Cook*

84 **Trade Unions in Asia**
An economic and sociological analysis
*Edited by John Benson and Ying Zhu*

85 **Trade Liberalisation and Regional Disparity in Pakistan**
*Muhammad Shoaib Butt and Jayatilleke S. Bandara*

86 **Financial Development and Economic Growth in Malaysia**
*James B. Ang*

# Financial Development and Economic Growth in Malaysia

James B. Ang

Routledge
Taylor & Francis Group
LONDON AND NEW YORK

Transferred to digital printing 2010

First published 2009 by Routledge
2 Park Square, Milton Park, Abingdon, Oxon OX14 4RN

Simultaneously published in the USA and Canada
by Routledge
270 Madison Ave, New York, NY 10016

*Routledge is an imprint of the Taylor & Francis Group, an informa business*



Typeset in Times New Roman by
RefineCatch Limited, Bungay, Suffolk



*British Library Cataloguing in Publication Data*
A catalogue record for this book is available from the British Library

*Library of Congress Cataloging in Publication Data*
A catalog record has been requested for this book

ISBN10: 0–415–46726–8 (hbk)
ISBN10: 0–415–59615–7 (pbk)
ISBN10: 0–203–88688–7 (ebk)

ISBN13: 978–0–415–46726–1 (hbk)
ISBN13: 978–0–415–59615–2 (pbk)
ISBN13: 978–0–203–88688–5 (ebk)

To my family

# Contents

# List of illustrations

# List of tables

# 1 Introduction

## 1.1 Introduction

The financial system comprises banking institutions, financial markets, other financial intermediaries such as pension funds and insurance companies, and a large regulatory body: a central bank, which oversees and supervises the operations of these intermediaries. Every economy requires a sophisticated and efficient financial system to prosper. A more efficient financial system provides better financial services, and this enables an economy to increase its real GDP growth rate. Conversely, a weakened financial system spills over unfavourably into the economy. An inadequately supervised financial system may be crisis-prone, with potentially devastating effects. The important role of financial intermediaries and financial markets therefore merits more attention from researchers and policy makers.

Although economists attach different degrees of importance to financial development, its role in contributing to long-term growth can be theoretically postulated, and this has been increasingly supported by the findings of growth empirics. Due to the lack of sufficient time series data for developing countries, empirical research on this subject has been dominated by cross-country studies. These studies have consistently shown a positive relationship between financial development and economic growth. However, economists have not reached a consensus with regard to the direction of causality between these two variables, nor do they provide a satisfactory solution on the endogeneity of the variables used in their analyses. Furthermore, the results may vary considerably due to different institutional and structural characteristics of each economy. Given the above, the assertion that financial development contributes to output growth may be an unqualified assumption, and its validity has to be tested within specific cases. For that reason, more empirical case studies are needed to throw light on the issue.

This chapter proceeds as follows:

- Section 1.2 describes the purpose, scope, and contribution of this study;
- Section 1.3 explains the motivation behind why Malaysia is chosen as the case study for this subject;

- Section 1.4 provides the definition for the key financial terms used in this research; and
- Section 1.5 provides an overview of the thesis structure.

## 1.2 Purpose and contribution of this study

This thesis seeks to provide some insight into how financial development and economic growth are related in the context of Malaysia. The central issue is how, and to what extent, improvement in Malaysia's financial system contributes to the process of economic development. It is hoped that this analysis will add to understanding of the evolutionary role of financial system and the interacting mechanisms between financial development and economic growth.

The purpose of this book is three-fold:

- to conduct a survey of both the theoretical and empirical evidence on this subject, and critically assess the evidence and validity of the theories. There is a vast literature on the issue of financial development and economic growth. It is essential, therefore, to identify studies that have made the greatest contribution to the understanding and development of this subject, and to try describing the relationship between each study. In doing so, the inadequacies and problems associated with the existing theories and empirical models will be identified, so that appropriate refinements can be introduced;
- to develop an analytical framework for examining the relationship between financial development and economic growth based on a critical survey of the existing literature. A well-specified model that explains the mechanisms of how financial development is linked to economic growth (and vice versa) is essential in understanding the underlying transmission channels of the finance–growth nexus;
- to conduct an in-depth case study for Malaysia using this analytical framework to gain a deep insight into the role of financial intermediation in the process of economic development. There must be serious doubt about the validity of any inference drawn based on the results of cross-country studies, given that each country has its own unique institutional setting and economic history. For that reason, only one country is chosen here as a case study as opposed to the conventional broad comparative examination that involves a much larger sample.

This book contributes to the existing body of finance and development literature in several aspects:

- it develops an analytical framework to provide an understanding of how financial development and economic growth are related by analysing the mechanisms linking them. Such a theoretical construct is often bypassed in many studies of this nature;

- the literature on this subject has been dominated by cross-country studies. Notwithstanding the contributions of these studies, they offer little guide for policy formulation. This study adds to the existing body of literature by providing further time series evidence on the issue and using this to help inform policy debates;
- it adopts a multi-equation approach by taking into account the possibility of financial development being an endogenous variable, rather than treating it as an exogenous variable, as is usually done in most cross-country studies. This ameliorates the serious problems of misspecification bias, and adequately deals with simultaneity bias;
- despite its status as a leading developing country, the economy of Malaysia remains substantially under-researched. It is hoped that the results of this study will serve as a useful guide in policy making for countries in the same region or for other less-developed countries.

Most of the available studies on the role of financial sectors in economic development in Malaysia are largely descriptive in nature (e.g. Drake, 1969; Lee, 1981; Rao, 1977). A more recent study by Yaakop (1988) employs a three-equation model to assess the impact of financial development on economic growth in Malaysia. However, the static regressions employed in his study fail to adequately explain the evolution of the economic behaviour of the key variables observed over time. With the advantage of using a longer time series, this study aims to disentangle the dynamics involved in the relationship between financial development and economic growth using recently developed time-series econometric techniques.

## 1.3 Why Malaysia?

Malaysia provides an interesting case study of this subject for several reasons. With rapid economic growth following the industrial transformation that took place in the 1970s and 1980s, Malaysia has evolved in recent years to be a leading country in the developing world. Accompanying this development has been a significant improvement in its financial system. Financial development, in terms of the emergence of more financial institutions and financial instruments, has improved tremendously. However, little attention has been paid to understanding the evolutionary development process of Malaysia's financial system.

Malaysia has a rich history of financial sector reform. Various financial restructuring programmes that aim to achieve a better financial system have been launched since the 1970s. However, there is little empirical evidence providing policy makers with the necessary information as to whether these reforms have had any impact on the financial system, and hence on economic growth. Such an interesting historical background provides the motivation behind using Malaysia as the case study for this subject.

The fact that Malaysia has a relatively good database by the standard of developing countries provides an added incentive for the research. The availability of a set of sufficiently long time-series data allows for a meaningful time series investigation. This is critical given that economic growth is a long-run phenomenon, which necessitates analysing the evolution of the variables of interest over time in order to relate the findings to policy designs (Solow, 2001).

## 1.4 Definition of key financial terms

Financial terms are sometimes inconsistently and ambiguously used in the literature.[1] It is therefore necessary to define the financial terms used in the context of this study:

- **Financial institution** refers to an individual member in the financial industry, such as the central bank, a commercial bank, or an insurance company (Tobin and Brainard, 1963). There are two broad categories of financial institutions: banking institutions including commercial banks, finance companies, merchant banks, national savings banks, etc.; and non-bank financial institutions, such as pension funds, insurance companies, etc.
- **Financial intermediary** refers to the entire industry of financial institutions. Thus, all commercial banks constitute one intermediary, all finance companies another, and so on.
- **Financial intermediation** is the process of transforming financial capital into more widely preferred types of financial assets by linking lenders and borrowers.
- **Financial markets** provide the exchange of capital and credit. They include stock markets, bond markets, money markets, future markets, foreign exchange markets, etc.
- **Financial instruments** refer to money, forwards, options, swaps, future contracts, etc.
- **Financial system** comprises financial intermediaries, financial markets, and financial instruments. Asymmetric information and transaction costs lead to the creation of a financial system. The primary function of a financial system is to ensure the efficient allocation of resources in the presence of an uncertain environment. Most literature focuses on a specific aspect of financial system by considering only banks, stock markets or money.
- **Financial structure** refers to the composition of a financial system, such as banks, stock markets, provident funds, etc., that makes up the whole financial sector. The extent of a financial system refers to how easy it is for firms and households to access financial services. The efficiency of a financial system refers to how effective financial markets and financial intermediaries are in reducing information and transaction costs for firms and households.

- **Financial deepening** is often referred to as the improvement in the extent or efficiency of a financial system. In the literature, a financial sector is said to deepen when:
    - the range of financial products and services broadens;
    - the accessibility to financial products and services improves;
    - the types of institutions operating in the financial sector expands;
    - the extent to which financial resources intermediated through the financial sector increases;
    - the amount of financial capital allocated to the private sector increases; and
    - the quality of regulation and stability of the financial sector is enhanced.

## 1.5 Organization of the book

The rest of the book is organized as follows:

- Chapter 2 reviews the theoretical and empirical works on financial development and economic growth. While the theory was initiated in the 1950s, most of the empirical counterparts have only been developed from the 1990s, following the seminal work of King and Levine (1993a). However, the focus has been largely on assessing the cross-country evidence. The chapter highlights the drawbacks of these broad comparative analyses by providing evidence on sensitivity of the results, and argues in favour of a country in-depth case study.
- Chapter 3 provides an overview of the Malaysian economy and development of its financial system in order to set the stage for the ensuing analyses. The policy context and growth experience of the Malaysian economy are discussed. Components of the Malaysian financial system are also described.
- Chapter 4 discusses data, variable construction, and econometric techniques. The autoregressive distributed lag (ARDL) bounds procedure is used as the cointegration test in favour of alternative tests given its desirable statistical features. An unrestricted error-correction model, which accounts for omitted lagged variable bias, is used to estimate the long-run relationships. An instrumental variable technique is adopted to correct for endogeneity bias so that reliable inference can be drawn from the estimated results.
- Chapter 5 examines the determinants of financial deepening by taking real per capita GDP, real interest rates, and a set of financial sector policies into consideration. The technique of principal component analysis is used to construct a summary measure of financial sector policies in order to account for the joint influence of interest rate controls,

reserve and liquidity requirements, and directed credit programs imposed on the Malaysian financial system.

- Chapters 6 and 7 then analyse the patterns and determinants of private saving and private investment respectively in Malaysia. In the former, the analytical framework is constructed using the life-cycle model with appropriate modifications to account for the structural and institutional features of the economy. In the latter, a static private investment function is derived from the neoclassical framework, with appropriate extensions to account for the features of the Malaysian economy. A cost-minimization problem, which assumes firms optimize investment level with respect to a quadratic loss function, is adopted to obtain a dynamic investment model suitable for estimation.
- Chapter 8 looks at the dynamic link between domestic saving and investment rates. The empirical specification of this dynamic relationship is derived based on an intertemporal current account model. Given that these two variables are cointegrated, the correlation is estimated using an error-correction model with a cointegrating framework to allow for an analysis of both the short-run and long-run dynamics of the saving–investment relationship.
- Chapter 9 examines the role of financial intermediation in the Malaysian economy. First, a growth accounting exercise is performed to shed light on the sources of growth by decomposing the growth rate of real GDP into TFP (total factor productivity) growth rate, and the growth rates of physical capital and labour input. The impact of financial development on economic growth, via the qualitative channel, is then tested using the standard neoclassical model, augmented with financial development.
- Chapter 10 provides some concluding remarks. The results of the five empirical results from Chapters 5 to 9 are summarized and analysed in this concluding chapter.

# 2 Finance and development*

## A survey of literature

### 2.1 Introduction

This chapter provides a survey of the theoretical and empirical evidence on the relationship between financial development and economic growth to provide a setting for the ensuing analyses. The chapter is structured as follows:

- Sections 2.2 and 2.3 explain the emergence and functions of financial systems, respectively;
- Section 2.4 describes the evolution of finance–growth thoughts;
- Section 2.5 surveys financial development and economic growth models;
- Section 2.6 provides a review of the empirical studies. The econometric techniques employed are critically appraised and some caveats on the interpretation of the results are highlighted;
- Section 2.7 discusses some key issues which remain unresolved in the literature and require further research;
- Section 2.8 is the conclusion.

### 2.2 The emergence of financial markets and intermediaries

Financial intermediaries emerge mainly due to information and transaction costs.[1] In an economy, some agents may have extra funds while some entrepreneurs may experience shortages of funds to finance investment projects. To raise the necessary funds in the absence of a sound financial system, entrepreneurs have to approach individual agents who have surplus funds to lend. Since the agents have very little knowledge about the investment projects involved, and the entrepreneurs have to find out which agents have surplus funds and how much each is willing to lend, this process turns out to be time consuming and costly.

In addition, when borrowers and lenders do not share common information, optimal financial contracts often involve agency costs, which are costs required in monitoring investment projects.[2] While borrowers typically

* This chapter was previously printed in Ang (2008c).

possess inside information about the investment projects, they have little incentive to disclose such information. Efforts made by a third party to obtain additional information are often costly. Furthermore, since lenders cannot distinguish between honest and dishonest borrowers prior to issuing loans, the incorporation of a lemons premium into the market interest rate discourages honest borrowers. Given that the necessary information is not available, credit rationing by way of limiting loan size arises in the market (Jaffee and Russell, 1976). As such, without proper information transfer, credit markets will perform poorly as loans are given to 'wrong' borrowers while genuine borrowers with good characteristics may sometimes be turned down.

Well-functioning financial markets and intermediaries ensure funds are allocated efficiently. Through economies of scale and economies of scope, financial markets and intermediaries are able to ameliorate the problems of asymmetric information and high transaction costs. The ability of financial markets and institutions to reduce these market frictions can lead to more efficient allocation of resources and thereby foster long-run growth.[3] Figure 2.1 summarizes how market imperfections are linked to long-run growth through the functions of financial systems, which are discussed in the next section.

## 2.3 The functions of financial systems

Growth theories suggest that there are two distinct, and yet complementary channels through which financial development can influence growth – the capital accumulation channel and the total factor productivity (TFP) channel. The capital accumulation channel, often known as the quantitative channel, is developed based on the 'debt-accumulation' hypothesis of Gurley and Shaw (1955). It focuses on the financial sector's ability to overcome

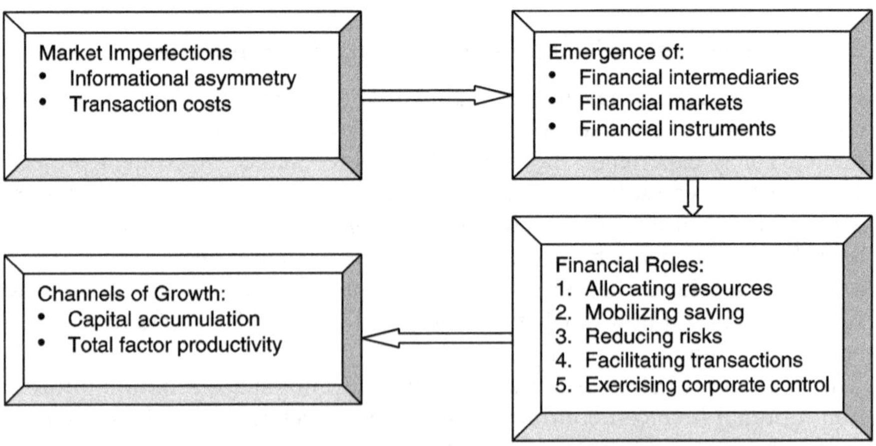


*Figure 2.1* A functional approach to financial systems.

*Source:* Adapted from Levine (1997)

indivisibilities through mobilizing saving. The mobilized saving is then channelled to productive sectors to fund investment projects, thereby leading to increased capital accumulation and higher output growth. The TFP channel, often known as the qualitative channel, emphasizes the role of innovative financial technologies in reducing informational asymmetries that hinder the efficient allocation of financial resources and the monitoring of investment projects.[4] An efficient financial system also facilitates the adoption of expensive new technologies.

These effects arise due to the key functions provided by the financial systems, which are fundamental in establishing the links between financial development and economic growth. In a comprehensive survey article, Levine (1997) classifies the functions of financial systems into the following five categories:

- A well-functioning financial system leads to more efficient allocation of resources. Tobin and Brainard (1963) argue that, with the ability to evaluate investment projects, financial intermediaries allow entrepreneurs to expand their business by borrowing at lower rates and with easier terms. Financial intermediaries evaluate different investment opportunities available by assessing the associated risks so that funds are channelled to the most promising projects. This leads to improved quality of investments that can have an expansionary effect on the economy. Financial markets may have a comparative advantage over financial intermediaries to fund new innovative investment projects since market participants can acquire relevant information on firms quickly, leading to more efficient allocation of resources.
- Financial intermediaries and financial markets perform an important role in coordinating the saving and investment decisions of households and firms, respectively (Wicksell, 1935). Savings from households may be insufficient to fully fund a borrower. Financial systems induce mobilization of saving by pooling the savings of diverse households and making this aggregate fund available for lending. Hence, as financial systems expand, more deposits will be attracted from savers, and more funds will be available for investments. This facilitates financial intermediating activities, and hence deepens the financial systems.
- Efficient financial systems allow investors to diversify their portfolios and hedge against risks. With the advantage of a large number of borrowers and lenders, financial intermediaries can effectively provide liquidity by properly matching the different maturity periods of loans (Diamond and Dybvig, 1983). Emergence of financial intermediaries significantly ameliorates the liquidity risks faced by individuals, and therefore facilitates investment activities. As a result, unnecessary liquidations can be avoided (Bencivenga and Smith, 1991). Financial markets also provide ample liquidity. Many potentially lucrative investment projects require long-term commitment of capital, but investors are often reluctant to tie

up their savings. Financial markets, particularly stock markets, offer a solution by allowing investors to invest in these high-return projects and yet be able to sell the investment quickly and obtain cash when necessary. This makes stock markets attractive avenues for some investors.

- Transactions are facilitated through offering credit facilities and guaranteeing payments. Gurley and Shaw (1960) argue that the main function of financial intermediaries is to transform primary securities into indirect securities. Financial intermediaries can obtain profits during the course of this transformation by exploiting economies of scale in lending and borrowing. Since financial intermediaries can manage and invest funds at a much lower cost, small individual depositors can avoid the hassles of having to evaluate every potential borrower, and firms seeking to borrow can save significant time and efforts to search for funds. This reduces the costs of information and therefore greatly facilitates transactions.
- Costs related to monitoring firms may fall with the increased availability of services provided by financial intermediaries. If it is costly for outside investors to verify project returns, firms will be discouraged from borrowing more, given that more borrowing implies a greater risk of default. Hence, these verification costs may impede efficient investment (Bernanke and Gertler, 1989). With the existence of financial intermediaries, Diamond (1984) shows that monitoring costs will be reduced through proper financial arrangements. From the financial market perspective, the valuation of company assets based on stock prices provides a yardstick to measure managers' performance. This leads to improved corporate controls, and may exert a positive influence on economic growth.

## 2.4 The evolution of the thinking on finance and growth

Economists hold different perspectives on the links between financial development and economic growth. The important role of credit markets in the process of economic development can be traced back to Schumpeter (1911), who contends that entrepreneurs require credit in order to finance the adoption of new production techniques. Banks are viewed as key agents in facilitating these financial intermediating activities and promoting economic development. Hence, well-developed financial systems can channel financial resources to the most productive use. The alternative explanation initiated by Robinson (1952) suggests that financial development does not lead to higher economic growth. Instead, financial development responds passively to economic growth as a result of higher demand for financial services. When an economy expands, households and firms demand more financial services. In response to this increased demand, more financial institutions, financial products and services emerge, thereby leading to an expansion in the financial systems.

The notable early works on finance and development along the Schumpeterian lines include Gurley and Shaw (1955), Goldsmith (1969) and

Hicks (1969). They argue that the development of a financial system is crucially important in stimulating economic growth. Underdeveloped financial systems retard economic growth. The policy implication of this view points to the importance of formulating policies aimed at expanding the financial systems in order to foster growth. The creation of more financial institutions and the provision of a greater variety of financial products and services generate a positive effect on the saving–investment process, and hence on economic growth. This was dubbed the 'financial structuralist view'. However, this view had little impact on development policy making in the early post-war decades, partly because it was not presented in a 'formal' manner, and partly because of the dominant influence of the Keynesian 'financial repressionist' ideology. Financial repression refers to various restrictive measures imposed on the financial systems, including interest rate controls, high reserve requirements, and directed credit programmes. These distortionary policies were popular in developing countries as ways of financing fiscal deficits without increasing tax or inflation. However, these measures weaken the incentive to hold money and other financial assets, and therefore reduce the credit available for investors. Hence, financial repression curtails the size of the banking system and suppresses financial intermediation.

In the 1970s, the applicability of the Keynesian view to analysing the role of financial intermediaries and financial markets in the development process was cogently challenged by McKinnon (1973) and Shaw (1973). The McKinnon model, which was further developed and popularized by its followers (i.e. Fry, 1988; Kapur, 1976; Mathieson, 1980; Pagano, 1993), assumes that investment in a typical developing economy is mostly self-financed. Given its lumpy nature, investment cannot materialize unless sufficient saving is accumulated in the form of bank deposits. Such a complementary role between money and physical capital is termed the 'complementarity hypothesis'. On the other hand, the 'debt-intermediation' view presented by Shaw (1973) postulates that financial intermediaries promote investment and raise output growth through borrowing and lending. These two arguments suggest that a higher level of financial development, which can be the result of financial liberalization, will lead to increased output growth.

Building upon the early works of Gurley and Shaw (1955),[5] Goldsmith (1969), Hicks (1969) and others, McKinnon (1973) and Shaw (1973) challenge the financial repression paradigm and provide a new paradigm in the design of financial policies. Their theories suggest that distortions in the financial systems, such as loans issued at an artificially low interest rate, directed credit programmes, and high reserve requirements are both unwise and unnecessary.[6] These can reduce saving, retard capital accumulation, and prevent efficient resource allocation. By allowing interest rates to adjust freely according to market mechanisms, entrepreneurs have more incentives to invest in high-yield projects. As such, higher economic growth is expected. Therefore, they called for financial liberalization, which refers to the process of eliminating or significantly alleviating financial system distortions. This was dubbed the 'financial liberalization view'.

In the early 1980s, the McKinnon–Shaw school of thought was severely criticized by a group of neo-structural economists led by van Wijnbergen (1982, 1983), Taylor (1983) and Buffie (1984).[7] Several key assumptions, which differed from the McKinnon–Shaw framework, were introduced. The most distinctive feature in their models of developing economies is the focus on competitive and efficient 'curb markets', or non-institution credit markets. Since commercial banks are subject to reserve requirements, which involve a leakage in the intermediation process, the neo-structuralists argue that curb markets perform more efficiently in intermediating savers and investors. Their models assume that households own three types of assets: gold, bank deposits, and curb market loans, which are substitutes for each other. A rise in the bank deposit rates induces households to substitute curb market loans for bank deposits, resulting in a fall in the supply of loanable funds. This discourages investment and dampens output. The neo-structuralists, therefore, claim that financial liberalization is unlikely to raise growth in the presence of efficient curb markets.

However, as Fry (1988) argues, curb markets are not necessarily as competitive and efficient as commercial banks. If this were the case, the neo-structuralists' claim that financial liberalization is likely to reduce economic growth by lowering credit supply may not hold. Furthermore, Owen and Solis-Fallas (1989) show that the relative efficiency of intermediation in formal and informal credit markets significantly influences the outcome of portfolio allocation effects generated through higher bank deposit rates. They contend that the characterization of unorganized credit markets as a perfectly efficient intermediation system by the neo-structuralists is highly unrealistic.

With the evolution in the growth literature in the 1980s, more complex types of models incorporating financial institutions into endogenous growth models emerged in the early 1990s.[8] Various techniques, such as externalities and quality ladders, were employed to model financial intermediation explicitly rather than taking it for granted as in the McKinnon–Shaw framework. These models support the finance-led argument by demonstrating that financial development reduces informational frictions and improves resource allocation efficiency. The policy implication of these views is that the abolition of government restrictions should foster real sector growth in developing countries.

The McKinnon–Shaw framework emphasizes the importance of financial liberalization in increasing saving and, hence, investment, whereas most endogenous finance and growth models focus on the role of financial intermediation in improving efficiency (rather than amount) of investment. Hence, their main distinction lies in the different focus of investment, i.e. quality versus quantity. Besides, unlike the McKinnon–Shaw models, which highlight the role of financial development in the process of economic growth, the endogenous finance and growth models show reciprocal interactions between these two variables. That is, on the one hand, a higher level of economic development stimulates more demand for financial services, leading to increased competition and efficiency in the financial intermediaries and financial markets. On the other hand, the provision of timely and valuable information by financial intermediaries to investors allows investment projects to be launched more efficiently, and this enhances capital accumulation and economic growth.

As an important extension to the existing body of knowledge, some studies have focused on the relative merits of a bank-based ('German–Japanese') financial system and a market-based ('Anglo-Saxon') financial system in promoting economic growth.[9] Although banks continue to play an important role in allocating resources to fuel economic growth, the increased importance of financial markets is widely observed especially in more advanced economies. A bank-based financial system typically has relatively less-developed financial markets. The main feature of this system is that firms rely more on finance provided by banks rather than on financial markets. As such, banks are more closely involved with firms where they can exercise a monitoring role. Firms are usually owned by a small number of shareholders with large share stakes and so hostile takeovers are also less likely to be seen in a bank-based system. This system tends to promote long-term growth as banks tend to offer longer-term loans. In contrast, a market-based financial system (such as in the UK and the US) is characterized by the presence of highly developed financial markets. Banks are less involved in the allocation of funds or ownership of financial assets, and long-term funds are usually raised through financial markets which are active, liquid and efficient. Firms are owned by a large number of shareholders with relatively small share stakes. Hence, mergers and takeovers are widely observed. A market-based financial system is more likely to have short-term effects as firms are primarily concerned with their immediate performance.

The model developed by Boyd and Smith (1998) shows that credit and equity markets function as complements rather than substitutes.[10] As Merton and Bodie (2004) argue, the issue is overall financial development and not which type of financial structure provides the financial services required to fuel growth. Given their diverse roles, it is possible for financial intermediaries and financial markets to have mutually reinforcing roles in the overall development of financial systems and economic growth.

## 2.5 Models of financial development and economic growth

This section provides an overview on different models of financial development and economic growth.

### *2.5.1 Keynesian model*

According to Keynes (1936), individuals hold money for three reasons: transactions, precautionary and speculative motives. The speculative demand for money arises from decisions about choosing between holding money and holding bonds. Bonds always yield the market interest rate ($i$). When the interest rate is low, individuals have more incentives to hold speculative money balances. In Keynes's model, there are some interest rates that individuals consider as 'normal' at a particular point in time. When the interest rates fall below their normal level, all individuals form the same expectation that the interest rate will rise in future. Hence, a rise in money supply will have no effect on interest rates since no one would want to purchase more bonds. This phenomenon is known as the 'liquidity trap', which has a crucial implication for the equilibrium level of output. Summing up, the money demand function can be expressed as:

$$(M / P)^D = \alpha + \beta /(i - \tilde{\imath}), \alpha > 0, \beta > 0 \tag{1}$$

where $i$ is the market interest rate, $\tilde{\imath}$ is the liquidity trap interest rate, and $i > \tilde{\imath}$. Hence, market interest rate is inversely related to the demand for real balances.

In this simple Keynesian model, planned investment is solely determined by the real interest rates. When the real interest rates increase, planned investment will be lower than planned saving at the full employment level in the presence of a liquidity trap, resulting in unintended inventory accumulation. Aggregate output must fall to restore equilibrium. The Keynesian framework, therefore, implies a high interest rate is not conducive for growth. However, the Keynesian model is criticized for its assumption on price rigidity and short-term orientation.

### 2.5.2 *Neoclassical model*

The neoclassical model assumes that capital markets operate costlessly and perfectly. Notwithstanding money has a role to satisfy the transactions motive, it has no direct role to play in capital accumulation. As such, it is not important to distinguish between currency and deposits, as money in this case can be considered as the outside fiat money. The key idea of the neoclassical model can be summarized as:

$$(M / P)^D = f(Y, R_{CAPITAL}, R_{MONEY})\ ; f_Y > 0, f_{R_{CAPITAL}} < 0, f_{R_{MONEY}} > 0 \tag{2}$$

where $(M / P)^D$ is the real money demand, $Y$ is the real income, $R_{CAPITAL}$ is the real rate of return on capital, and $R_{MONEY}$ is the real return on money. $Y$ is positively related to $(M / P)^D$ due to the transactions motive demand for money. The main assumption of this model is that money and capital are substitutes. Hence, an increase in $R_{MONEY}$ reduces demand for physical capital. In other words, holding large real cash balances will prevent the accumulation of capital. This implies that $R_{CAPITAL}$ is negatively associated with $(M/P)^D$ whereas $R_{MONEY}$ is positively associated with $(M / P)^D$.

### *2.5.3 The McKinnon-Shaw model*

The two financial liberalization models developed by McKinnon (1973) and Shaw (1973) emphasize different aspects of the effects of raising interest rates. McKinnon's model stresses the relationship between the deposit rate and investment, whereas Shaw's model focuses on the importance of lending and borrowing activities. The main difference between these two models lies in the assumption about the way finance is raised. In McKinnon's outside money model, all finance is raised internally, whereas Shaw (1973) postulates an inside money model that considers externally raised funds.[11] For practical considerations, most projects are financed by a combination of own funds (outside money) and borrowed funds (inside money), so these two models should be viewed as complementary (Molho, 1986).

The McKinnon–Shaw model has strong implications for financial development, which can begin by allowing the real interest rates to free flow according to market mechanisms. However, it is criticized on the ground that the use of interest rates as a key indicator of financial development is unconvincing. As De Gregorio and Guidotti (1995) put forward, this is misleading since high interest rates may reflect a lack of confidence in economic policy and the banking system, and the adoption of more risky behaviour in investment undertakings.

McKinnon (1973) criticizes both the Keynesian and neoclassical models for assuming that capital markets function competitively with a single rate of interest governing the markets. These views cannot adequately explain the operation of capital markets in poor countries, which are often characterized by fragmented rates of interest. The complementarity hypothesis of McKinnon (1973) states that money and capital are complements in developing countries in the absence of efficient financial systems. The hypothesis is derived from an outside money model where it is assumed all economic units are confined to self-finance and money is essentially the fiat currency issued by the public sector. Because of fragmented economic conditions and the lack of external finance to firms, physical capital has a lumpy nature. Entrepreneurs must accumulate sufficient funds in monetary assets to finance investment projects. As such, money and capital are viewed as complementary assets where money serves as a channel through which capital accumulation takes place.

Using the complementarity hypothesis as the basis, McKinnon (1973) develops an alternative monetary model that can better explain the relationship between the monetary process and capital accumulation in less developed economies. The complementarity hypothesis is a joint hypothesis where the demand for real money balances, $(M / P)^D$, depends positively on the real average return on capital ($R_{CAPITAL}$), and the investment ratio ($I / Y$) rises with the real deposit rate of interest ($R_{MONEY}$). This joint hypothesis implies that both $(M / P)^D$ and $I / Y$ react positively to a rise in $R_{CAPITAL}$ and $R_{MONEY}$, which can be summarized as:

$$(M / P)^D = f(Y, R_{CAPITAL}, R_{MONEY}) \; ; f_Y > 0, f_{R_{CAPITAL}} > 0, f_{R_{MONEY}} > 0 \quad (3)$$

and

$$I / Y = g(R_{CAPITAL}, R_{MONEY}) \; ; g_{R_{CAPITAL}} > 0, g_{R_{MONEY}} > 0 \quad (4)$$

The debt–intermediation view of Shaw (1973) is based on an inside money model, where money created as loans to the private sector is based on the internal debt of the private sector. The higher the money stock in relation to economic activity, the greater the extent of financial intermediation between savers and investors through the financial systems. Shaw (1973) argues that high interest rates are essential in attracting more saving. With a larger supply of credit, financial intermediaries may promote investment and raise output growth through borrowing and lending. Shaw (1973) stresses the importance of raising funds externally where money plays the role of credit and tangible medium of exchange. Complementarity has no role to play here as investors are not constrained to self-finance. If institutional credit is not available, non-institutional credit will appear. This model can be summarized as:

$$(M / P)^D = f(Y, R_{OPP}, R_{MONEY}, T) \; ; f_Y > 0, f_{R_{OPP}} < 0, f_{R_{MONEY}} > 0, f_T > 0 \quad (5)$$

where $Y$ is real income, $R_{OPP}$ is a vector of opportunity costs of holding money in real terms, $R_{MONEY}$ is the real deposit rate of interest, and $T$ is the technological improvement in the financial industry. Technological advancement is assumed to have a positive impact on money demand.

### *2.5.4 Endogenous finance and growth models*

In the neoclassical growth model, production in an economy depends on the amount of capital stock and labour, and the level of technological progress. Assuming that there is no technological progress and the labour force grows at a constant rate, per capita production depends only on per capita capital stock. The law of diminishing marginal returns results in less and less output produced as per capita capital stock increases. As such, higher capital accumulation due to higher saving can only have a temporary impact on growth. Achieving long-run growth requires continuous technological progress. This consideration leads to the emergence of endogenous growth models following the seminal work of Lucas (1988).

As highlighted previously, development in the financial systems can lead to higher economic growth through technological progress, given that expansion in the financial systems allows more innovative projects to be carried out. However, long-term growth is only possible with continuous technological development. Since technological progress is treated as an exogenous factor, financial development cannot be a determinant of long-run growth in the neoclassical framework. The endogenous growth models are models in which long-run growth is an endogenous variable. These models provide a theoretical framework, demonstrating that financial intermediation can have both growth and level effects.

For an illustration, consider the model developed by Pagano (1993) to highlight the relevance of financial factors in the process of economic growth. Pagano assumes the simplest endogenous growth setting, i.e. the $AK$ model of Rebelo (1991). It is postulated that only capital ($K_t$) is used in production, and it exhibits constant returns to scale. Capital depreciates at a rate of $\delta$ and there is no population growth so that $K_{t+1} = I_t + (1-\delta)K_t$. It is also assumed that a certain proportion of saving, the size of $(1 - \phi)$, is lost during the process of financial intermediation. Only the fraction ($\phi$) of total saving can be used to finance investment. Such a saving leakage indicates inefficiency in the financial systems. Therefore, the saving–investment relationship can be described as $I_t = \phi S_t$, and the steady state growth rate ($g$) expressed as:

$$g = \frac{K_{t+1} - K_t}{K_t} = \frac{I_t + (1-\delta)K_t - K_t}{K_t} = \frac{\phi S_t}{K_t} - \delta = A\phi s_t - \delta \qquad (6)$$

where $s_t = S_t / Y_t = S_t / AK_t$. From the above, it can be seen that there are three ways in which finance can influence growth:

- increasing the marginal productivity of capital ($A$);
- raising the proportion of saving channelled to investments ($\phi$); and
- influencing saving rates ($s$).

The rate of depreciation ($\delta$) is assumed to be constant. The two limitations of this model are that this is a closed economy model, which does not account for capital inflows, and the model is restricted to financial intermediation activities while ignoring stock markets activities and other components in the financial system.

## 2.6 Empirical evidence

Building upon the early works of Schumpeter (1911), Gurley and Shaw (1955), Patrick (1966), Goldsmith (1969), McKinnon (1973), Shaw (1973) and others, there has been a number of empirical studies focusing on examining the relationship between financial development and economic growth using data for various countries and time periods. Although most of these studies document a positive association between financial development and economic growth, this does not necessarily imply that financial development is always exogenous to economic growth (Levine, 1997). The empirical results nonetheless have a far-reaching influence on the policy prescriptions adopted by many developing countries during the 1970s and 1980s, which tended to encourage more financial saving by increasing real interest rates.

The empirics on this subject can be broadly categorized into three groups based on the nature of the data employed: pure cross-country; time series; and panel studies. Pure cross-country and panel analyses typically use growth equations in the style of Barro (1991), while time-series analyses mainly adopt either a VAR framework or a single equation error-correction framework. All types of study are subject to some limitations.

### *2.6.1 Pure cross-country evidence*

The positive relationship between financial development and economic growth was documented in an early study by Goldsmith (1969). However, empirical studies on this subject only burgeoned in the 1990s, following the prominent work of King and Levine (1993a). They study 80 countries over the period 1960–89 by controlling for other factors that affect long-run growth. Their results imply that the initial level of financial development is a good predictor of the subsequent rates of economic growth. Their empirical specifications, especially the measures of financial development, have been widely used with some modifications in many recent studies.

While King and Levine (1993a) focus on using banking variables to proxy the level of financial development, some studies attempt to examine the role of stock markets in promoting economic growth. The results of Atje and Jovanovic (1993) show that stock markets have both positive levels and growth effects on economic activity. Subsequent studies by Demirguc-Kunt and Maksimovic (1998) and Levine and Zervos (1998) confirm these results.

There is also considerable interest in examining the relative importance of a bank-based or a market-based financial system in economic growth. The cross-country results of Levine (2002) indicate that although there is a strong connection between financial development and economic growth, there is no overall empirical support for either the bank-based or the market-based view. By exploiting firm-level data for 40 countries, Demirguc-Kunt and Maksimovic (2002) show that overall financial development helps explain the growth of firms; however, firms do not tend to grow faster in either bank-based or market-based systems.

Quite apart from the general findings of the literature, Ram (1999) shows that financial development and economic growth are negatively correlated based on the results of 95 countries. The correlation between financial development and economic growth in these countries is found to be weakly negative or even negligible. Similar results are obtained when the analyses are performed on each individual country and on each sample grouped by the level of growth rates.

The main findings of pure cross-country analyses are summarized in Table 2.1. On the whole, the results of a majority of these studies seem to suggest that financial development exerts a positive impact on economic growth. Although these studies have made significant contributions to the

*Table 2.1* Pure cross-country evidence on finance and growth: a summary

| *Study* | *Sample* | *Method* | *Key findings* |
|---|---|---|---|
| Goldsmith (1969) | Annual data for 35 countries over the period 1949–63. | Ordinary least squares (OLS) and graphical analysis | The regression results show a clear relationship between financial development and economic growth. However, the relationship is statistically weak in the sense that the correlation coefficients are low and negative for developed countries. |
| Atje and Jovanovic (1993) | Annual observations for 94 countries during the period 1960–85. | OLS | Stock markets have both positive levels and growth effects on economic activity. However, a similar effect of bank lending is not observed. |
| King and Levine (1993a) | Annual data for 80 countries over the period 1960 to 1989. | OLS | Various indicators of financial development are found to be positively and strongly associated with real per capital GDP growth, the rate of physical capital accumulation and TFP growth. The empirical results provide some support for the Schumpeterian view that finance matters for growth. |
| Harris (1997) | Annual data for 39 countries over the period 1980–88. | Two stage least squares (2SLS) | In contrast to the results reported by Atje and Jovanovic (1993), the paper finds little support for the argument that stock market activity helps explain growth in per capita output. For less developed countries, the stock market effect is rather weak. However, stock market activity is found to have some effect on growth in developed countries. |
| Demirguc-Kunt and Maksimovic (1998) | Annual data for 30 developing and developed countries for the period 1980–91. | OLS | The analysis shows that in countries with better and more efficient legal systems, more firms use long-term external finance. A larger banking sector, a more active stock market and a well-developed legal system enable firms to obtain external funds more easily, which in turns facilitate firms' growth. These firms typically report lower returns on capital and profits. Government subsidies do not appear to play a role in these economies. |
| Levine (1998) | Annual data for 42 countries covering the period 1976–93. | OLS and Generalized method of moments (GMM) | Countries with more efficient legal systems tend to have better developed banking systems. Banking sector development contributes positively to per capita GDP growth. |
| Levine and Zervos (1998) | Annual data for 47 countries over the period 1976–93. | OLS | The results are consistent with the view that financial development leads to higher economic growth. Stock market liquidity and banking sector development both positively affect real per capita GDP growth, capital accumulation and productivity growth. Stock market size, volatility and international integration are robustly related to growth. |

(*Continued Overleaf*)

*Table 2.1* Continued

| *Study* | *Sample* | *Method* | *Key findings* |
|---|---|---|---|
| Levine (1999) | Annual data for 49 countries over the period 1960–89. | GMM | The results show that financial systems are better developed in countries with sound legal and regulatory systems. Furthermore, financial development is found to be positively associated with economic growth. |
| Ram (1999) | Annual data for 95 countries over the period 1960–89. | OLS | Based on the data for 95 individual countries, the correlation between financial development and economic growth is found to be weakly negative or negligible. Similar patterns are observed when regression analyses are performed on each individual country, and on each sample grouped according to the level of growth rates. |
| Deidda and Fattouh (2002) | Annual data for 80 countries over the period 1960–89. | Threshold OLS model | Using initial per capita income as the threshold variable, the authors find that higher levels of financial development are positively related to higher growth rates. In the model without threshold effects, the results only hold for high-income countries but not for low-income countries. |
| Demirguc-Kunt and Maksimovic (2002) | Firm level data for the largest publicly traded manufacturing firms in 40 countries over the period 1989–96. | 2SLS | The impact of the stock market and banking sector development on firms' growth is closely related to the level of development of the country's legal environment. There is no evidence that development of a market-based or bank-based financial system *per se* affects firms' access to financing. |
| Levine (2002) | Annual data for 48 countries over the period 1980–95. | OLS and IV | The results provide no evidence for either the bank-based or market-based view. The overall level of financial development helps explain cross-country growth variations. The legal system is an important factor which influences financial development, and this in turns influences long-run economic growth. |
| McCaig and Stengos (2005) | Annual data for 71 countries from 1960 to 1995. | GMM | The results indicate a strong positive effect of finance on growth when private domestic credit or liquid liabilities is used as the measure of financial development. However, the link is considerably weaker when the ratio of commercial bank assets to central bank assets is used as the indicator of financial development. |

literature for understanding the finance–growth nexus, the results are subject to the several criticisms outlined below.

### *2.6.2 Limitations of pure cross-country studies*

While many empirical studies have tried to investigate the link between financial development and economic growth, the standards of the econometric techniques employed are often subject to criticism. Pure cross-country regressions typically construct observations for each country by averaging out the variables over the entire period of study. The empirical specification is often adopted from Barro's (1991) regression model, augmented with financial development indicators. However, there are several econometric problems associated with this specification.

Most studies take the finance-leading view for granted and so focus explicitly on how the financial system affects growth, while little effort has been given to examining the reverse. As a result, these studies typically employ a single equation approach in specifying the finance–growth relationship. While such an empirical specification is intuitively appealing for its simplicity, its use may pose some conceptual problems. Since potential endogeneity has not been properly controlled for, this is likely to yield biased and inconsistent estimators.

Researchers often include instrumental variables in the estimation to deal with the problems of endogeneity bias. However, as demonstrated by Ahmed (1998) and Ericsson *et al.* (2001), this technique is inadequate to account for the possible reverse causality from economic growth to financial development when data are averaged over decades. Averaging data over long periods may mask the important features of the growth path of the economy and eliminate all dynamics. It may also introduce a spurious contemporaneous correlation between time-averaged variables, although the original series may not be contemporaneously correlated. Both the sign and size of the induced correlation may differ from those of the original series.

Indeed, when financial development is specified as the dependent variable instead, individual country studies have shown that economic development has a positive impact on financial development (see Demetriades and Luintel, 1997, 2001). Hence, in a single equation framework, the empirical specification derived from any a priori theoretical belief has limited use for disentangling the causal relationship of the variables. A more promising approach is to formulate a set of simultaneous equations, which explicitly provides a specification for the financial development equation.

The static assumption of the econometric models adopted in pure cross-country studies reflects a one-period comparative static framework. Hence, the assertion made by these studies that the results represent the long-term economic behaviour is ungrounded. As Ericsson *et al.* (2001) argue, these analyses omit levels of relationship in the specification. Thus, they estimate the short-run rather than the long-run relationship. Thiel (2001) stresses the importance of having long time series for analysis of the finance–growth link. Given that cash flows or profits of firms are pro-cyclical in nature, firms' demand for external funds may be subject to the same cyclical patterns. As such, financial development measures may not necessarily be associated with growth on a short-term basis. Since economic growth is a long-term phenomenon, sufficiently long time series are required for the analysis of the finance–growth link.

The danger of grouping countries together has been highlighted clearly in an early study by Gupta (1970). Using the same source of data, Gupta (1970) re-estimates the saving functions of Rahman (1968) for all 50 available countries, instead of just 31 as arbitrarily selected by Rahman (1968). His results show that the coefficient of capital flow changes sign and becomes statistically insignificant. In another example, Harris (1997) shows that the results of Atje and Jovanovic (1993), which find a significant correlation between economic growth and stock market transactions over the period 1980–88 for 40 countries, are not robust. Harris (1997) argues that the use of lagged investment as an instrument in their study is inappropriate to deal with the endogeneity issues since lagged investment is not highly correlated with current investment and so it is not a good instrument. Upon re-examining the results of Atje and Jovanovic's (1993) study, Harris (1997) finds only a weak impact from stock market activity on growth in per capita output.

Furthermore, Garretsen *et al.* (2004) find that once legal and other societal factors have been controlled for, the positive association between the stock markets and economic growth found in Levine and Zervos (1998) disappears. By dividing the sample countries into several groups based on the level of financial development, Rioja and Valev (2004) obtain a different impact of financial development on economic growth. The findings of these studies suggest that the results obtained from cross-country studies are at best ambiguous and fragile. They are subject to the sample countries included in the estimation, the control variables used, the time period covered and the econometric techniques employed. Hence, these studies are unlikely to yield robust results.

Empirical research on the finance–growth nexus burgeons in recent years with the availability of new data sets compiled by the World Bank. Such data sets involve a large sample of countries and have been widely employed by many empirical analyses. However, the lack of high quality data with a sufficient degree of comparability across countries is a fundamental hindrance for the applicability of the findings of these broad comparative studies. These broad comparative analyses conducted at the aggregate level are unable to capture and account for the complexity of the financial environments and histories of each individual country. This is because the finance–growth nexus is largely determined by the nature and operation of the financial institutions and policies pursued in each country (Arestis and Demetriades, 1997). Therefore, without an in-depth understanding of the financial historical context and the financial environment of each individual country, the cross-country evidence provides little policy guidance. In view of these limitations, a number of researchers have put forward strong arguments for time-series country-specific in-depth studies (see Demetriades and Hussein, 1996; Edwards, 1996; Neusser and Kugler, 1998; Ericsson *et al.*, 2001; Kenny and Williams, 2001; Kirkpatrick, 2005; Ang, 2008a).

### *2.6.3 Time series studies*

Using quarterly industrial output data to measure the level of economic development, Gupta (1984) conducts the first time-series investigation to study the finance–growth nexus for 14 developing countries. The results indicate that causality runs from financial development to economic growth, suggesting a catalyst role of the financial sector in the process of economic development. However, due to a lack of better alternatives, industrial output is used in Gupta's (1984) study. This measure represents only a small portion of total output in most developing countries and is therefore not a satisfactory indicator for economic development.

Patrick (1966) contends that the direction of causality between financial development and economic growth changes over the course of development. At the beginning of the growth process, the creation of financial institutions leads to higher growth by transferring resources from traditional sectors to modern sectors (dubbed 'supply-leading hypothesis'). However, in the second stage, higher growth creates more needs for financial services and modern financial institutions (dubbed 'demand-following hypothesis'). In an attempt to test the validity of Patrick (1966), Jung (1986) conducts Granger causality tests for 56 countries from 1950 to 1981. While the results provide more support for the supply-leading hypothesis, they yield inconclusive results for reverse temporal causality patterns. As in Gupta's (1984) study, Jung's (1986) results suffer from degrees of freedom problems in the estimation.

More recently, Neusser and Kugler (1998) study the finance–growth relationship by using financial sector GDP and manufacturing GDP as proxies for financial development and economic growth, respectively. The findings of their causality tests are consistent with the supply-leading view that finance plays an important role in economic development. Similar findings are obtained by Demetriades and Luintel (1996), Choe and Moosa (1999), Luintel and Khan (1999), Xu (2000), Bell and Rousseau (2001) and Rousseau and Vuthipadadorn (2005).

Demetriades and Hussein (1996) and Arestis and Demetriades (1997) assess the finance–growth causal links in developing and developed economies, respectively. Their results exhibit substantial variation across countries even when the same variables and estimation methods are used, highlighting the limitations of cross-country studies for treating different economies as a homogeneous entity. Arestis and Demetriades (1996) provide several accounts for the variation of causality results from country to country:

- different financial systems may have different institutional structures and certain institutional structures may be more conducive to economic growth;
- financial sector policies play an important role in determining whether financial development fosters economic growth;
- two countries with identical financial systems and financial sector policies may still differ due to the effectiveness of those institutions that design and implement the policies.

Using time series data from 1960 to 2001, Ang and McKibbin (2007) conduct multivariate cointegration and several causality tests to assess the finance–growth link in the small open economy of Malaysia. To deal with the issue of multicollinearity and over-parameterization problems, they propose the use of principal component analysis to construct a financial development index using the appropriate financial development indicators. Since Malaysia has more features of a bank-based financial system, only banking variables are used in constructing the index. Contrary to the conventional findings, the results strongly support the view that output growth causes financial development in the long run, but not the hypothesis that a bank-based financial system induces long-term growth in real sector. In a study that explicitly examines the causal impact of stock market developments on economic growth, Caporale *et al.* (2005) find strong evidence that stock market development in Malaysia enhances economic growth through raising investment efficiency, which in turn increases the productivity of the economy at the aggregate level.

Attempts have also been made to examine the relative importance of banks and stock markets in contributing to economic growth in the time-series context. Arestis *et al.* (2001) find that banks are more powerful in promoting economic growth. They argue that the role of stock markets has been overemphasized by cross-country studies. Their results show that in two of the five developed economies examined, stock markets tend to have negative effects on economic growth. However, contrasting findings are obtained by Thangavelu and Ang (2004) using Australia as the case study. In their study, the empirical test results using financial development indicators related to financial intermediaries suggest that the banking sector is reactive to the demand generated from the economic development, i.e. economic growth causes banking development in the Granger sense. On the other hand, the results of using financial market indicators are consistent with Schumpeter's (1911) view that development of the stock market is essential in fuelling economic growth.

Several studies have also attempted to examine the impact of financial repression on the development of the financial system. Using India as the case study, Demetriades and Luintel (1997) find that financial repression (measured by a summary of repressionist controls) has substantial negative effects on financial development. Ang and McKibbin (2007) report similar findings for Malaysia. However, contrasting findings are obtained by Demetriades and Luintel (2001) for the Korean experience. The authors attribute these results to the presence of a sound institutional framework in the Korean financial system. In fact, in their sample of six developing countries, Arestis *et al.* (2002) find that the effects of financial liberalization on financial development vary considerably across countries. The main findings of the time series studies are provided in Table 2.2.

### 2.6.4 Limitations of time series studies

Owing to data constraints, the estimation period used in many time series studies is often short. This problem is particularly severe for most developing countries where data are scarce. A meaningful time series analysis requires long series in order to properly account for the persistent dynamics, a feature common in most macroeconomic time series. In order to preserve the degrees of freedom, some studies arbitrarily select only one lag in their empirical model specification. This casts doubt on the reliability of the results, since sufficient lags are required to model short-run dynamics and properly deal with the problems of serial correlation. The results may also be sensitive to the choice of lag length and the inclusion of trend terms in the econometric specification. Furthermore, using quarterly data to increase the sample size does not fully resolve the problem as a sufficiently long time span is required to make inference on the long-run results.

A majority of the available time series studies are subject to omitted variable problems. In the light of limited data points available for most developing countries, most studies typically specify a time series model, whether a single equation or simultaneous equations, with usually not more than four variables. This involves a real income variable ($Y_t$), a financial development indicator ($F_t$) and some control variables ($Z_{it}$), such as real interest rate, inflation, investment, etc. The variables in the time series model are always kept to a minimum in order to preserve degrees of freedom. However, there is no compelling reason to believe that $F_t = f(Y_t, Z_{it})$ and $Y_t = g(F_t, Z_{it})$ are an adequate specification of the relationship between financial development and output. This simple specification may be subject to model misspecification problems and is of limited use in identifying the transmission mechanisms linking financial development and economic growth. This problem is particularly more pronounced in analyses that make use of VARs, which are often deemed to be *atheoretical* since no restrictions are imposed using economic theory.

Analyses based on Granger causality tests may misinterpret the results. This is because expectation about future economic development may induce financial development. If firms anticipate stronger economic performance in the near future, indicating higher demand for financial services, they may invest more in financial services related investments in anticipation of higher future profits. In this sense, financial development is simply a leading indicator

*Table 2.2* Time series evidence on finance and growth: a summary

| *Study* | *Sample* | *Method* | *Key findings* |
|---|---|---|---|
| Gupta (1984) | Quarterly time series data from 1961Q1 to 1980Q4 for 14 developing countries. | VARs and Granger causality | The results indicate that causality runs from financial systems to the economic sector, suggesting a catalyst role of the financial sector. There is some evidence of reverse causality but lesser evidence for a two-way causality. |
| Jung (1986) | Annual data on 37 less developed countries and 19 developed countries. | VARs and Granger causality | Overall, the results provide some support for the Patrick's supply leading hypothesis that causality runs from financial development to economic development in less developed countries, but a reverse causal pattern is observed in developed countries. |
| Demetriades and Hussein (1996) | Annual data for 16 countries (Costa Rica, El Salvador, Greece, Guatemala, Honduras, India, Korea, Mauritius, Pakistan, Portugal, South Africa, Spain, Sri Lanka, Thailand, Turkey and Venezuela) with at least 27 observations. | VARs, VECM, Engle–Granger cointegration, Johansen cointegration and Granger causality | Based on the causality results, the study finds little support for the view that finance is a leading factor for economic development. On the whole, the results seem to suggest that financial development and economic growth are jointly determined. |
| Demetriades and Luintel (1996) | Annual observations for India from 1961 to 1991. | Error-correction model (ECM), exogeneity tests and principal component analysis (PCA) | Banking sector controls are found to have negative effects on the process of financial development. On the basis of exogeneity tests, financial development and economic growth are found to be jointly determined. |

| | | | |
|---|---|---|---|
| Arestis and Demetriades (1997) | Quarterly data for Germany and the US for the period 1979Q1 to 1991Q4. | Johansen cointegration, VECM and weak exogeneity tests | The results vary substantially across countries, highlighting the limitations of cross-country analyses. In Germany, causality runs from financial development to real GDP whereas for the case of the US, a reverse causal pattern is found. |
| Demetriades and Luintel (1997) | Annual data for India for the period 1960–91. | Engle–Granger cointegration, Stock–Watson cointegration, PCA and weak exogeneity tests | Financial repression, measured by a summary of repressionist controls, has substantial negative effects on financial development. Raising real deposit rate contributes to development of the financial sector. Financial development and economic growth are found to be jointly determined. |
| Neusser and Kugler (1998) | Annual data for 13 OECD countries for the period 1970–91. | Johansen, Stock–Watson, Horvath–Watson, Phillips–Ouliaris, Engle–Granger cointegration and Granger causality | Cointegration between financial sector GDP and manufacturing GDP is found only in half of the sample countries examined. Causality results show, in general, that finance Granger-causes manufacturing TFP. Some feedback relationships are also found in several countries. |
| Choe and Moosa (1999) | Annual data for Korea covering the period 1970–92. | VARs and Granger causality | The causality tests show that financial development leads to higher economic growth for the Korean experience. Financial intermediaries are more important than capital markets in this causal relationship. |
| Luintel and Khan (1999) | Annual data for 10 developing countries with 36–41 observations (Costa Rica, Colombia, Greece, India, Korea, Malaysia, the Philippines, Sri Lanka, South Africa and Thailand). | VARs, VECM, Johansen cointegration, weak exogeneity and Granger causality | A bidirectional causality between financial development and economic growth is found in all 10 sample countries. Finance and output are also positively related in the long run. |

(*Continued Overleaf*)

*Table 2.2* Continued

| *Study* | *Sample* | *Method* | *Key findings* |
| --- | --- | --- | --- |
| Xu (2000) | Annual data for 41 countries over the period 1960 to 1993. | VARs and impulse response analyses (IRA) | The results provide evidence that financial development stimulates growth, and investment is an important channel through which finance affects growth. Out of 41 countries examined, 27 countries are found to have positive effects of financial development on investment growth and economic growth. |
| Arestis *et al.* (2001) | Quarterly data for 5 developed countries, including Germany, the US, Japan, UK and France over the period 1972–98. | Johansen cointegration, VECM and weak exogeneity tests | The results indicate that overall both banks and stock markets promote economic growth. However, the contributions from stock markets are relatively small compared to that of banks. The results also suggest that stock market volatility has negative real effects in Japan, France and the UK. |
| Bell and Rousseau (2001) | Annual data for India from 1951 to 1995. | Johansen cointegration, VECM, Granger causality and IRA | The results show that financial sector plays an important role in stimulating the economic performance of India. Increases in financial aggregates have preceded increases in both investment and growth. However, financial sector has no influence on the TFP of manufacturing industries. |
| Demetriades and Luintel (2001) | Annual data for South Korea from 1956 to 1994. | ECM and PCA. | The effects of financial restraints on the financial development in South Korea are positive and large. However, the effects of real interest rate on financial development are insignificant. |
| Arestis, Demetriades, Fattouh and Mouratidis (2002) | Annual data for six developing countries, i.e., South Korea, the Philippines, Thailand, Greece, India and Egypt for the period 1955–97. | VECM, Johansen cointegration and PCA. | The effects of financial liberalization are found to vary considerably across the six developing countries under study. Real interest rate has positive and significant effects in four out of the six countries examined. |

| | | | |
|---|---|---|---|
| Thangavelu and Ang (2004) | Quarterly data for Australia from 1960Q1 to 1999Q4. | VARs and Granger causality | The empirical results using financial development indicators related to financial intermediaries suggest that the banking sector is reactive to the demand generated from the economic development, i.e., economic growth causes banking development in Granger's sense. On the other hand, the results of using financial market indicators are consistent with the Schumpeterian view that development of the stock market is essential in fuelling economic growth. |
| Caporale, Howells and Soliman (2005) | Quarterly data from 1979Q1 to 1998Q4 for Chile, Malaysia, Korea and the Philippines. | VARs and Modified-WALD (Toda–Yamamoto) tests | The study explicitly examines the causal impact of stock market developments on economic growth. The evidence points to the causality running from stock market development to economic growth through increasing investment efficiency. |
| Rousseau and Vuthipadadorn (2005) | Annual data for 10 Asian countries over the period 1950–2000. | Johansen cointegration, VECM, Granger causality tests, Modified-WALD (Toda–Yamamoto) tests and variance decomposition analyses | The results show that finance is a key driving force for investment, supporting the factor accumulation channel. However, the role of financial factor in expanding output is found to be weaker. |
| Ang (2008a) | Annual data for Malaysia from 1965 to 2004. | VECM, Johansen cointegration, Granger causality and PCA. | This study examines the FDI–growth nexus in Malaysia by controlling for the level of financial development. Financial development is measured by a composite index, which is a summary measure of four financial development indicators. The results show that FDI and financial development are positively related to output in the long run. The impact of FDI on output is enhanced through financial development. |
| Ang and McKibbin (2007) | Annual data for Malaysia from 1960 to 2001. | VECM, Johansen cointegration, Granger causality and PCA | Based on the causality results, the findings support the view that output growth leads to financial development in the long run but not the hypothesis that a bank-based financial system induces long-term growth in real sector. Finance and output are positively related in the long run. |

rather than a causal factor (Ahmed, 1998). Such evidence of 'causality', therefore, must be interpreted with caveats. Furthermore, the Granger causality test is merely an examination of whether the past values of one variable are useful in predicting the current value of another variable. Since causality is assessed relative to the information set at hand, if a variable helps predict another variable, this does not necessarily imply one causes another (Demetriades and Andrianova, 2004). As Diebold (2004) explains, '*X* causes *Y*' is simply the abbreviated expression for '*X* contains useful information for predicting *Y*'. Therefore, the causality results should be interpreted in the probabilistic rather than the deterministic sense.

Although individual country case studies provide an important insight, which can be used as a reference for policy formulation, the findings of these case studies are not sufficient to confirm or refute the existing views on the finance–growth relationship. The results obtained from any particular country cannot be readily generalized or extended to other countries to make inference. Hence, the use of single country time series analysis may be limited to policy formulation for the particular country under investigation.

### *2.6.5 Panel studies*

In more recent years, researchers have tried to ameliorate the econometric shortcomings associated with pure cross-sectional studies by taking into account the time dimension with the use of dynamic panel estimation techniques. The empirical results of Levine (1999), Beck *et al.* (2000), Benhabib and Spiegel (2000), Levine *et al.* (2000), Rousseau and Wachtel (2000), Beck and Levine (2004) and Rioja and Valev (2004) consistently point to the same conclusion that the measures of financial development have a positive impact on economic growth.

In view of the issues of limited data points and 'spurious' regressions, Christopoulos and Tsionas (2004) propose the use of panel unit roots and panel cointegration techniques to examine the causality patterns. They find strong evidence of causality running from financial development to economic growth but no evidence of a feedback relationship. Similarly, using the Geweke decomposition test on pooled data of 109 developing and developed countries from 1960 to 1994, Calderon and Liu (2003) find a bi-directional causality between financial development and economic growth. However, financial development contributes more to the causal relationships in developing countries than in developed countries.

Some attempts have been made to examine the issue at the micro level by exploiting firm- or industry-level data, supplementing the findings of these cross-country studies. Rajan and Zingales (1998) contend that better-developed financial intermediaries and financial markets help reduce market frictions. This provides lower costs of external finance to facilitate firms' expansion and encourage new firm formation. Using industry-level data for a large sample of countries over the 1980s, they demonstrate those industries which are more reliant on external finance prosper more in countries with better-developed financial intermediaries and financial markets. The results suggest that financial development may play a beneficial role in firms' growth and the rise of new firms by easing the flow of external finance. The seminal work of Rajan and Zingales (1998) has stimulated much research interest in using micro-level data to gain more insight into the relationship between financial development and economic growth beyond country level (see Wurgler, 2000; Cetorelli and Gambera, 2001; Demirguc-Kunt and Maksimovic, 2002; Fisman and Love, 2003; Bertrand *et al.*, 2004; Allen *et al.*, 2005). The key features of the studies that have used pooled time series and cross-sectional data in a panel setting are summarized in Table 2.3.

Although the use of dynamic panel analysis is an attempt to incorporate the time dimension, they may still be subject to the econometric problems discussed in Section 7.2. This type of regression analysis is also subject to omitted variable problems or heterogeneity bias when the unobserved country-specific effects are included in the error term, and this leads to biased and inconsistent estimates (Pesaran and Smith, 1995). Wachtel (2003) argues that holding country-specific effects constant in panel regressions would generate a spurious aggregate relationship as the reported relationship between financial development and economic growth is due to between-country differences rather than within-country differences over time. Hence, it appears it is difficult to draw any reliable policy inferences from these broad comparative analyses (Demetriades and Andrianova, 2004).

## 2.7 Key issues

Having discussed the cross-country and time series findings, and the weaknesses associated with these studies, there are still some important unresolved issues in the literature, as outlined below.

Until recently, a major constraint impeding research on the dynamic relationship between financial development and economic growth has been the lack of sufficient time series data for developing countries. As a result, cross-country studies have dominated the literature. Although these studies have made significant contributions to the literature and spurred much research, as Ahmed (1998) points out, the issue of causality cannot be satisfactorily addressed in a simple broad comparative framework. While the findings of these studies provide a useful guide to the finance–growth relationship, they cannot be generalized since such a causal link is largely determined by the nature and operation of the financial institutions and policies pursued in each country.[12] As Solow (2001) proposes, while a group of economies may share some common features, each has its own distinctive characteristics. Explaining the evolution of the economic behaviour observed over time requires an economic model that is dynamic in nature. Hence, it is important to carry out country-specific studies in order to relate the findings to policy designs within specific cases.

*Table 2.3* Panel evidence on finance and growth: a summary

| *Study* | *Sample* | *Method* | *Key findings* |
|---|---|---|---|
| De Gregorio and Guidotti (1995) | Annual data for 99 countries during 1960–85, and panel data for 12 Latin American countries during 1950–85. | OLS and panel data random effects | The empirical findings suggest that financial development leads to improved economic performance. However, for the case of Latin American countries, unregulated financial liberalization and expectation of government bail out can lead to negative effect of finance on growth. |
| Odedokun (1996) | Annual data for 71 less developed countries, spanning the 1960s to 1980s. | Generalized least squares (GLS) | Regression results for each country show that financial development promotes economic growth in about 85% of the sample countries. The growth-enhancing effects of finance are more prominent in low-income than in high-income less-developed countries. The panel data estimation results show that the results are invariant across regions and the levels of economic development. |
| Rajan and Zingales (1998) | 41 countries with industry-level data for the period 1980–90. | OLS and panel data fixed effects | The results indicate that those industries which are more reliant on external finance prosper more in countries with better-developed financial intermediaries and financial markets. Financial development may play a beneficial role in firms' growth and the rise of new firms by easing the flow of external finance. |
| Beck, Levine and Loayza (2000) | Annual data for 77 countries for the period 1960 to 1995. | Instrumental variable (IV) and GMM | Financial sector development is found to be robustly and positively correlated with both real per capita GDP growth and TFP growth. The results also provide some support for the positive role of financial development on both capital accumulation and private saving rate; but these links are statistically weaker. |
| Benhabib and Spiegel (2000) | Annual observations for Argentina, Chile, Indonesia and Korea from 1965 to 1985. | GMM | The results show that financial development positively affects both investment rates and TFP growth. However, the results are sensitive to the inclusion of country fixed effects and different indicators of financial development. |

| | | | |
|---|---|---|---|
| Henry (2000) | Annual data for 11 developing countries (Argentina, Brazil, Chile, Colombia, India, Korea, Malaysia, Mexico, the Philippines, Thailand and Venezuela), spanning the 1970s and 1990s. | Panel data techniques | The empirical evidence shows that stock market liberalization leads to increased private investment in 9 out of 11 countries studied. The average growth rate of private investment was 22 percentage points higher than the sample mean three years after the liberalization. |
| Levine *et al.* (2000) | Annual data for 74 countries spanning from 1960 to 1995. | IV and GMM | Using both instrumental variable and dynamic panel techniques, the results show that financial intermediary development is positively related to economic growth. The results also suggest that legal systems and accounting standards help explain differences in the level of financial development. |
| Rousseau and Wachtel (2000) | 47 countries with annual data for the period 1980–95. | Panel VARs | The analysis shows that stock market liquidity and financial intermediation lead to higher per capita output. The effects of stock market capitalization on output are found to be weaker. |
| Beck and Levine (2002) | Annual data from 1980 to 1990 on a panel of 42 countries and 36 manufacturing industries. | OLS and panel data techniques | Industries that rely more on external finance tend to grow faster in countries with more advanced financial systems and more efficient legal systems. However, having a bank-based or market-based financial system *per se* does not seem to matter for growth. |
| Rousseau and Wachtel (2002) | Annual data for 84 countries from 1960–95. | Panel data fixed effects | The results show that there is an inflation threshold of 13–25% for the finance–growth link. Finance does not seem to increase growth when inflation exceeds this threshold level. The effects are significantly positive when inflation falls below the threshold of 6–8%. |
| Calderon and Liu (2003) | Pooled data of 109 developing and industrial countries from 1960 to 1994. | Panel VAR, Geweke decomposition and Granger causality | A bidirectional causality is found between financial development and economic growth. Finance exerts a stronger effect in developing countries. The longer the sample period, the larger the effects of finance. Finance affects growth through both channels of capital accumulation and productivity growth, with the latter channel being more prominent. |
| Beck and Levine (2004) | A panel data set on 40 countries over the period 1976–98. | OLS and GMM | Overall financial development contributes positively to economic growth. Both stock market and banking sector development enter the growth regressions significantly and positively, suggesting that stock markets provide financial services different from that of banks. |

(*Continued Overleaf*)

*Table 2.3* Continued

| *Study* | *Sample* | *Method* | *Key findings* |
|---|---|---|---|
| Christopoulos and Tsionas (2004) | Annual data for 10 developing countries, i.e., Colombia, Paraguay, Peru, Mexico, Ecuador, Honduras, Kenya, Thailand, Dominican Republic and Jamaica from 1970 to 2000. | Panel VECM, panel cointegration, threshold cointegration and fully modified OLS | Based on panel cointegration analysis, the results show that there is a long-run equilibrium relationship between financial development and economic growth. The long-run causality runs from finance to growth, but there is no feedback relationship observed. There is also no evidence of short-run causality. |
| Rioja and Valev (2004) | Panel data of 74 countries for the period 1961–95. | GMM | By dividing all countries into three groups according to their levels of financial development, the evidence suggests that finance has a strong positive impact on economic growth mainly in countries with more developed financial systems. In financially less developed countries, the effect of finance on growth is ambiguous |
| Ketteni *et al.* (2005) | Panel data of 74 countries for the period 1961–95. | Semiparametric partial linear model | They authors find that the finance–growth nexus is only linear when the non-linearities between economic growth and initial per capital income, as well as economic growth and human capital, are taken into account. The relationship appears to be non-linear when these non-linearities are ignored. Therefore, it appears that the alleged non-linear finance–growth relationship is not robust. |
| Ndikumana (2005) | Annual data for 99 countries for the period 1965–97. | OLS and panel data fixed effects | The evidence shows that various financial development indicators are positively related to domestic investment, suggesting that as financial systems grow, capital becomes more easily available and cheaper, which is conducive to capital accumulation. On the other hand, the results find no support for either a bank-based or a market-based financial system being better at promoting investment. Hence, financial structure does not seem to matter. |
| Stengos and Liang (2005) | Panel data of 66 countries for the period 1961–95. | IV augmented semiparametric partial linear model | The authors employ a semiparametric approach to study the potential non-linearity of the effect of finance on growth. Their results indicate that a non-linear effect exists in the relationship but the results are sensitive to the choice of the measures for financial development. |

The selection of key variables to indicate the level of financial services produced in an economy and measuring the extent and efficiency of financial intermediation are the main problems in an empirical study of this nature. As Edwards (1996) put forward, 'defining appropriate proxies for the degree of financial development is, indeed, one of the challenges faced by empirical researchers.' Some studies try to include as many financial proxies as possible in the estimation in order to present a more 'complete' picture of financial development. This is particularly obvious in studies that examine the relative importance of a bank-based and a market-based financial system. However, this leads to the problems of multicollinearity in both cross-sectional and panel data investigations, as well as over-parameterization in time series analyses.

In addition, Cole (1988) notes that the commonly used financial development measures (i.e. M2/GDP and bank credit/GDP) are unable to provide a comprehensive picture of the size of the financial systems because there are many types of financial claims which are not recorded. The treatment and classification of these financial claims also differ over time and across countries. This problem is more pronounced in less-developed countries with poor financial infrastructure.

Even if data quality is ignored, it is still hard to be sure that any single rudimentary aggregated financial measure would be sufficient to capture most aspects of financial development. This is because countries differ in terms of their financial structure, degree of concentration of financial institutions, size of financial institutions and instruments, efficiency of financial intermediaries, volume of financial transactions, and effectiveness of the financial regulatory framework.

M2/GDP and bank credit/GDP are highly aggregated measures of financial development. They are often used to proxy financial development for convenience, despite the possibility that different components of financial system (stock markets, banks, insurance companies, etc.) may have different impacts on economic growth. As noted by Gurley and Shaw (1955), in the early stages of financial development, financial intermediaries are predominantly banks, providing lending and transactions services. Under such circumstances, money stock is a reliable proxy to measure the extent of financial intermediation. However, as the financial systems evolve, the use of money stock becomes inappropriate with the emergence of other types of more complex financial intermediaries. Furthermore, it appears that using different measures of financial development may give rise to different conclusions about how financial development and economic growth are related. These crude measures of financial development must be interpreted with caveats. For example, a high ratio of private credit/GDP or M2/GDP does not necessarily indicate a high level of sophistication in the financial systems. In the case of Malaysia, while these ratios were relatively high before the Asian financial crisis, they do not necessarily indicate the existence of a sound and efficient financial system (Athukorala, 2001; Hill, 2005).

Thiel (2001) highlights that a significant portion of the bank loans issued to the private sectors may be used to finance housing loans instead of being channelled to fund productive activities. Furthermore, with increasing global financial integration, domestic financial indicators are not sufficient to capture development in the financial systems. In recent years, increasing merger and acquisition activities have been an important force for raising funds from stock markets. Thus, funds raised from stock markets are not necessarily used to finance investment projects, casting doubt on the reliability of financial development indicators based on stock market measures.

While examining the importance of financial markets, research has so far mainly focused on the role of banks. These studies play down the contributions from other components of the financial system, such as pension funds, insurance companies, bond markets, share markets, etc., on the grounds that these intermediaries are relatively new and small and therefore provide little funds to spur growth. Ignoring the rapid development of these intermediaries may lead to significant underestimation of the level of financial development. Furthermore, informal finance (curb markets) is also often neglected in the discussion as some economists view the informal sector as an unorganized and immaterial sector in generating resources to spur economic growth (Chandavarkar, 1992). Although informal finance may play a substantial role in intermediating resources in developing countries, it is difficult to gather these data.[13]

Institutional factors have largely been ignored by most empirical studies. Since each country differs in terms of the quality of their regulatory authorities, the legal system and contract enforcement, barriers to participation of foreign banks, the perceived importance of the financial sector as an instrument of growth by the government, etc., financial intermediaries and financial markets are only as good as the environment in which they operate. Driffill (2003) highlights that while some of the empirical results on the positive influence of financial development look convincing, they must be interpreted with caveats since they may just be picking up other features of the countries involved e.g. legal factors, institutions, geography, etc. Although it is often argued that the success of any financial sector policy critically depends on the existence of good governance, most studies take no account of institutions in their analysis, mainly because it is very difficult to find an appropriate proxy for institutions. Hence, the results obtained from these studies are far from complete. As Morck and Steiler (2005) argue, 'financial development is not a given, but depends on politics and history.' This also raises concerns about treating financial development as a purely exogenous variable.

Empirical studies generally suffer from a fundamental limitation in their approach to understanding the finance–growth nexus. Cross-country studies typically employ Barro's (1991) regression model and augment it with some financial development indicators. Even though attempts have been made by using 2SLS or instrumental variables estimators to account for the potential endogeneity of financial variables, this single equation approach does not capture the full interaction between financial development and economic growth. A more promising way of describing the finance–growth relationship is to use a system of equations by explicitly modelling for economic growth, financial development and other variables concerned. Although time series approaches with a VAR specification treat all variables in the model as endogenous, these reduced form equations contain little theoretical backing.[14] Structural VARs were invented to deal with this problem. However, they are accused of imposing too stringent (often zero) restrictions on the model. As a result, empirical researchers often struggle in choosing an appropriate approach.

## 2.8 Conclusions

There is ample cross-country empirical evidence pointing to a positive impact of financial development on economic growth. This chapter highlights some methodological reservations about these empirical findings. In addition, it is well known that there are significant differences among developing countries in which various structural features and institutional aspects may have a direct bearing on the impact of financial development in the process of economic growth. Hence, this thesis proposes a country-specific in-depth case study to examine the issue at hand. The next chapter provides an overview of the Malaysian economy and its financial system before proceeding to examine the channels that link financial development and economic growth.

# 3 The Malaysian economy and its financial system

## 3.1 Introduction

In order to set the stage for the later analyses, this chapter provides an overview of the Malaysian economy and the development of its financial system from a historical perspective. The chapter focuses on a number of key 'stylized facts' about the Malaysian economy which have a direct bearing on the subject at hand. Firstly, Malaysia is a relatively small but high growth economy which relies heavily on international trade for its growth dynamics. Secondly, throughout the post-independence era Malaysia has maintained a relatively open foreign trade and investment regime. The rapid growth of the economy has had much to do with its openness and trade orientation. Thirdly, during most of the period under study, Malaysia has maintained an impressive track record of pursuing prudential macroeconomic policies. The central bank has been able to maintain price stability in the economy where inflation has always been very well-managed, except during period of external shocks, such as oil crises. Fourthly, with the exception of the racial riots in 1969, Malaysia has been able to enjoy a stable political environment.

The chapter is structured as follows:

- Section 3.2 discusses the policy framework of the Malaysian economy;
- Section 3.3 gives an overview of the Malaysian growth experience;
- Sections 3.4 and 3.5 discuss financial sector development and financial sector reforms in Malaysia, respectively;
- section 3.5 discusses components of the financial system;
- Sections 3.6 and 3.7 discuss saving behaviour and investment patterns, respectively;
- Section 3.8 analyses the saving and investment relationship; and
- Section 3.9 provides a conclusion.

## 3.2 The policy framework: an overview

Malaysia achieved independence on 31 August 1957. At the time of independence, economic conditions in Malaysia appeared conducive to sustained economic growth. The newly independent government inherited from the British colonial administration a well-developed infrastructure, an efficient administrative system, and a growing primary export sector with ample potential for expansion. In terms of educational attainment and standard of living, Malaysia was well ahead of most of its neighbouring countries (Snodgrass, 1980).

Economic performance was generally regarded as very good after independence, as reflected by the rapid expansion of the economy. The First Malaysia Plan (1966–70), a five-year economic development plan, was outlined in the early 1960s to promote the welfare of all citizens. Increasing concern about income inequality among major ethnic groups accompanied this development, threatening the political and economic stability of the country.[1] Although political power was dominated by Malays, who accounted for more than half of the population in the 1960s, they were relatively poor and mainly engaged in low productivity agricultural activities. Ethnic Chinese, who accounted for about one-third of the population, were relatively well off and controlled most of the modern-sector productive activities. As a result, sustainable economic growth was questioned by native Malays, who felt the benefits of income growth were being concentrated in the hands of ethnic Chinese (Snodgrass, 1980; Bhalla and Kharas, 1992). Income inequality over the 1960s continued to worsen and resulted in growing interracial tension. In fact, from independence in 1957 to the general election in 1969, household incomes of the *bumiputras* grew least rapidly, while those of ethnic Chinese grew most rapidly (Chee, 1990; Lucas and Verry, 1996). This deteriorating situation eventually led to the bloody racial riot following the outcome of the general election in May 1969.

In response to the May 1969 riot, the New Economic Policy (NEP) was instituted in 1970 to improve inter-ethnic relations through the eradication of poverty by raising income levels and increasing opportunities for all Malaysians, irrespective of race, and through rapid reordering of the society to correct economic imbalances, so as to reduce, and eventually eliminate, the identification of race with economic function. Specifically, this twenty-year programme aimed to expand the corporate shareholding, employment and education opportunities of the *bumiputras* so they would be able to improve their standard of living. The NEP became the key reference for the formulation of economic development policies, remaining in place for the next two decades and beyond. Given that the main political and economic objectives of the NEP were to redistribute the financial wealth of the minority non-*bumiputras* to the *bumiputras*, implementation of the NEP inevitably involved a series of pro-*bumiputra* affirmative action programmes. Since its inception, the inter-ethnic gaps in household incomes have narrowed significantly (Snodgrass, 1980; Lucas and Verry, 1996).

A series of privatization and restructuring of state-owned enterprise activities took place from the mid-1980s. Alongside this development was an emphasis on promoting heavy industry through government involvement under the fourth Prime Minister Mahathir's 'Look East' policy (Crouch, 1996). Huge saving and export growth, coupled with political stability, ethnic harmony, and effective reforms in the financial system, raised the status of Malaysia to middle-income level in the 1980s. This remarkable economic performance coincided with implementation of the NEP and the five-year economic plans.

The Malaysian economy was hit by the collapse of commodity prices at the end of 1985 (Corden, 1996). As a result, aggregate output fell dramatically by 4 per cent in 1985, unemployment increased from 5.8 per cent in 1984 to 8.3 per cent in 1986, and the economy entered a recession. In response to this adverse situation, the government carried out a privatization policy to promote the private sector as the key engine of economic growth. The government also spent massively on infrastructure to accelerate industrialization in line with the aim to transform Malaysia into a newly industrialized economy. At the same time, regulations on foreign equity participation in Malaysia were relaxed. Other measures introduced to stimulate growth and reduce unemployment included low-cost housing schemes, speedier approval of licences for small business, new public infrastructural projects, retraining programmes for the unemployed, etc. (Yusof *et al.*, 1994).

The NEP was extended for another decade in 1990 with some modifications, under the new label of the National Development Policy (NDP) (Snodgrass, 1995). This policy was complemented by Vision 2020 formulated in 1991, which projected Malaysia to be a fully industrialized nation within the next three decades. Most of these proposals were related to providing a sound infrastructure base, maintaining macroeconomic stability, and developing human capital. Throughout the 1991–96 period, budget deficits were well-managed at a low level and mainly financed by a non-inflationary source – the Employee Provident Fund (EPF). The government was also able to service external loans and reduce borrowing due to the sound performance of the economy (Khan, 2002). In addition, the unemployment rate, prices and the exchange rate were well-managed and remained stable. There was also a considerable reduction in the incidence of poverty, where the *bumiputra* racial group made significant progress in the modern sectors of the economy.

Malaysia was severely hit by the Asian financial crisis in 1997–98, but rebounded quickly in 1999–2000 (Athukorala, 2001). The Asian financial crisis initially started off as a currency crisis, but rapidly translated into a financial crisis following the weakening of the banking system. This subsequently deteriorated into an economic recession.[2] It is widely believed imprudent supervision and sustained strong credit growth prior to 1997 were partly accountable for the crisis.[3]

While Malaysia's initial approach to crisis management was to follow the measures prescribed by the IMF, the government eventually chose an unconventional route by adopting a capital control regime. Capital controls were deemed necessary by policy makers to prevent massive capital flight. For a small open economy like Malaysia, a drastic movement in short-term capital can lead to volatility in the financial system. Macroeconomic policies were aimed at reducing current account deficits, combating inflation, and managing the excess demand triggered by high credit growth. The National Economic Action Council (NEAC) was set up in January 1998 to address the deteriorating economic conditions and revitalize the economy. Six months later, the National Economic Recovery Plan was launched to provide a comprehensive framework for economic recovery (BNM, 1999). BNM took further action to deal with the adverse consequences of the crisis on the financial system by providing a deposit guarantee to depositors and liquidity support to banks to strengthen stability. Two special agencies, *Danaharta* (an asset management company) and *Danamodal* (a recapitalization agency), were set up to buy non-performing loans at a discount and inject new capital in certain institutions, respectively. These two agencies were complemented by the Corporate Debt Restructuring Committee (CDRC), which provided an opportunity for ailing banking institutions and debtors to work out feasible restructuring schemes without having to resort to legal proceedings. In addition, BNM was prompted to introduce selective capital controls and fix the exchange rate at US$1=RM3.80 effective from 2 September 1998. These measures brought about a stable domestic economic environment and remained in place until July 2005.

After the crisis, NDP was replaced by the National Vision Policy 2001–2010 (NVP), emphasizing achievement of rapid economic growth as the key policy for development. However, the new policy still contains some strong elements of affirmative action programmes, mainly targeted at improving the living standards of the *bumiputras*. Malaysia has largely relied on its five-year economic plans to implement its development strategy throughout the last few decades.[4] These plans have been aimed basically at charting the government development strategy to achieve a high level of economic growth and reducing economic disparities and poverty (Khan, 2002). To a large extent, they were designed to complement the objectives of other core policies, such as NEP, NDP and NVP. All of these national economic plans place strong emphasis on developing the infrastructure base, which has greatly facilitated the undertaking of investment activities. It is important to note that they are basically 'public sector investment plans' whereas plans for the private sector are largely 'indicative plans'. The government has never been directly involved in planning private sector investment activities. This is one of the key reasons behind the success story of Malaysia's economic development.

## 3.3 The Malaysian growth experience

This section provides an overview of Malaysia's growth experience, segregated into five distinct phases:

- the early post-independence period (1957–70);
- the soaring 1970s;

- the structural adjustment period in the 1980s;
- investment booms in the 1990s; and
- Asian financial crisis and the recovery period (1997–2005), as illustrated in Figure 3.1.

During the post-independence era, Malaysia provided a fundamentally sound environment to attract investment. This was based on a rich natural resource base, the ample availability of financial resources due to the huge presence of foreign banks, the supply of a relatively well-trained labour force, and the provision of an adequately developed infrastructure base. These factors, together with the presence of a large plantation sector, were important in generating rapid industrial growth in the 1960s, which had a far-reaching impact on economic development for the next two decades. Real GDP growth accelerated from a negative rate of –0.1 per cent in 1957 to a respectable rate of 7.8 per cent in 1966, but slowed slightly to 6.0 per cent in 1970. Economic growth in the 1960s was accompanied by an improvement in living standards, better access to health and education, and a higher level of urbanization (Yusof, Hussin, Alowi, Lim and Singh, 1994; Narayanan, 2004).

### *3.3.1 An overview of economic growth*

The 1970s marked a significant improvement in the performance of the manufacturing sector. During the period 1971–80, the manufacturing sector grew by an average annual rate of 22.9 per cent, accounting for 21.6 per cent of GDP in 1980. This was underpinned by a boom in export-oriented and

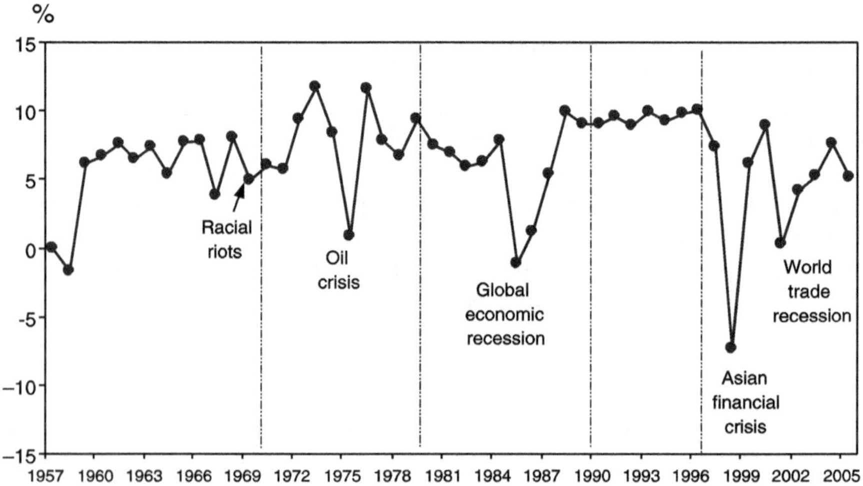


*Figure 3.1* GDP growth of Malaysia, 1957–2005.

*Sources:* compiled from Nazrin (2000) and World Development Indicators.

labour-intensive industries, such as electronics, textiles and wool products. This impressive performance was largely the result of government efforts in attracting and promoting export-oriented industries through the establishment of free trade zones from the early 1970s. The economy grew strongly at an average annual rate of 7.9 per cent due to the exceptional performance of these industries (Yusof *et al.*, 1994).

However, the performance of the economy was severely affected by the oil crisis that led to the world recession of 1975. Real GDP growth declined sharply from 8.3 per cent in 1974 to 0.8 per cent in 1975. Inflation increased rapidly from 3.2 per cent in 1972 to 17.3 per cent in 1974. The government responded to this marked decline in growth by massive spending on public investment projects. Average public investment spending grew nearly threefold between the periods 1971–75 and 1976–80, providing a strong impetus to fuel economic recovery. As a result, the growth rate of real GDP had rebounded to 9.3 per cent by 1979.

GDP in the 1980s registered an average annual growth rate of 6.0 per cent, about 2 percentage points lower than the previous decade. This was mainly due to a sharp fall in commodity prices, following a prolonged global economic recession in the early 1980s. By the end of 1982, the government faced a twin deficit situation: a fiscal deficit at 18 per cent of GNP and a current account deficit at 14 per cent of GNP. In view of these problems, external borrowing was sought, resulting in a significant increase in external debt from RM 10 billion (19.5 per cent of GNP) in 1980 to RM 24.3 billion (40.7 per cent of GNP) at the end of 1982 (Othman, 1987; Lin and Chung, 1995).

The economy entered a recession when the prices of several main export commodity prices collapsed in 1985. Total export income fell by 1.6 per cent and 6.2 per cent in 1985 and 1986, respectively. This had an adverse impact on the economy when deflation followed, and share prices and property prices fell dramatically. As a result, real GDP contracted by 1 per cent. Following an improvement of external conditions which led to a spectacular performance in the export sector, the economy recovered rapidly from 1987, achieving a high annual growth rate of more than 9 per cent during the period 1988–90.

The 1990s saw exceptional growth in the Malaysian economy, with an annual average growth rate of 9.6 per cent during the period 1991–96. This strong growth record was mainly due to active promotion of the private sector as the main driver of economic development. Alongside this development was a massive influx of foreign direct investment (henceforth FDI), where the average ratio of FDI to GDP increased two-fold from 3.3 per cent during the period 1981–90 to 6.6 per cent during the period 1991–96. The share of FDI in total investment reached a record high of about 23 per cent in 1992. This remarkable increase in FDI was partly due to the government granting of attractive FDI incentives, including location incentives, tax allowances, and double deduction for promotion of exports, etc.[5]

The performance of the Malaysian economy was severely affected in the wake of the Asian financial crisis, which led to a corresponding decline in the growth rate of GDP. In 1998, the economy recorded a negative growth rate of 7.4 per cent. From 1998 to 2005, the average annual real GDP growth rate was much lower at 3.8 per cent. As highlighted earlier, macroeconomic and financial sector policies were formulated to deal with this adverse situation. The economy recovered rather quickly and, in 1999, real GDP grew by 6.1 per cent from the previous year. However, the growth rate was moderated to 0.3 per cent due to the world trade recession in 2001. In the subsequent four years, the economy grew at an average rate of 5.6 per cent.

### *3.3.2 Comparison with other Asian countries*

In 1961, Malaysia was one of the highest per capita income countries in the Asian region, after Japan, Hong Kong, Singapore, and South Korea (see Table 3.1). This ranking remained unchanged over the next three decades. Annual real GDP growth during the period 1961–80 averaged 7.2 per cent, above the performance of many other Asian developing countries. The growth rate increased marginally to 7.4 per cent during the period 1981–96, prior to the Asian financial crisis. Over the entire period of 1961–2005, Malaysia's average real GDP growth rate was higher than Indonesia, the Philippines, Japan, Bangladesh, India, Pakistan and Sri Lanka, but lower than that of Singapore, Thailand, China, Hong Kong and South Korea.

*Table 3.1* Per capita income and economic growth

| *Country/Region* | *GDP per capita, constant 2000 US$* | | | | *Real GDP growth (%)* | | | |
|---|---|---|---|---|---|---|---|---|
| | *1961* | *1980* | *1996* | *2005* | *1961–1980* | *1981–1996* | *1997–2005* | *1961–2005* |
| **Malaysia** | 818 | 1,848 | 3,763 | 4,437 | 7.2 | 7.4 | 4.2 | 6.6 |
| **Southeast Asia** | | | | | | | | |
| Indonesia | 204 | 397 | 878 | 942 | 6.0 | 6.9 | 2.3 | 5.6 |
| Philippines | 627 | 989 | 948 | 1,136 | 5.4 | 2.2 | 4.0 | 4.0 |
| Singapore | 2,478 | 9,043 | 20,039 | 25,968 | 9.4 | 7.9 | 4.9 | 8.0 |
| Thailand | 336 | 804 | 2,154 | 2,446 | 7.5 | 8.0 | 2.5 | 6.7 |
| **East Asia** | | | | | | | | |
| China | 78 | 186 | 716 | 1,449 | 5.5 | 10.3 | 9.0 | 7.9 |
| Hong Kong | 3,428 | 11,522 | 23,049 | 30,010 | 9.6 | 6.1 | 3.9 | 7.2 |
| Japan | 7,883 | 23,917 | 36,137 | 39,075 | 7.5 | 3.1 | 1.1 | 4.6 |
| South Korea | 1,132 | 3,221 | 9,707 | 13,240 | 7.8 | 8.3 | 4.3 | 7.3 |
| **South Asia** | | | | | | | | |
| Bangladesh | 258 | 249 | 321 | 433 | 2.6 | 4.0 | 5.4 | 3.6 |
| India | 179 | 223 | 393 | 588 | 3.6 | 5.7 | 6.3 | 4.9 |
| Pakistan | 192 | 327 | 522 | 598 | 6.0 | 5.7 | 4.0 | 5.5 |
| Sri Lanka | 274 | 442 | 723 | 1,010 | 4.5 | 4.6 | 4.6 | 4.5 |

*Source:* compiled from WDI (2005).

### *3.3.3 Structural change of the economy*

The discussion now turns to the structure of the Malaysian economy. Trade had a significant impact on economic structure of the country. At independence, the primary sector accounted for 45 per cent of GDP, the tertiary sector, which mainly played a supporting role for the primary sector, accounted for another 44 per cent, and the manufacturing sector made up the remaining 11 per cent. Exports constituted about 46 per cent of GDP, indicating a huge export sector primarily dominated by the rubber and tin industries. The country's highly open economy was responsible for a standard of living among the highest in Asia (Lim, 1975).

The structure of the Malaysian economy has undergone a remarkable transformation since independence. With the adoption of a sound policy mix and effective implementation of these development policies, Malaysia has successfully shifted the structure of its economy from an agriculture-based economy to one based on industries that produce a variety of manufactured goods. Figure 3.2 shows that the share of agriculture value-added has declined gradually over the years and the manufacturing sector has become increasingly important. Between 1961 and 2005, the manufacturing sector grew by an average of 14 per cent per year, with the share of manufacturing in GDP increasing from 7 to 23 per cent as a result of the aggressive export-oriented strategy pursued by the country. The industry sector has also grown significantly over the last few decades. Its share in output increased by more than double from 19 per cent in 1960 to 40 per cent in 2005. In contrast, the share of agriculture in GDP declined from 33 to 7 per cent during the same period.

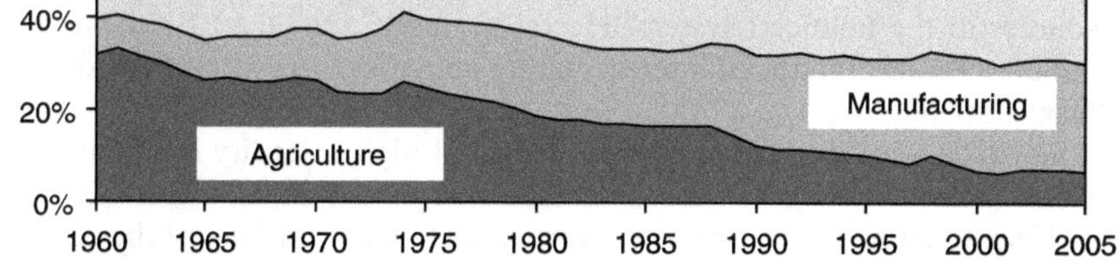


*Figure 3.2* The economic structure of Malaysia, by share of value-added, 1960–2005.

*Notes:* 'Services' includes value-added in wholesale and retail trade (including hotels and restaurants) and transport, and government, financial, professional, and personal services such as education, health care, and real estate services. 'Industry' comprises value-added in mining, construction, electricity, water, and gas.

*Source:* compiled from World Development Indicators.

The importance of the services sector, in terms of GDP share, has remained more or less unchanged over the years.

## 3.4 Financial sector development

The development of Malaysia's financial system evolved mainly through the channel of international trade during the colonial period. A simple and stable monetary regime – the currency board system – emerged during this time, providing the necessary currency exchange service to facilitate the expansion of trade and foreign capital inflow (BNM, 1989). The gold-exchange standard incorporated the Malayan currency by fixing it to the gold-based British currency at the exchange rate of one Malayan dollar equal to 2s.4d. (Drake, 1969b; Huff, 2003). Bank Negara Malaysia (the Central Bank of Malaysia, henceforth BNM) was set up in 1959 alongside the currency board system. However, it had little role to play in the monetary system before 1967, when the currency board stopped issuing currency. Since then, it has been playing a pivotal role in promoting development of the financial sector. A list of the financial sector policies adopted in Malaysia since the establishment of the Central Bank is provided in Appendix 1.

The financial structure in the early 1960s mainly comprised the commercial banks, which were basically set up to provide the services of trade financing. Hence, the primary development force in the financial system in these early days was the volume of international trade. During this period, commercial banks were owned mostly by foreigners and headquartered in London. The key objective of BNM in the 1960s was to establish a basic infrastructure for the domestic financial system. This was achieved by developing domestic banks to complement the well-established foreign banks.

These efforts were carried into the 1970s, when other financial intermediaries, such as finance companies, merchant banks and development finance institutions, were set up by BNM to cater for other financial services not provided by commercial banks. New legislation was passed to bring these financial intermediaries under the supervision of BNM (BNM, 1999). At the same time, the informal financial sector was able to mobilize substantial resources in the financial system. However, due to the lack of reliable data, these unorganized financial intermediating activities were not reflected in the official statistics.

The 1980s were characterized by a period of high volatility in the financial system. Following failure of the Overseas Trust Bank (OTB) in Hong Kong in July 1985, there had been many rumours regarding the stability of the banking system in Malaysia. In September 1985, the first deposit-taking institution in Malaysia failed, causing severe anxiety among depositors. Three months later, the failure of a large public listed company in Singapore, Pan-Electric, led to a three-day closure of the Kuala Lumpur Stock Exchange (KLSE). As a result, there were sporadic runs throughout the following year against the weaker financial institutions (Lin and Chung, 1995). A few cooperative finance companies and banks failed and were bailed out by BNM. Laws were passed to bring them under close supervision by BNM (Ariff and Khalid, 2000). In view of this, most of BNM's efforts in the late 1980s were focused on restoring confidence in the financial system and further strengthening the regulatory framework in the banking system.

The 1990s were characterized by rapid development in the financial sector due to strong economic growth, a high saving rate, and advancements in telecommunications. These changes have had a significant impact on the functioning of financial institutions and financial markets, and led to the emergence of a variety of financial products and services. However, this rapid development was interrupted when the economy was hit by the 1997–98 Asian financial crisis. The crisis highlighted the importance of maintaining financial stability for the sustained development of an economy. It put BNM under great pressure to promote a competitive banking system while preserving financial stability. The key challenge faced by BNM in the aftermath of the crisis, therefore, was to improve financial stability.

Financial instability emerges when the failure of one or more financial institutions triggers adverse effects on the financial system (e.g. price misalignment, resource misallocation) as well as on the economy as a whole. These negative consequences can spill over to destabilize financial systems in other countries, as was clearly illustrated in the case of the 1997–98 Asian financial crisis (BNM, 1999). Financial stability ensures that the functions of the financial systems are effectively carried out, resulting in effective allocation of resources and promoting sustained economic development. Financial stability is also important for the reason that it is vital for the effective conduct of monetary policy, which is mainly carried out through the banking system. However, this would not be possible without the presence of a sound supervisory framework. In this regard, the functional role of BNM in strengthening the regulatory framework in the financial system is indispensable. To achieve financial stability, various reforms have been carried out by BNM in the Malaysian financial system, as will be seen below.

## 3.5 Financial sector reforms

The existence of an effective prudential regulatory framework is critical as it minimizes the risk of financial instability. In 1988, supervision of the insurance industry was brought under the purview of BNM, with the aim of streamlining supervision of the entire financial system and realizing economies of scale. In October 1989, the introduction of the Banking and Financial Institution Act 1989 marked an important step by BNM to strengthen the prudential and regulatory framework in the financial system (Hussein, 1994). The Act enhances the powers and duties of the auditors of licensed institutions. In September 1996, the Insurance Act 1996 came into force to further enhance the legislative framework governing the supervision of the insurance industry (BNM, 1999).

BNM has also consistently reviewed its supervisory approach by concentrating on high risk areas that may have an undesirable impact on the financial system. In this connection, minimum standards on risk management for derivatives were introduced in 1996, and guidelines on minimum audit standards implemented in 1997. These measures were aimed at enhancing the soundness of corporate governance. Furthermore, disclosure requirements were improved by requiring banking institutions to publish key indicators of financial soundness on a more regular and timely basis. Measures were also introduced in the financial markets to improve transparency and protect the interests of minority shareholders (BNM, 1999).

BNM has actively pursued interest rate liberalization, with the objective of developing a more market-driven financial system. BNM followed a gradual approach in interest rate reforms, beginning in the 1970s by cautiously liberalizing interest rates. The major phase occurred in 1978 when commercial banks were allowed to set deposit and lending rates freely (Hussein, 1994). However, the market-determined interest rate mechanism was interrupted from October 1985 to January 1987 when BNM imposed controls on interest rates to mitigate the impact of the world economic recession on Malaysia. In February 1987, BNM abandoned the pegged deposit rate regime and, in September 1987, turned to the use of the base lending rate (BLR) to control interest rates. These interest rate controls remained in force until 1991 (Yusof *et al.*, 1994).

From February 1991, the BLR of banking institutions was completely freed from administrative control. All commercial banks and finance companies were allowed to set their own deposit and lending rates (Yusof *et al.*, 1994). Lending rates were subject to a maximum of 4 percentage points above the declared BLR. As a result of this policy, deposit and lending rates were competitively determined by market forces. Furthermore, in 1995, a new BLR framework was introduced to reduce time lag by linking the BLR to the weighted monthly average of the 3-month interbank rate. In order to further reduce the transmission lag, in 1998 the BLR was linked to the 3-month BNM intervention rate instead of to the 3-month interbank rate (BNM, 1999).[6]

In the past, Malaysia has been reluctant to relax foreign ownership restrictions in the financial sector. However, with the view that opening the financial sector to foreign institutions will introduce international standards of best practice and increase competitiveness, Malaysia has gradually recognized the importance of opening up the domestic financial sector to foreign competition. This has allowed the financial system to play a more efficient role in mobilizing and channelling financial resources to fuel economic development. At the same time, it is important to note that potential undesirable effects might have followed if liberalization had not been carried out in a prudent manner. In this connection, Malaysia has adopted a gradual and progressive approach to liberalize its financial sector. The pace of financial liberalization has been compatible with the prevailing economic conditions and regulatory framework (BNM, 1999).

These liberalization policies have resulted in a high level of foreign participation in the domestic financial sector. For instance, in 2003 there were 11 fully foreign-owned commercial banks in the financial system, which accounted for about 25 per cent of the total assets of commercial banks (BNM, 2004). Stiff competition in the banking industry has resulted in narrowing of the gross interest margins of commercial banks, from 4.1 percentage points in 2001 to 3.7 percentage points in 2003. Foreign banking institutions have expanded their loan market share, mainly in housing loans, whereas the domestic banking institutions have continued to be the key provider of financing for business, particularly for small and medium-sized enterprises (BNM, 2004). There has also been a strong foreign presence in the insurance industry following liberalization of the insurance sector in the early 1960s. In 2003, there were 28 foreign-owned insurers in the financial system. The foreign market shares of life insurance premiums and general insurance premiums were about 76 per cent and 39 per cent, respectively (BNM, 2004).

Malaysia remains very committed to further liberalizing its financial sector. This was reflected by the signing of the Interim Agreement on the financial services sector in 1995 and the Fifth Protocol of the General Agreement on Trade in Services (GATS). In the latter, Malaysia has committed to increase the aggregate foreign equity limit in insurance companies to 51 per cent and to open up offshore investment banking, offshore insurance, and offshore financial leasing (BNM, 1999). In 2000, the maximum foreign equity in a stockbroking company and a financial leasing company was increased from 30 to 49 per cent. The maximum credit that could be obtained by a non-resident controlled company from foreign-owned banking institutions was raised from 40 to 50 per cent, and this constraint was subsequently removed in 2003. Furthermore, foreign banks were allowed to provide Internet banking services in 2002 (BNM, 2004).

The liberalization policies adopted by BNM seem to have worked well at the early stage of development, when financial development was observed. The monetization ratio (M2/GDP), which is commonly used as a crude indicator of financial development, increased remarkably from 31 per cent in 1970 to 52 per cent by 1980. In the 1980s, the Malaysian financial sector underwent a radical transformation and deepening, along with expansion in the economy. The upshot of this transformation was the emergence of a broader, deeper, more organized and better-structured financial system.

Nevertheless, Malaysia has never completely and consistently liberalized its financial sector. In the past, the main components of reform policies have been liberalization of the interest rates, improvement of the regulatory and supervisory framework, and opening up of the domestic financial sector. The reform programmes also appear to have been narrow in scope, where much of BNM's efforts have been focused on eliminating interest controls (Bascom, 1994). In addition, some of the liberalization measures were introduced as instruments to tackle certain problems in the economy during specific time periods. For example, Malaysia experienced an acceleration of capital account opening in the 1990s following the stock market booms. However, capital controls were put in place temporarily in 1994 and 1998–2005 to manage exchange rate fluctuations. Furthermore, although measures have been introduced to enhance banking sector competition, restriction of foreign banks participation still prevails. It appears, therefore, that the financial sector policies adopted by Malaysia are not consistent, given that the liberalization measures taken did not represent a continuous and steady policy to liberalize the financial system (Hussein, 1994).

Quite apart from the financial liberalization policies pursued, a series of directed credit programmes were implemented in 1975. These strong financial commitments were made mainly for the advancement of the indigenous Malaysians (Haggard, 2004). During that year, at least 50 per cent of total lending made by banks had to be advanced to the *bumiputra* community. The requirement was reduced to 20 per cent in the following year, and then adjusted upward to 30 per cent in 1996. The programmes also include minimum lending to other priority sectors, including agriculture, manufacturing and small and medium-sized enterprises, and to individuals for housing loans. These programmes are currently in force.

In sum, it appears that repressionist measures, such as interest rate controls, banking sector restrictions, and directed credit programmes, coexist with a structuralist policy of promoting the creation of more financial institutions (Yaakop, 1988).[7] These financial sector policies, liberalization or repression, and the development that follows, can have a significant impact on the relationship between financial development and economic growth. Consequently, the relationship of these two variables must be examined in the context of the financial environment.

## 3.6 Financial structure

The financial system in Malaysia can be broadly classified into financial institutions and financial markets (Table 3.2). The former consists of the banking system and non-bank financial intermediaries, of which the banking system is the largest component in the financial system. The latter comprises money and foreign exchange markets, capital markets, derivatives markets and offshore markets.

The compositions of major financial intermediaries by assets in 1970 and 2003 for Malaysia are presented in Figure 3.3. As is evident, the financial system in Malaysia has grown rapidly over the past few decades. Total assets in the financial system increased from RM 11 billion at the end of 1970 to RM 1,564 billion at the end of 2003, an average annual growth rate of 16 per cent. The dominance of the banking sector in the Malaysian financial system is also evident. The total assets of banking institutions accounted for more than half of total assets at the end of 2003, of which commercial banks alone accounted for 40 per cent. Finance companies and merchant banks were relatively insignificant, accounting for 9 per cent and 3 per cent,

*Table 3.2* Structure of the Malaysian financial system

| *Financial Institutions* | *Financial Markets* |
|---|---|
| <u>Banking System</u> | <u>Money and Foreign Exchange Markets</u> |
| ■ Bank Negara Malaysia | ■ Money Market |
| ■ Banking Institutions | ■ Foreign Exchange Market |
| —Commercial Banks[1] | |
| —Finance Companies | <u>Capital Markets</u> |
| —Merchant Banks | ■ Equity Market |
| ■ Others | ■ Bond Market |
| —Discount Houses | —Public Debt Securities |
| —Representative Offices of Foreign Banks | —Private Debt Securities |
| —Offshore Banks in Labuan International Offshore Financial Centre (IOFC) | |
| <u>Non-Bank Financial Intermediaries</u> | <u>Derivatives Markets</u> |
| ■ Provident and Pension Funds | ■ Commodity Futures |
| ■ Insurance Companies[2] | ■ KLSE CI Futures |
| ■ Development Finance Institutions | ■ KLIBOR Futures |
| ■ Saving Institutions | |
| —National Savings Bank | |
| —Co-operative Societies | |
| ■ Other Non-Bank Financial Intermediaries | <u>Offshore Market</u> |
| —Unit Trusts | ■ Labuan International Offshore Financial Centre (IOFC) |
| —Housing Credit Institutions | |
| —Cagamas Berhad | |
| —Credit Guarantee Corporation | |
| —etc. | |

*Notes:* 1. including Islamic Banks; 2. Including Takaful.

*Source:* adapted from BNM (1999) p. 67.

respectively. BNM constituted another 13 per cent of the total assets in the financial system. Among the major groups of non-bank financial institutions, the provident and pension funds and insurance funds remained the largest, accounting for more than 20 per cent of the financial system at the end of 2003. The share of commercial bank assets in the financial system has remained more or less unaltered over the past three decades. However, the relative importance of the central bank and the EPF has diminished over time due to the expansion of other financial intermediaries, such as finance companies, development financial institutions, and insurance funds.

### *3.6.1 Banking system*

The banking system is the largest component of the financial system. It mainly includes commercial banks, finance companies and merchant banks,

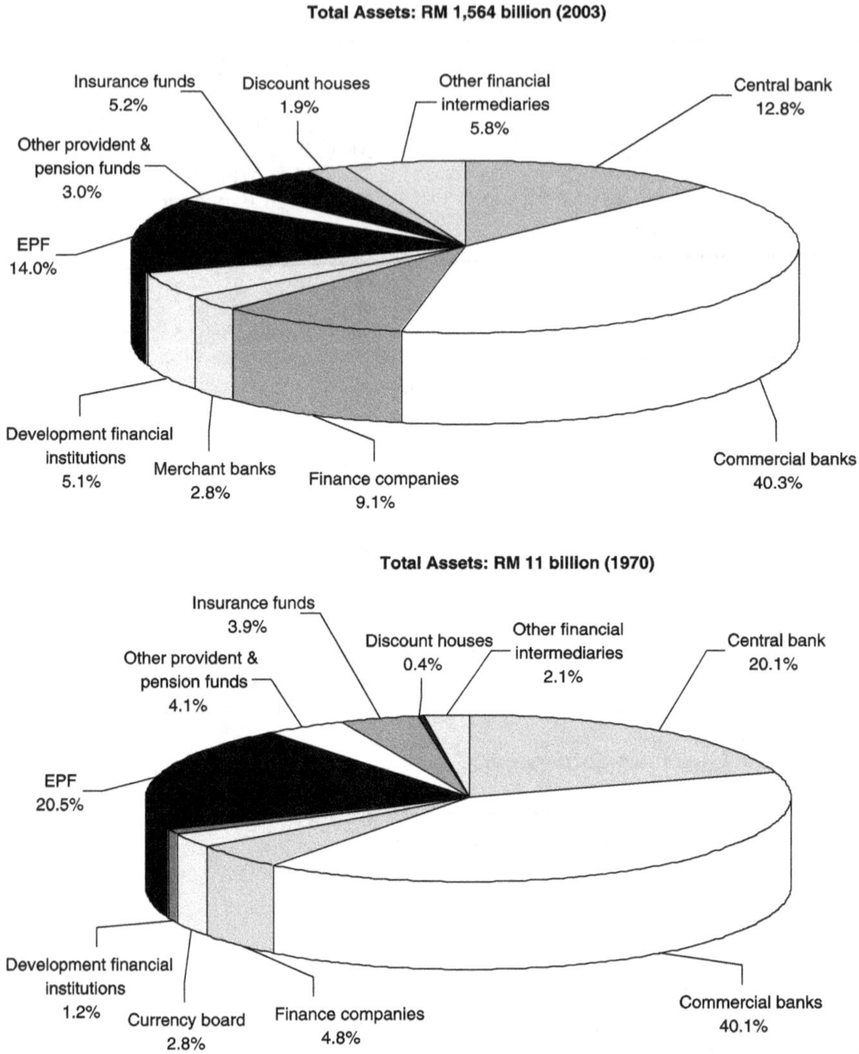


*Figure 3.3* Asset distribution of financial intermediaries (per cent share).

*Notes:* The Currency Board ceased functioning in November 1979. The first merchant bank was set up in 1970.

*Source:* compiled from BNM (1994, 2004).

which are governed by BNM.[8] Other smaller institutions include discount houses, the representative offices of foreign banks and offshore banks in Labuan. BNM is responsible for the regulation and supervision of the banking system. However, the offshore banks operating in the Labuan International Offshore Financial Centre come under the purview of the Labuan Offshore Financial Services Authority (LOFSA).

Growth in the banking system over the past few decades has been remarkable. Total assets of the banking system rose from RM 7 billion in 1970 to RM 1,046 billion in 2003, an average annual growth rate of 16 per cent. It appears that the increase in the size of the financial system over the last few decades is largely attributable to expansion in the banking system. This significant development in the banking system has been achieved mainly through the wider spread of bank branch networks, the acceleration of credit growth, and the proliferation of banking products and services. Close supervision by BNM is also partly responsible for this development.

### *(a) Bank Negara Malaysia (BNM)*

BNM was set up in 1959 to oversee the operation of the financial sector. It plays an important role in stimulating growth of the financial sector and stabilizing the economy with respect to curbing inflation and combating recession. It is also responsible for the formulation and implementation of monetary and credit policies to achieve financial and economic objectives. The progress of BNM can be assessed in terms of its assets, which increased from RM 151 million in 1959 to RM 12,994 million in 1980, and RM 323,028 million in 2005.

The key objectives of BNM are to:

- issue currency and keep the reserves that safeguard its value;
- act as banker and financial adviser to government;
- promote monetary stability and a sound financial structure; and
- influence the credit situation to the advantage of Malaysia.

These objectives are, by and large, complementary. Various legislative powers have been granted to regulate and supervise the financial system, allowing BNM to meet these objectives. These include the Central Bank of Malaysia Act 1958, the Islamic Banking Act 1983, the Banking and Financial Institutions Act 1989, the Essential (Protection of Depositors) Regulations 1986, and the Insurance Act 1996. This regulatory framework empowers BNM to play a fundamental role in overseeing the financial system in Malaysia, as illustrated in Figure 3.4 (BNM, 1999).

Malaysia has historically been able to maintain price stability, with an inflation rate averaging 3.3 per cent per annum over the past four decades. A wide range of monetary instruments, including open market operations, intervention in the interbank money market, issuance of BNM papers, and variations of the statutory reserve requirement have been used to achieve the objective of maintaining price stability (BNM, 1999). Price stability is a common goal pursued in most economies because it provides a platform towards sustained economic growth. Without price stability, the functions of resource mobilization and efficient allocation of resources would be retarded.

A high level of central bank independence is generally associated with a

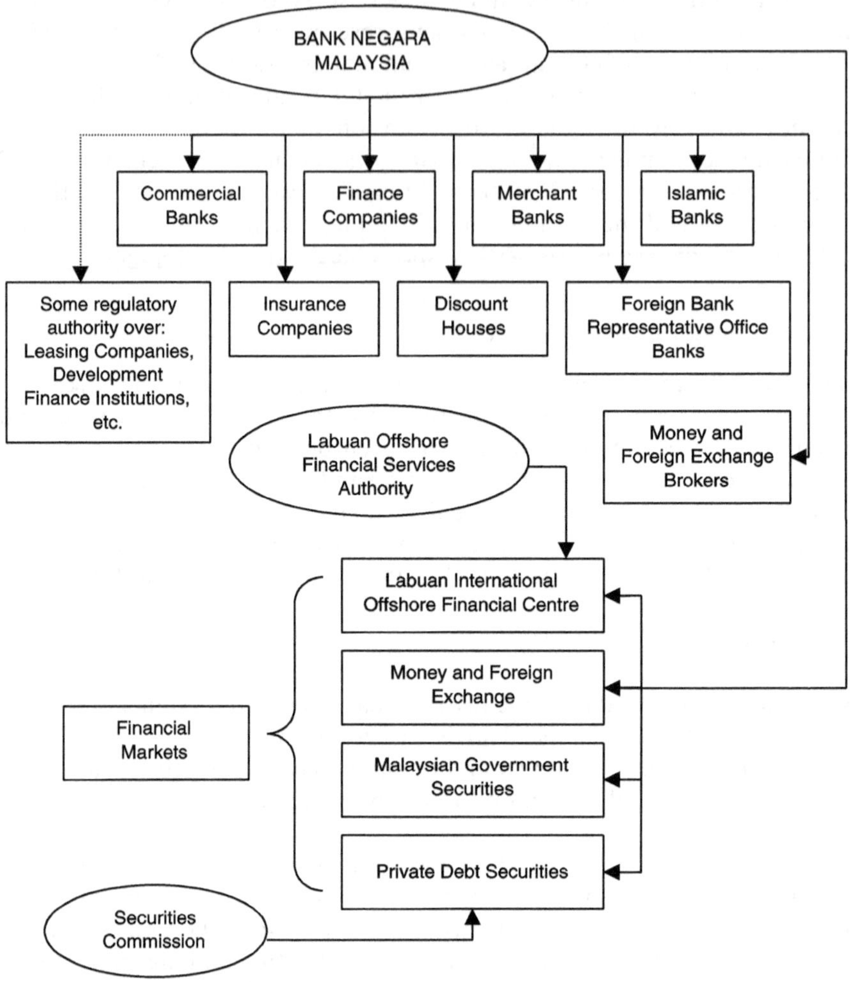


*Figure 3.4* Financial institutions and markets regulated by BNM.

*Source:* adapted from BNM (1999).

central bank's ability to achieve the objective of price stability. In an influential study, Cukierman (1992) develops broad-based measures of central bank independence by using several legal proxies to characterize independence. A composite index is used to rank central banks by their degree of independence. Independence in this context is defined as a central bank's ability to achieve price stability, even at the expense of other short-term objectives. The degree of central bank independence is of significant interest since it influences the rates of credit growth, inflation and fiscal conditions (Cukierman, Webb and Neyapti, 1992). The index of legal aspects of central bank independence for selected Asian countries is summarized in Table 3.3. In the compilation of the

*Table 3.3* Ranking of central banks for selected Asian countries

| *Country* | *Overall legal independence* | *Ranking* |
|---|---|---|
| Philippines | 0.42 | 21 |
| Malaysia | 0.34 | 33 |
| India | 0.33 | 35 |
| Indonesia | 0.32 | 36 |
| China | 0.29 | 41 |
| Singapore | 0.27 | 47 |
| Thailand | 0.26 | 50 |
| Korea | 0.23 | 56 |
| Pakistan | 0.19 | 60 |
| Japan | 0.16 | 64 |

*Source:* compiled from Cukierman (1992, p. 381).

*Notes:* the range of overall legal independence is from zero (minimum independence) to one (maximum independence).

legal independence index for 68 developed and developing countries by Cukierman (1992), the ranking ranges from a minimum of 0.10 for Poland to a maximum of 0.68 for Switzerland during the period 1980–89. It is evident that Malaysia fares reasonably well in terms of central bank legal independence among Asian countries.

In terms of relations with international organizations, BNM has maintained an active role in international financial matters. BNM has established a tradition of regional cooperation through the Conference of Governors of South-East Asian Central Banks and the Conference of South-East Asia, New Zealand and Australia Central Banks and Monetary Authorities. BNM also maintains close working relationships with international financial institutions, such as the International Monetary Fund (IMF), The World Bank, the Asian Development Bank (ADB), the Islamic Development Bank (IDB), the World Trade Organization (WTO) and the Bank for International Settlements (BIS) (BNM, 1999).

### *(b) Banking institutions*

The banking industry consists mainly of three institutions: commercial banks, finance companies and merchant banks, with total assets of RM 8,480 million, RM 1,184 million and RM 123 million, respectively, as of 1973. Until the 1970s, the banking sector was largely dominated by foreign banks (Aziz, 1984). Domestic banks have since become more influential. While commercial banks play a dominant role in the mobilization of saving, the roles of finance companies and merchant banks have become increasingly important over time due to the need for different financial services. In 2003, the total assets of these three major banking institutions recorded dramatic increases to RM 629,975 million, RM 141,911 million and RM 44,104 million, respectively, with an average annual growth rate of 16 per cent, 18 per cent and 26 per cent, respectively, since 1973.

Domestic commercial banks are key players in the banking system. They are the largest providers of funds with total loans amounting to more than RM 600 billion at the end of 2003. There were 23 commercial banks operating in the economy with a network of 1,684 branches (BNM, 2004). Finance companies are the second largest group of deposit-taking institutions. They specialize mainly in hire-purchase finance, leasing finance, housing loans, car loans, and secured personal loans. At the end of 1997, there were 39 finance companies with a total of 1,144 branches. However, following the undertaking of the merger programme, the number of finance companies had shrunk significantly at the end of 2003 to only 11 companies with a total of 729 branches. Total loans issued by finance companies amounted to more than RM 100 billion at the end of 2003. As the Malaysian economy prospers, the country's banking needs have become more sophisticated. This has led to the emergence of merchant banks to complement the financial products and services provided by commercial banks and finance companies. They play an important role in providing corporate finance services, management consultancy services, and investment management advisory services. There were 10 merchant banks at the end of 2003, and all were domestically controlled.

### *(c) Islamic banking*

One distinctive feature of the Malaysian financial system is the presence and promotion of Islamic banking, which has become an increasingly important component of the financial structure. Malaysia is the pioneer of the dual banking system, where Islamic banking operates in parallel with conventional banking. Malaysia is also the only country that has an Islamic interbank money market (Kader and Hashim, 2005).

The introduction of Islamic Banking in 1983, following the enactment of the Islamic Banking Act 1983, was an important development in the evolution of the banking system in Malaysia. During that year, Bank Islam Malaysia Berhad (BIMB) was established as the first Islamic bank under the legislation. It had a paid up capital of RM 80 million and a branch in Kuala Lumpur. The bank was created for Malaysian Muslims who wanted the services of a modern banking system but did not want to pay or receive interest, which is forbidden by their religion.[9] As with other banking institutions, BIMB is supervised and regulated by BNM. BIMB carries out conventional banking services based on Islamic principles. For example, saving and current deposits are offered under the concept of *Al-Wadiah* (guaranteed custody) and investment deposits are offered based on the principle of *Al-Mudharabah* (profit sharing).

The bank was listed on the main board of the Kuala Lumpur Stock Exchange (KLSE) in 1992. In 1999, the total assets of the bank were RM

7.1 billion, with a network of 80 branches throughout the country. Islamic banking activity has experienced rapid growth in recent years. In 2003, the Islamic banking system was represented by 33 Islamic banking institutions, comprising two Islamic banks and 31 conventional banking institutions (nine commercial banks, four foreign banks, seven finance companies, four merchant banks and seven discount houses), offering a wide range of Islamic banking products and services under the Islamic Banking Scheme. It accounted for about 10 per cent of the total assets of the banking system in 2003, representing a 2.8 percentage point increase from 2000 (BNM, 2004). Rapid expansion of the Islamic banking sector has been fostered by the introduction of a variety of Islamic financial products and the promotion of Kuala Lumpur as a regional Islamic financial centre.

With the launching of the Financial Sector Master Plan (FSMP) in 2001, in which clear strategies to develop the Islamic financial system have been set out, the government is committed to expanding the Islamic banking system. The plan explicitly sets a target for Islamic banking to capture at least 20 per cent of the banking market share by 2010 (Kader and Hashim, 2005). In addition, the Islamic Financial Services Board (IFSB) was established in 2002 to promote the development of Islamic banking. Its objective was to develop international prudential regulatory standards in accordance with the distinct features and risks of Islamic financial institutions. Since its inception, the IFSB has attracted wide participation. At the end of 2003, the number of IFSB members had increased to 13 full members, three associate members and 20 observer members (BNM, 2004). As part of the efforts to promote Malaysia as an International Islamic Financial Centre, BNM issued a sizeable amount of RM 400 million of Sukuk Islamic bond in 2006.

### *3.6.2 Non-bank financial intermediaries*

Non-bank financial intermediaries include provident and pension funds, insurance companies, saving institutions, development finance institutions, unit trusts, Credit Guarantee Corporation, leasing companies, etc. Of these, provident and pension funds, and insurance companies are the largest intermediaries as measured by their asset bases. They are supervised by various government departments and agencies. The insurance companies are under the supervision of BNM.

The provident and pension funds are a group of financial intermediaries designed to provide members and their families with a measure of social security and welfare. The key provident and pension funds operating in Malaysia are the Employees Provident Fund (EPF), the Social Security Organization (SOCSO), the Armed Forces Fund and the Teachers Provident Fund (Aziz, 1984). The EPF is the largest amongst the provident and pension funds in the country. It accounted for about 83 per cent of the total resources of provident and pension funds at the end of 2003 (BNM, 2004). The growth of other private provident funds and insurance funds has been rather limited due to the dominance of this forced saving scheme. This is because individuals are left with less savings after contributing to the EPF.

### *(a) The Employees Provident Fund (EPF)*

The presence of the EPF marks an important feature of the Malaysian financial system. This statutory fund was established under the Employees' Provident Fund Ordinance 1951, with the objective of providing members with a retirement plan. Since its inception, the EPF has been a very powerful vehicle in mobilizing compulsory savings. It is important for the government to maintain an effective EPF, since the fund is instrumental in generating resources to finance public investment projects at low cost (Gillam, 1982; Tracy, 1995). Hence, such an institutional investor provides long-term funding, which is influential in ensuring the long-term success of Malaysia.

The EPF is a publicly managed pension fund that operates under a fully funded pay-as-you-earn (PAYE) scheme with a defined contribution plan. Contributors get back their contributions plus accumulated returns at the point of retirement. The pension benefits take the form of one lump sum payment or a series of periodic payments. The government does not contribute, unless it is an employer. Some partial withdrawals are allowed for education, housing and medical expenses before contributors reach the retirement age of 55.

Under this scheme, both employees and employers are required to contribute to the provident fund to help provide for employees retirement benefits. In 1975, the statutory rate of contribution was raised from 10 per cent (5 per cent from the employer and 5 per cent from the employee) of the employees' monthly salary to 13 per cent (7 per cent from the employer and 6 per cent from the employee). In 1980, the rate was increased to 20 per cent (9 per cent from the employer and 11 per cent from the employee). Currently, the scheme requires a mandatory contribution of 12 per cent of an employee's income by the employer and 11 per cent by the employee.

The fund is managed by the Employees' Provident Fund Board. The investment policy of the EPF is determined by the EPF Board in accordance with the provisions of the EPF Ordinance 1951, the Trustee Act 1949 and the Trustee Investment Act 1965. Permission must be sought from the Ministry of Finance for investment overseas. Apart from the retirement benefits, members are permitted to withdraw a portion of their EPF contributions for the acquisition of housing, subject to certain conditions. The last few decades saw an upward trend in the dividend rate paid by the EPF prior to the Asian financial crisis. It increased steadily from 2.5 per cent in the 1950s to a high of 8.5 per cent per annum in the 1980s (Merican, 1992). However, after the crisis, the rate declined to 6 per cent in 2000 and just 4.5 per cent in 2003. Nevertheless, these returns were still generally higher than the 12-month fixed deposits rate of commercial banks.

The coverage of the programme is extensive. Almost all formal sector employees are covered by the programme, except for those on government pensions and those contributing to the Armed Forces Provident Fund (Merican, 1992). As a result of the improvement in coverage and an increase in the labour force, the fund has grown significantly in size over the years. Its total accumulated contributions increased from RM 594 million in 1960 to RM 209,380 million in 2005, growing at an average annual rate of 14 per cent. Its importance is also reflected in the number of its members, increasing from 1.1 million to 11.1 million during the same period (see Table 3.4). Its assets in the financial system rose from RM 2 billion in 1970 to RM 265 billion in 2005 (see Figure 3.3).

In many developed economies, savings in the private sector are channelled into private provident funds and insurance companies. Most of these funds are then invested in equities, and the balance in government and corporate bonds. However, in Malaysia, a substantial portion of private savings are formed by compulsory contributions to the EPF. These funds are invested mostly in government securities (Merican, 1992; Queisser, 1999). The EPF was required to hold more than 70 per cent of government securities before the rule was relaxed in the 1990s, acting as a lender of the federal government. It has also been used as a non-inflationary tool to finance government budget deficits. However, as shown in Table 3.4 the share of total investment in government securities has decreased gradually over the years due largely to the government's effort in promoting the private sector and reducing fiscal deficits. The greater emphasis on various market instruments, such as Negotiable Certificates of Deposit (NCD), fixed deposits, foreign securities, etc., has also contributed to this development.

### *(b) Insurance*

One aspect of a country's financial system often neglected in discussion of finance and development is the element of risk and its effect on the economy.

*Table 3.4* The Employee Provident Fund (EPF)

| *Year* | *Amount contributed (RM million)* | *Total accumulated contributions (RM million)* | *No. of contributors (million)* | *Total Investment (At book value RM million)* | *Malaysian Government Securities, MGS (RM million)* | *MGS in total investment (%)* |
|---|---|---|---|---|---|---|
| 1960 | 85 | 594 | 1.1 | 619 | 558 | 90.1 |
| 1970 | 207 | 2,149 | 2.1 | 2,218 | 2,062 | 93.0 |
| 1980 | 1,068 | 9,129 | 3.8 | 9,261 | 8,582 | 92.7 |
| 1990 | 4,139 | 46,179 | 5.9 | 45,642 | 36,129 | 79.2 |
| 2000 | 20,954 | 167,485 | 9.8 | 179,047 | 61,766 | 34.5 |
| 2005 | 26,280 | 209,380 | 11.1 | 265,210 | 97,768 | 36.9 |

*Sources:* compiled from BNM (1994) and BNM (various issues) *Monthly Statistical Bulletin*.

Insurance is not only a means for diversifying risks, it is also potentially an effective tool for mobilizing saving. Until the 1970s, the insurance industry was dominated by foreign companies. Since then, domestic insurance companies took over the role and began to provide an important source of funds for development of the economy.

Total assets of life insurance funds increased from RM 111 million in 1962 to RM 60,195 million in 2003, representing an average annual growth rate of 13 per cent. The combined premium income of the life and general insurers registered an annual growth of 18 per cent over the period 1989–99 to reach RM 10,857 million. The insurance products offered have also become increasingly more sophisticated to serve the diversified needs of consumers (BNM, 1999). The last decade has also witnessed an impressive development of Islamic insurance business in Malaysia.

### *3.6.3 Money and foreign exchange markets*

The money market provides an avenue to channel short-term funds with maturities usually less than 12 months. It provides liquid funds for market participants who face temporary shortages of funding and serves as an investment outlet for those with temporary surplus funds. The openness of BNM's policy since the 1980s has resulted in little intervention in the Malaysian money market (Lin and Chung, 1995). The money market instruments mainly include deposits and short-term securities (e.g. bankers acceptances, NCD, treasury bills, Cagamas notes). The key players in the money market are commercial banks, merchant banks, discount houses, and other eligible finance companies. Thus, development in the financial system and money market are closely related.

The foreign exchange market is a wholesale interbank market for the sale and purchase of foreign currencies. It provides a facility for the trading of foreign currencies, which can be conducted through the spot market or the forward and swap markets. The key participants in the foreign exchange market are commercial banks and some designated merchant banks. The Kuala Lumpur Foreign Exchange market has long been dominated by transactions in US dollars against the ringgit. However, in recent years there has been a significant increase in the share of euro and yen transactions against the US dollars (BNM, 2004).

### *3.6.4 Capital markets*

Capital markets are the markets for longer-term financial assets. They include a primary securities market, which offers the issues of government and corporate securities for sale, and a secondary securities market, which offers the trading of securities.

### *(a) Stock market*

Although the Malayan Stockbrokers' Association was formed in 1937, actual share trading was not done publicly until 1960 (Drake, 1969a). Capital market development in Malaysia was initiated in 1960, with trading in Kuala Lumpur of stocks and bonds that were also listed in Singapore (double listing). Stock exchange activities have operated in Malaya and Singapore since the late nineteenth century, facilitating the trading of shares for companies incorporated locally or abroad. In 1973, the combined stock exchange for Malaysia and Singapore was reconstituted as the Kuala Lumpur Stock Exchange (KLSE) and the Stock Exchange of Singapore (SES), respectively. Listed companies could continue to be traded on both markets if they wished. At the end of 1982, there were 261 firms listed in the KLSE with a total nominal paid-up capital of RM 9,177 million (Lee, 1986).

In 1989, all Malaysian companies were delisted from the SES. Following this, the 'over-the-counter' market, Central Limit Order Book (CLOB), was established by the Singapore government to facilitate the trading of shares from Hong Kong, Thailand, Australia and Malaysia. In 1998, more than 100 Malaysian companies were traded on the SES on an unlisted basis through the CLOB computer-based trading system (Lau and McInish, 2002). However, the trading of CLOB was discontinued in September 1998, following the outbreak of the Asian financial crisis.

Malaysian policy makers have put much effort into developing the stock market to reduce reliance on the banking sector and diversify the sources of finance. Since the late 1980s, the stock market in Malaysia has undergone robust development and has gradually evolved to be one of the fastest growing markets in the region. During the period 1988–96, the KLSE experienced significant expansion with market capitalization rising from RM 98.7 billion in 1988 to RM 806.8 billion in 1996, before declining to RM 374.5 billion in 1998, following the Asian financial crisis. Nevertheless, the market rebounded to RM 640.3 billion in 2003. The number of companies listed on the KLSE increased from 295 to more than 900 over the period 1988–2003 (BNM, 2004).

Although the stock market was severely affected during the crisis, private enterprises benefited significantly from the availability of cheap finance through the issuance of initial public offerings and new shares. Funds raised in capital markets have increased steadily over the last few decades, reflecting a growing demand for long-term funds for both the public and private sectors (see Table 3.5). Funds can also be raised through the Kuala Lumpur Stock Exchange (KLSE) and the Malaysian Exchange of Securities Dealing and Automated Quotation (MESDAQ), which are secondary markets. The KLSE is the largest segment in capital markets whereas the MESDAQ is a separate market established in 1997 for small, high-growth potential and high-technology companies. The average annual funds raised from the stock market over the period 1971–2005 accounted for about 25 per cent of total

*Table 3.5* Average funds raised in capital markets (RM million)

| *Year* | *Public net issues of debt securities* | *Private new issues of shares/warrants* | *Private net issues of debt securities* | *Total* |
|---|---|---|---|---|
| 1971–1980 | 1,323 | 91 | 8 | 1,422 |
| 1981–1990 | 4,629 | 1,907 | 684 | 7,220 |
| 1991–1996 | 1,490 | 8,834 | 15,624 | 25,949 |
| 1997–2005 | 13,165 | 8,026 | 21,958 | 43,148 |
| 1971–2005 | 5,341 | 4,149 | 8,522 | 18,013 |

*Sources:* compiled from BNM (1994) and BNM (various issues) *Monthly Statistical Bulletin.*

*Table 3.6* Comparative stock market indicators for selected Asian countries

| *Country/ Region* | *Stock market capitalization to GDP* | | | | *Stock market turnover ratio* | | | |
|---|---|---|---|---|---|---|---|---|
| | *1980* | *1990* | *1996* | *2002* | *1980* | *1990* | *1996* | *2002* |
| **Malaysia** | 40.7 | 99.7 | 264.7 | 128.8 | 25.8 | 24.7 | 65.0 | 22.6 |
| **Southeast Asia** | | | | | | | | |
| Indonesia | 0.1 | 4.5 | 34.9 | 16.5 | 18.6 | 77.2 | 40.3 | 45.4 |
| Philippines | 9.1 | 18.9 | 85.3 | 53.4 | 21.0 | 14.0 | 36.1 | 7.6 |
| Singapore | – | 95.8 | 162.5 | 125.0 | – | 57.4 | 28.5 | 50.8 |
| Thailand | 4.1 | 29.1 | 67.0 | 33.1 | 23.1 | 91.9 | 36.4 | 113.7 |
| **East Asia** | | | | | | | | |
| China | – | – | 9.5 | 39.2 | – | – | 327.2 | 67.0 |
| Hong Kong | 107.0 | 107.2 | 241.0 | 302.1 | 11.7 | 42.8 | 44.1 | 43.2 |
| Japan | 29.8 | 121.2 | 72.3 | 55.2 | 50.2 | 43.3 | 36.8 | 71.4 |
| South Korea | 7.1 | 49.9 | 29.2 | 43.0 | 42.4 | 59.9 | 109.0 | 336.6 |
| Taiwan | 13.5 | 107.3 | 82.6 | 98.9 | 80.0 | 419.7 | 203.4 | 225.3 |
| **South Asia** | | | | | | | | |
| Bangladesh | – | 1.3 | 7.2 | 2.4 | – | 1.4 | 24.6 | 57.4 |
| India | 3.4 | 10.1 | 32.5 | 23.5 | 46.3 | 66.8 | 76.4 | 164.9 |
| Pakistan | 3.1 | 6.7 | 17.4 | 12.3 | – | 8.7 | 59.1 | 345.8 |
| Sri Lanka | – | 8.2 | 14.0 | 9.1 | – | 5.9 | 6.9 | 21.2 |

*Source:* compiled from WDI (2005).

funds sourced from capital markets. A majority of the funds raised in capital markets were used to finance private sector development. This is in line with the government's objective of promoting the private sector as the key engine of growth.

The comparative statistics presented in Table 3.6 highlight the position of Malaysia among the Asian countries. In terms of the extent of stock market development, which can be measured by stock market capitalization to GDP, Malaysia topped the ranking in 1996 before the Asian financial crisis. However, it is not clear whether this was a sign of strength or vulnerability. The stock market turnover ratio, which measures the liquidity of the stock markets, also shows that the Malaysian stock market performed favourably in comparison with other Asian stock markets in the same year.

### *(b) Bond market*

In contrast to the stock market, the bond market provides an opportunity for the private and public sectors to raise funds through the issuance of private and public debt securities, respectively. It comprises mainly the government securities market and the private debt securities market. Listed bonds are traded in the KLSE whereas unlisted bonds are traded through the over-the-counter (OTC) market.

The bond market has traditionally been dominated by the government securities market. Until the second half of the 1980s, there was virtually no private debt securities market in Malaysia. The Malaysian government securities (MGS) market is the largest component of the bond market. In terms of the amount of funds raised, the size of this component is subject to the fiscal condition of the government. For instance, between 1980 and 1982 when budget deficits were large, the size of the government debt grew rapidly. Most MGS bonds are held by social security institutions and the banking system. The EPF, which is the largest pension saving funds in Malaysia, has been the principal investor in MGS (Lin and Chung, 1995).

From the mid-1980s, the need to develop the market became quite clear, given the intention of the government to reduce public expenditure. Thus, in line with the policy to promote the private sector as the key engine of growth in the economy during the 1980s, the private debt securities market was set up to complement the government securities and equity market. The first move to achieve this objective was the setting up of Cagamas Berhad in 1986, the first national mortgage corporation. Its role was to buy housing loans and restructure these loans into fixed rate bonds (Yusof, 1992).

In addition, BNM published new guidelines on the issue of private debt securities (PDS) in 1988, aimed at encouraging firms to raise funds through this channel. Since the mid-1990s, the government has strongly encouraged private and public entities to issue bonds as an alternative to raise finance. During the post-crisis period, significant funds were raised by the public sector to finance expenditure on massive infrastructure projects to stimulate economic recovery (see Table 3.5). Another major step taken was the incorporation of the Rating Agency of Malaysia Berhad (RAM) in 1990, providing the function of rating all issues of bonds and commercial papers and disseminating timely information to all potential investors.

Although the bond market in Malaysia is still relatively immature and requires further development, its performance has been impressive in terms of the increase in asset base. The size of its market increased from RM 49.7 billion at the end of 1987 to RM 165.7 billion at the end of 1999, growing at an average annual rate of about 10 per cent. The increasing size of the Islamic bond market has also contributed to development of the bond market. The PDS market has since emerged as an important segment in the bond market, accounting for 27 per cent of the total assets in 1999.

Table 3.7 shows the relative level of development of the bond markets in Asia. It is clear that the private bond market performs better than the public bond market in Malaysia. Development of the private bond market, as measured by the ratio of market capitalization to GDP, has increased from just 14.5 per cent in 1990 to 53.5 per cent in 2002. However, development of the public bond market seems to show a declining trend over the years, which is consistent with the analysis presented earlier. In terms of the level of development relative to other Asian countries, Malaysia fared relatively well in the development of its private bond market. In 2002, Malaysia appeared to have had the highest level of private bond market development compared with other Asian countries. Turning to the public sector, Malaysia had the highest public bond market development in 1990 among Asian countries. However, this level of development has diminished over time. In 2002, the public bond market development was ahead of the Philippines, Thailand, China, Hong Kong, South Korea, Taiwan and India, but behind Singapore and Japan.

In sum, there seems to be less development in Malaysian capital markets in relation to other components in the financial system. Nevertheless, consistent with its national economic policies that view the financial sector as the facilitator of economic growth, the Malaysian government is committed to providing the necessary support for creation of an efficient capital market in order to foster a favourable investment climate for both domestic

*Table 3.7* Comparative bond market indicators for selected Asian countries

| *Country/ Region* | *Private bond market capitalization to GDP (%)* | | | *Public bond market capitalization to GDP (%)* | | |
|---|---|---|---|---|---|---|
| | *1990* | *1996* | *2002* | *1990* | *1996* | *2002* |
| **Malaysia** | 14.5 | 36.2 | 53.5 | 55.3 | 31.2 | 35.0 |
| **Southeast Asia** | | | | | | |
| Philippines | – | – | 0.1 | 22.1 | 32.8 | 26.7 |
| Singapore | 15.7 | 10.7 | 23.5 | 12.2 | 15.1 | 35.5 |
| Thailand | 6.5 | 8.9 | 14.3 | 3.2 | 0.7 | 18.7 |
| **East Asia** | | | | | | |
| China | 4.7 | 3.8 | 9.9 | 3.9 | 5.6 | 17.6 |
| Hong Kong | 0.3 | 12.2 | 18.4 | 1.3 | 6.2 | 9.2 |
| Japan | 40.1 | 45.2 | 46.3 | 45.4 | 52.1 | 102.9 |
| South Korea | 26.3 | 34.3 | 46.0 | 8.1 | 7.7 | 15.9 |
| Taiwan | 14.0 | 19.6 | 25.3 | 3.0 | 12.0 | 22.0 |
| **South Asia** | | | | | | |
| India | 0.3 | 1.1 | 0.4 | 19.6 | 18.7 | 27.8 |

*Source:* compiled from the World Bank's Financial Structure Database.

entrepreneurs and foreign investors. This was reflected in the 10-year Capital Market Master Plan (CMP) published in February 2001. The key objectives of the plan were to improve liquidity, ease fund raising, reduce transaction costs, and develop a broader stock market and bond market (BNM, 2004).

### *3.6.5 Derivatives markets*

Derivatives include forwards, futures, options and swaps. The trading of derivatives in Malaysia began with the establishment of the Kuala Lumpur Commodity Exchange (KLCE) in 1980. In 1995, financial futures emerged in the market following the introduction of the Kuala Lumpur Stock Exchange Composite Index Futures (FKLI) on the Kuala Lumpur Options and Financial Futures Exchange (KLOFFE), and the 3-month Kuala Lumpur Interbank Offered Rate Futures on the Commodity and Monetary Exchange (COMMEX) in 1996. Although KLOFFE and COMMEX are allowed to operate on a self-regulatory basis, these markets are supervised by the Securities Commission, which was set-up in 1993 as the market watchdog to oversee the regulation and supervision of the securities industry (Hussein, 1994).

### *3.6.6 Offshore financial market*

The offshore financial market in Malaysia was set up following the establishment of the Labuan International Offshore Financial Centre (IOFC) in 1990, with the aim of promoting Malaysia as a regional financial centre. The Labuan IOFC is regulated under the Labuan Financial Services Authority Act 1996. It is an integrated financial offshore centre, which seeks to provide a wide range of offshore financial products and services to customers worldwide, particularly those in Asia. These include banking services, insurance activities, trust business, capital market activities, Islamic finance, etc. At the end of 1999, more than 2,100 offshore and supporting companies had been set up. There were 63 offshore banks, 50 insurance-related companies, 20 trust companies, seven offshore leasing companies, and six fund managers operating in Labuan (BNM, 1999).

### *3.6.7 Bank-based or market-based?*

Financial systems can be broadly classified into bank-dominated (German–Japanese model) and capital market-dominated systems (Anglo-Saxon model).[10] One of the key features of the Malaysian financial system is the presence of a large number of small and medium-sized firms. In most private firms, families still retain significant control of management, which is a phenomenon not very common in an advanced financial system (Claessens *et al.*, 1999).

Another feature is the limited development in the Malaysian capital markets over the last 30 years. A majority of the companies in Malaysia are not listed and hence the more plausible source of finance is from banks rather than from financial markets. The market concentration ratio is rather high for Malaysia, compared with other more advanced financial markets, as market capitalization is highly concentrated in the hands of the ten largest firms. As Kohsaka (2004) maintains, development of the financial systems in the East Asian economies (including Malaysia) has mainly been supported by financial intermediation through commercial banks and other financial intermediaries rather than by bonds and equities through capital markets. Although the ratio of stock market capitalization to GDP has been relatively high over the years (see Table 3.6), the composition diagram illustrated in Figure 3.5 clearly highlights that a majority of funds raised by the private sector are from the banking sector. On these grounds, the Malaysian financial system can be described as a bank-based system rather than a capital market-based system.

## 3.7 Trends and patterns of savings

Economic growth is sustainable only if domestic resources can be mobilized efficiently and transformed into productive uses. Therefore, mobilization of saving is an important vehicle for capital formation, and hence economic development. Historically, Malaysia has been able to maintain a high saving record. Over the past four decades, the country has saved an average of 25.5 per cent of GDP. In 2003, Malaysia became one of the top savers in

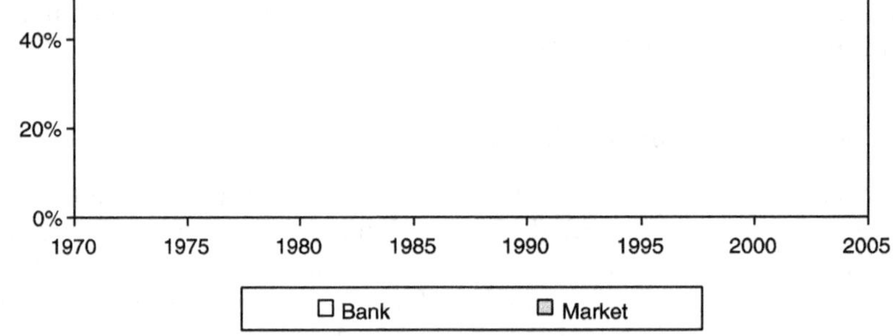


*Figure 3.5* Composition of funds raised by the private sector, 1970–2005.

*Notes:* 'Bank' = domestic bank lending to the private sector; 'Market' = new issues of shares and warrants plus new issues of debt securities.

*Sources:* compiled from BNM (1994) and BNM (various issues) *Monthly Statistical Bulletin*.

the world, after China and Singapore. This impressive saving record is an important contributing factor to the high growth rates achieved by Malaysia.

### *3.7.1 The role of government*

The government has consistently promoted high saving as part of national development policy. Over the past four decades, various measures have been taken to promote saving, as outlined below:

- The Insurance Act enacted in 1963 subjected all life insurance companies to a set of comprehensive legislation, aimed at enhancing the sound operation of insurance business. Under this legislation, insurance companies were required to back up their liabilities with a minimum of 55 per cent (Lee, 1971). Since then, investment in life insurance products has largely been encouraged by the government as a method to save for retirement. In 2003, the annual premium income was equal to 5.1 per cent of GNP, signifying the effectiveness of the government efforts (BNM, 2004).
- Malaysia has a relatively well-developed banking system, comprising commercial banks, finance companies, merchant banks, and other smaller banking institutions. Of these, commercial banks are the most crucial deposit-taking institutions. These banking institutions have served as an effective vehicle for deposit mobilization in the past few decades. Another important development during this period was the establishment of Post Office Savings Bank (POSB) in 1948. The Bank was later restructured and renamed as the National Savings Bank in 1974. POSB was set up to provide adequate banking facilities and promote saving, particularly among small savers in both urban and rural areas. A large number of bank branches ensure basic banking facilities reach the majority of the general public. In addition, the Agriculture Bank of Malaysia was set up in 1969 to provide credit to the rural sector. Its ability in mobilizing resources in rural areas has led to substantial credit expansion in the rural areas and enabled agricultural activities to be carried out effectively.
- Promoting saving by way of education has always been a very effective tool. In the past, various ad hoc saving schemes, such as the *Amanah Saham National* in 1979, the *Amanah Saham Bumiputra* in 1991, the National Saving Campaign in 1996, and the *Amanah Saham Vision 2020* in 1996, have been provided by the government with the key objective of expanding saving. The implementation of these schemes has promoted the virtues of thrift and the saving habit in the Malaysian community. This may have largely mobilized domestic private saving in the economy.
- With respect to the institutional setting, the mandatory contribution of the labour force to the Employees Provident Funds (EPF) is an important factor in accounting for this high saving record. The EPF, set up in 1951

to serve as a nationwide old age retirement scheme for employees, is the largest compulsory saving institution operating in Malaysia. The resources of the EPF have mostly been invested within Malaysia, particularly in the public sector. This provides substantial resources to finance economic development. Its importance is reflected by the size of the annual EPF contribution, which made up 6.1 per cent of GNP in 2003 (BNM, 2004).

Given the above, it appears that one common explanation for the high saving rate observed in Malaysia has been the presence of an effective forced saving policy in the form of a broad based EPF scheme. Thus, in order to shed some light on the behaviour of private saving, the separation of provident fund contributions from private saving is necessary, since the proportion of compulsory saving is determined by government policy. As shown in Figure 3.6, the share of EPF contribution in private saving has persistently increased over time. Thus, the saving function in Chapter 6 is estimated for two saving variables, i.e. private saving and private saving net of annual EPF contributions.

### *3.7.2 Composition of saving*

From Table 3.8, it can be seen that Malaysia's GDP growth was mainly attributable to the increase in saving from the private sector, most notably in

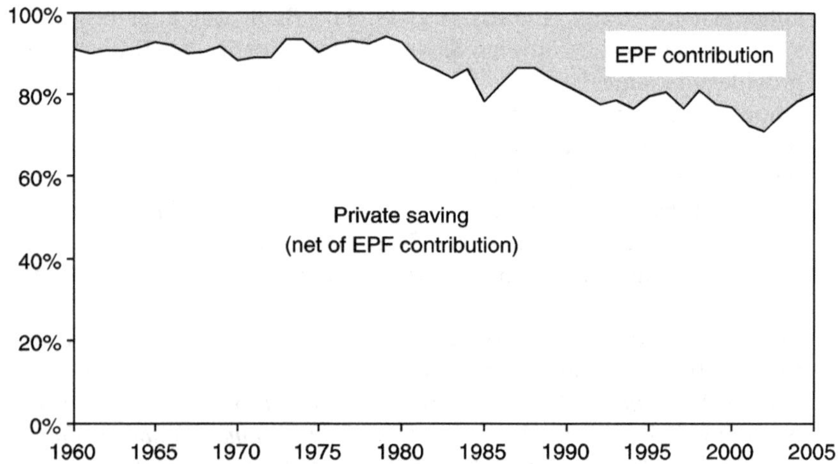


*Figure 3.6* Composition of private saving and EPF.

*Notes:* Public saving refers to total public sector current surpluses/deficits, which can be defined as government revenue minus operating expenditure, plus non-financial public enterprise surplus. Private saving equals to gross national saving minus public saving.

*Sources:* compiled from BNM (1994) BNM (various issues) *Annual Report* and *Monthly Statistical Bulletin* and Ministry of Finance Malaysia (various issues) *Economic Report*.

*Table 3.8* Contribution of saving to GDP increment (%)

| | *1961–70* | *1971–80* | *1981–90* | *1991–96* | *1997–05* |
|---|---|---|---|---|---|
| Private saving | 13.2 | 29.6 | 9.7 | 27.0 | 28.1 |
| Public saving | 3.7 | 3.1 | 22.4 | 19.5 | 4.7 |
| Total | 16.8 | 32.7 | 32.2 | 46.5 | 32.8 |

*Sources:* compiled from BNM (1994), BNM (various issues) *Monthly Statistical Bulletin* and Ministry of Finance Malaysia (various issues) *Economic Report*.

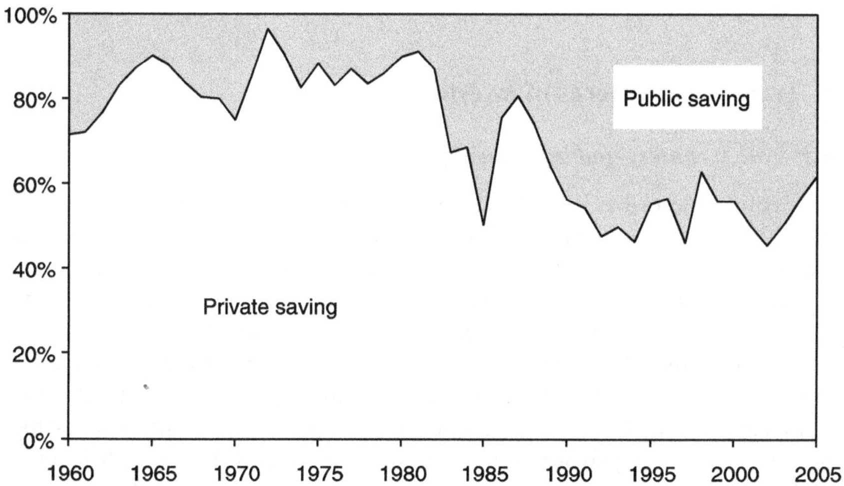


*Figure 3.7* Composition of saving in Malaysia: 1960–2005.

*Sources:* compiled from BNM (1994), BNM (various issues) *Annual Report* and *Monthly Statistical Bulletin* and Ministry of Finance Malaysia (various issues) *Economic Report*.

the 1970s and the early 1990s. The contribution of saving to output expansion from the private sector declined dramatically in the 1980s, mainly due to the global economic recession in 1985, when corporate earnings were curtailed significantly. During this period, the shrinkage in private saving was compensated by a corresponding increase in public saving. However, saving from the public sector plunged in 1998 following the Asian financial crisis.

Figure 3.7 shows the relative contribution of private and public saving to total domestic saving. Private saving accounted for more than three-quarters of total domestic saving in the 1960s. This share declined steadily over the next three decades to about 50 per cent by 2003. Since the mid-1980s, the relative contribution of public saving to total domestic saving has increased persistently.

This pattern of change highlights the importance of treating private and public saving separately in examining the determinants of domestic saving, since the analysis of total saving per se may be subject to aggregation bias. However, as Newlyn (1977) pointed out, there is no theory available for public saving given that the government can determine its own income. The public saving decision is therefore part of the tax policy, which depends on the country's capacity to tax and other policy factors that hardly change over time. The lack of an established theory for public saving prompts the assumption that public saving is exogenous. Hence, the analysis of saving behaviour in Chapter 6 is mainly concerned with the determinants of private saving. Unfortunately, a further segregation of private saving into household saving and corporate saving is not possible due to the lack of sufficient time series data.

## 3.8 Trends and patterns of investment

### *3.8.1 Policy context and investment patterns*

This section describes investment behaviour in Malaysia over the period 1960–2005. After achieving independence in 1957, the country inherited a relatively well-developed infrastructure and an efficient administrative system from the British government, which appeared to be conducive for capital formation. Given that capital formation is an important driver for sustained economic development, the Malaysian government enacted the Pioneer Industries Ordinance of 1958 to stimulate private investment. Malaysia started 1960 with a moderate level of both private and public investment, where the shares of private and public investment in GDP were 8.2 per cent and 1.9 per cent, respectively (see Figure 3.8). However, this total investment rate of 10.1 per cent was much lower than the average of lower and middle-income countries, which stood at 21.3 per cent in the same year. The total investment rate increased rapidly to about 17 per cent by the mid-1960s, prior to declining in the late 1960s due to the higher macroeconomic uncertainty triggered by the racial riots of 1969.

The government attributed the poor performance of investment activities to inadequacies of the 1958 Ordinance, and many of the weaknesses were corrected in the Investment Incentives Act of 1968. The 1970s saw a massive increase in capital formation, reaching a peak in the early 1980s. Investment rates were curtailed significantly when the global economic recession hit the country in 1985. Confronted with huge government budget deficits and current account deficits following the recession, as well as decreasing domestic and foreign investment, Malaysia began to grant attractive investment incentives to attract local and foreign investors through the Promotion of Investment Act 1986.[11]

As Figure 3.8 makes clear, the total investment rate, which consists of private and public investment rates, shows an overall increasing trend over the period 1960–84. The series declines sharply following the global economic recession in 1985. After the recession, private and public investment rates show

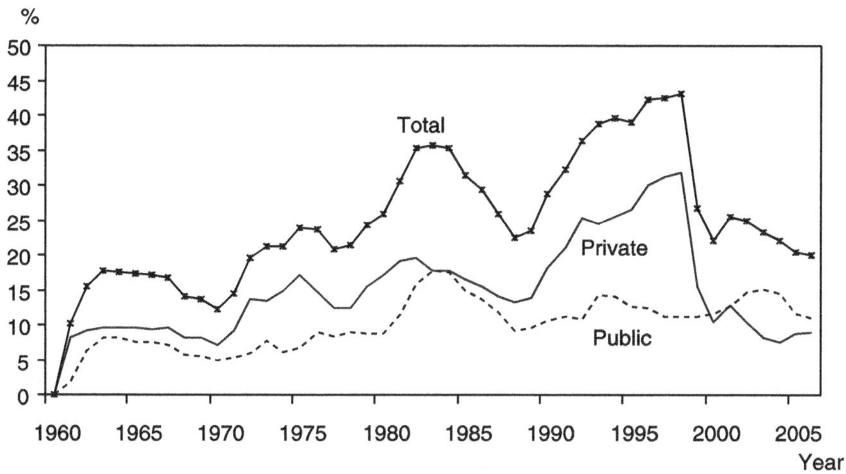


*Figure 3.8* Trends of private and public investment rates, 1960–2005.

*Notes:* Private investment rate is gross private fixed capital formation as a percentage of GDP. Public investment rate is gross public fixed capital formation as a percentage of GDP. The total investment rate is the sum of private and public investment rates.

*Sources:* compiled from BNM (1994) and BNM (various issues) *Monthly Statistical Bulletin*.

a rather different pattern of development. Private investment rate showed an upward swing in 1987, and increased at a rapid pace for a few years whereas little change was observed in public investment rate during the same period. Malaysia's impressive saving record has enabled the total investment rate to increase gradually over the years, reaching a peak in 1997, before the onset of the Asian financial crisis.

Notwithstanding these past strong records, the private investment rate declined sharply in the aftermath of the crisis. This sharp contraction in private investment resulted in a downward trend in the total investment rate. Since then, capital formation has been mainly supported by public investment and it is not clear whether this will be sustainable in the long run. Hence, understanding the patterns and behaviour of private investment is of direct interest to policy makers aiming at raising output in the long run.

### *3.8.2 Composition of investment*

Figure 3.9 reflects the shares of private and public investment in total investment. Private investment accounted for more than 80 per cent of the total in 1960. This share showed a declining trend over the next two decades before picking up again in the 1980s. On the whole, private investment dominated total investment in Malaysia prior to the 1997–98 crisis. However, as would be expected, the share of private investment declined sharply after the crisis.

From the above analysis, it appears that the behaviour of investment in

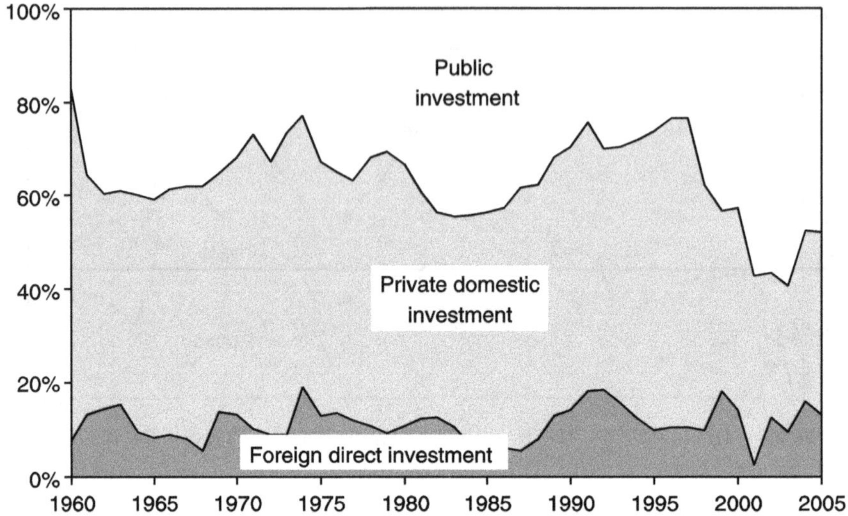


*Figure 3.9* The composition of investment 1960–2005.

*Sources:* compiled from BNM (1994) and BNM (various issues) *Monthly Statistical Bulletin.*

Malaysia is predominantly influenced by private rather than public investment (except when the latter is counter-cyclical). This suggests that in order to avoid aggregation bias, a decomposition of aggregate investment is necessary. It is important to focus on private investment in order to understand the behaviour of investment, given that public investment is primarily driven by policy objectives, which are empirically difficult to quantify and estimate.

### *3.8.3 Foreign direct investment*

FDI constitutes an important component of total investment, given that Malaysia is one of the most successful developing countries in attracting a large amount of FDI inflows. According to the inward FDI potential index (a measure of the attractiveness of the host economy to foreign investors) published by UNCTAD (2004) in 2003, Malaysia was ranked first among the Asian developing countries. The importance of FDI to domestic economic development is therefore undeniable. As pointed out by Athukorala and Menon (1995), FDI is an important contributing factor to Malaysia's growth-led industrialization.

Policy reforms, including the introduction of the Investment Incentives Act 1968, the establishment of free trade zones in the early 1970s, and the provision of export incentives, together with the acceleration of open policy in the late 1980s, all led to a surge in FDI. Apart from these policy factors, it is generally believed sound macroeconomic management, sustained economic growth, relatively low set-up costs, political stability, a sufficiently trained labour force, and a well-functioning financial system make Malaysia an attractive prospect for FDI.

Notwithstanding the importance of FDI for Malaysia, an examination of the determinants of FDI is not straightforward. This is because FDI depends upon a quite different set of determinants from that of private investment.[12] For instance, the cost of capital for FDI may depend on the cost of raising funds in the source country, rather than the host country. Foreign investors are likely to bring in their own sources of funding rather than raise funds in the host country. However, given the above considerations and the objectives of this book, the examination of what determines FDI in Malaysia is beyond the scope of this study and is therefore not pursued here.[13]

As depicted in Figure 3.9, the share of FDI in total gross domestic capital formation has not changed significantly over the period 1960–2005, averaging at about 13 per cent per year. Therefore, the inclusion of FDI in the estimation of private investment is unlikely to make much difference to the results. However, keeping the caveat in mind that FDI depends on a set of factors quite different from those captured in the standard private investment function, it is necessary to estimate for both private investment and private domestic investment, where the latter is defined as private investment net of FDI. An econometric analysis of the determinants for private investment and private domestic investment is provided in Chapter 7.

## 3.9 The saving–investment dynamics

This section looks at the development experience of Malaysia in managing the saving–investment gap to achieve sustained economic growth. Table 3.9 and Figure 3.10 show how the average rates of saving and investment interacted with the current account balance over the period 1961–2005. Gross

*Table 3.9* Saving, investment, and current account balance (% of GDP)

| *Period* | *S/Y* | *I/Y* | *CA/Y* |
|---|---|---|---|
| 1961–1965 | 20.1 | 17.1 | 3.1 |
| 1966–1970 | 19.5 | 14.9 | 4.6 |
| 1971–1975 | 23.4 | 22.1 | 1.3 |
| 1976–1980 | 32.2 | 25.4 | 6.7 |
| 1981–1985 | 31.0 | 33.6 | –2.7 |
| 1986–1990 | 35.0 | 27.4 | 7.6 |
| 1991–1996 | 38.3 | 39.8 | –1.5 |
| 1997–2005 | 44.6 | 25.7 | 18.9 |
| 1961–2005 | 31.9 | 26.1 | 5.9 |

*Sources:* compiled from BNM (1994), BNM (various issues) *Monthly Statistical Bulletin* and Ministry of Finance Malaysia (various issues) *Economic Report*.

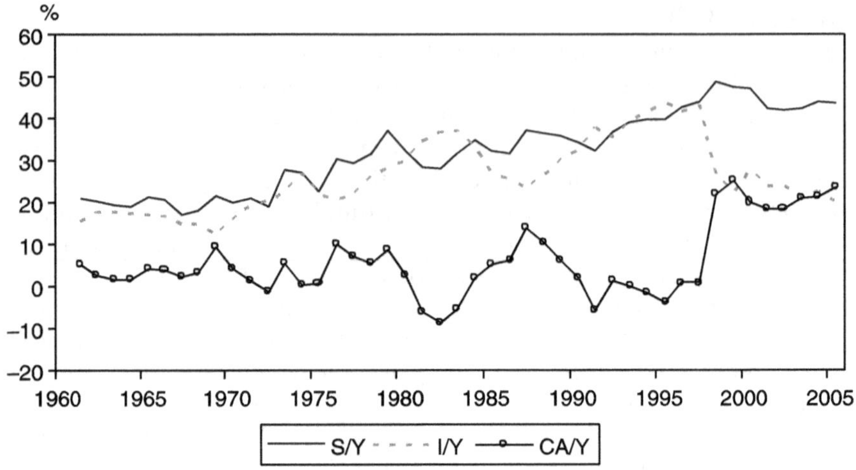


*Figure 3.10* Trends of saving, investment and current account balance (per cent of GDP).

*Sources:* compiled from BNM (1994), BNM (various issues) *Monthly Statistical Bulletin*, and Ministry of Finance Malaysia (various issues) *Economic Report*.

domestic saving (*S*), gross domestic investment (*I*), and current account balance (*CA*) are expressed as a ratio of GDP (*Y*), denoted as *S*/*Y*, *I*/*Y* and *CA*/*Y*, respectively. The current account balance equals gross domestic saving minus gross domestic investment ($CA = S - \text{I}$).[14]

It is evident that Malaysia has been very successful in mobilizing saving. The average annual share of gross domestic saving to GDP rose from just 20.1 per cent in 1961–65 to 44.6 per cent in 1997–2005. Gross domestic investment was primarily funded by domestic saving (which includes household saving, corporate saving and government saving) and was supplemented by foreign saving. That is, when investment was greater than saving, the resource gap was financed by current account deficits. Its average annual rate increased from 17.1 per cent of GDP in 1961–65 to a record high of 39.8 per cent of GDP in 1991–96, before the onset of the 1997–98 Asian financial crisis.

Although investment increased rapidly during the period 1961–80, Malaysia was able to finance much of the investment projects without significant recourse to external financing. Consequently, there were no large current account deficits recorded in the balance of payments. However, this pattern of development was not continued in the 1980s. During the period 1981–85, a current account deficit averaging 2.7 per cent of GDP was recorded. This historically high level of current account deficit was due mainly to the counter-cyclical pump-priming efforts of the government, following deterioration in the prices of several major export commodities. The government initiated a 'big push' programme that contributed to a significant rise in investment. As a result, the investment to GDP ratio rose from 14.9 per cent during the period 1966–70 to a high level of 33.6 per cent during the period 1981–85. With increasing commodity prices in the next few years, 1986–90 saw an improvement in the saving–investment gap, which narrowed further through restraining fiscal spending by government. Following this structural adjustment policy, excessive consumer spending was curbed, resulting in a higher saving rate.

With rapid expansion in investment activities, the resource gap emerged once again during the period 1991–96, when some investment activities were financed by foreign capital. However, gross domestic investment was severely affected in the wake of the Asian financial crisis and has remained sluggish. Hence, the post-crisis period saw a huge current account surplus.

In sum, it appears that the high saving rate recorded in Malaysia throughout the past four decades has enabled investment activities to be carried out without much reliance on foreign capital, although inflows of FDI have been high in Malaysia. In most periods, domestic saving has been sufficient to fund expansion in investment activities. Thus, the current account has been in surplus most of the time.

A further breakdown of saving and investment rates into public and private components shows that public saving were insufficient to support public investment prior to the 1990s (see Table 3.10). The public sector became a net saver from the 1990s onwards due to a significant increase in public saving. At the same time, the government actively promoted the private sector as the main driver of economic development. This was augmented by the introduction of the Promotion of Investment Act 1986 (BNM, 1999). In contrast, the private sector was a net saver during the period 1961–90. However, this surplus in private saving turned negative during the period 1991–95 when there was a massive increase in private capital formation. Following a fall in private investment from 1996, a surplus in the private sector was again recorded.

*Table 3.10* Average savings and investment gap (% of GDP), 1961–2005

| *Period* | *Public saving* | *Public investment* | *Surplus/ Deficit* | *Private saving* | *Private investment* | *Surplus/ Deficit* |
|---|---|---|---|---|---|---|
| 1961–1965 | 0.029 | 0.076 | –0.047 | 0.132 | 0.095 | 0.037 |
| 1966–1970 | 0.030 | 0.058 | –0.027 | 0.133 | 0.085 | 0.048 |
| 1971–1975 | 0.022 | 0.071 | –0.049 | 0.167 | 0.148 | 0.019 |
| 1976–1980 | 0.039 | 0.092 | –0.053 | 0.239 | 0.153 | 0.086 |
| 1981–1985 | 0.070 | 0.160 | –0.090 | 0.184 | 0.174 | 0.010 |
| 1986–1990 | 0.086 | 0.104 | –0.019 | 0.202 | 0.161 | 0.041 |
| 1991–1995 | 0.152 | 0.128 | 0.024 | 0.156 | 0.264 | –0.108 |
| 1996–2000 | 0.167 | 0.116 | 0.051 | 0.209 | 0.204 | 0.005 |
| 2001–2005 | 0.160 | 0.130 | 0.030 | 0.189 | 0.096 | 0.093 |

*Sources:* compiled from BNM (1994), BNM (various issues) *Monthly Statistical Bulletin* and Ministry of Finance Malaysia (various issues) *Economic Report*.

## 3.10 Conclusions

Malaysia's economic performance in the post-independence era was relatively impressive by developing country standards. For the period 1961–96, real GDP growth rate averaged 7.3 per cent. Changes in the economic environment have given rise to different needs for financial products and services. Together with the financial liberalization policies undertaken, these changes have led to the emergence of a much more sophisticated financial system. Today, the financial system plays a more important role in mobilizing and channelling resources effectively to productive sectors rather than merely serving the needs of trade financing. However, due to limited development in the capital markets, the Malaysian financial system is predominantly bank-based. Rapid economic growth and ongoing deepening in the financial sector suggest financial development and economic growth in Malaysia may be strongly related.

# 4 Data, variable construction and estimation methodology

## 4.1 Introduction

The purpose of this chapter is to discuss the sources of data, the construction of variables, and the estimation methodology:

- Section 4.2 describes the sources of data used in this study;
- Section 4.3 sets out the details on how to construct the variables used in the regression analyses;
- Section 4.4 describes the proposed time series econometric techniques for the empirical tests.

## 4.2 Sources of data

Annual data for the period 1960–2005 are used in the estimation. The national economic database of Malaysia is considered relatively good by developing country standards. The data have been collected from various sources. Most of the data series are directly obtained or compiled from domestic sources, including Economic Reports of the Malaysian Ministry of Finance, Yearbook of Statistics of the Malaysian Department of Statistics, BNM Annual Reports, Money and Banking in Malaysia (1989, 1994), Quarterly Bulletin and Monthly Statistical Bulletin. Some data series are also obtained from the international sources, such as World Development Indicators of the World Bank and International Financial Statistics of the International Monetary Fund, where the compiled data are originally collected from domestic sources. In the data compilation, the most recent publication of the above-mentioned sources has been referenced to ensure that the most up-to-date data are used in the empirical analyses.

Some of the data used in this study are not directly available. For instance, private savings, macroeconomic uncertainty, user cost of capital, etc., cannot be directly obtained from the above-mentioned sources. In these cases, the data are derived by proxies using the standard conversion procedures. The following section defines the variables used in each of the empirical specifications and explains how each has been derived. Sources of data are described in Appendix 2.

## 4.3 Construction of variables

*(a) Financial deepening*

Choosing variables to indicate the level of financial deepening in an economy and measuring efficiency of the financial systems are perplexing problems in an empirical study of this nature due to a diverse array of agents and institutions involved in the financial intermediation activities. The extent of financial deepening is best measured by the intermediaries' ability to reduce information and transaction costs, mobilize savings, manage risks and facilitate transactions. However, there are no directly measurable and reliable data available. Consequently, an indirect approach to measuring financial deepening using an appropriate indicator has been the standard practice adopted in this field of study. This study considers two commonly used measures of financial deepening, defined as:

$$M2Y_t = \frac{M2_t}{GDP_t} \tag{1}$$

$$BCY_t = \frac{\textit{Bank credit to the private sector}_t}{GDP_t} \tag{2}$$

Although it has been widely used in the literature of financial development, the monetization ratio ($M2Y_t$) in Equation (1) is not a particularly good indicator of financial deepening since it reflects the extent of transaction services provided by financial systems, rather than the ability of financial systems to channel funds from depositors to investment projects. The alternative measure of financial deepening in Equation (2), bank credit to the private sector as a ratio of GDP ($BCY_t$), is often argued to be a more superior measure (Levine *et al.*, 2000). Since the private sector is able to utilize funds in a more efficient and productive manner compared with the public sector, the exclusion of credit to the public sector better reflects the extent of efficient resource allocation.

*(b) Real interest rate*

Real interest rate ($RI_t$) is defined as the 12-month commercial banks deposit interest rate minus the expected inflation rate ($\pi_t^*$). Since $\pi_t^*$ is not directly observable, the adaptive expectations model is proposed to explain how expectations are formed. This model, popularized by Cagan (1956), postulates that economic agents adapt their expectations based on past experience by learning from their mistakes. The model $\pi^*_t - \pi^*_{t-1} = \lambda(\pi_t - \pi^*_{t-1})$ states that expectations are revised each period by a proportion $\lambda$ of the difference between the inflation rate observed today ($\pi_t$) and its anticipated value in the previous period ($\pi^*_{t-1}$). We follow the standard practice by assuming $\lambda = 1$, implying that expectations are realized instantly in the same period. Hence, the expected inflation rate equals the current inflation rate. The rate of inflation is constructed using the consumer price index (CPI). Therefore, the real interest rate is given as:

$$RI_t = Deposit\ interest\ rate_t\ (DIR_t) - inflation\ rate_t\ (\pi_t) \quad (3)$$

*(c) Financial liberalization index*

To measure the level of financial liberalization ($FL_t$), it is necessary to take interest rate policies, statutory reserve and liquidity requirements, and directed credit programmes into consideration. However, using all these variables in the equation of financial development may pose some econometric problems since the underlying policy variables may be highly correlated. On the other hand, using them individually may also lead to omitted variables bias since the central bank may impose some of these controls concurrently. Thus, this study proposes to construct an index for financial liberalization following the approach adopted by Bandiera *et al.* (2000) and Demetriades and Luintel (1997, 2001). Nine series are collected for repressionist policies. Six are interest rate controls, including a maximum lending rate for priority sectors, a policy intervention rate, a minimum lending rate, a maximum lending rate, a minimum deposit rate, and a maximum deposit rate. These policy controls are translated into dummy variables, which take the value of 1 if a control is present and 0 otherwise. The remaining three policies are directed credit programmes, statutory reserve ratio, and liquidity ratio, measured in percentages.[1]

Using these nine variables, a summary measure of financial liberalization, which represents the joint impact of the financial repressionist policies, is developed by employing the method of principal component analysis.[2] The inverse of this measure can be interpreted as the extent of financial liberalization. Theoretically, this new index for financial liberalization is able to capture most of the information from the original data set that consists of nine policy variables. Given its conciseness, this approach sufficiently deals with the problems of multicollinearity and over-parameterization.

Table 4.1 presents the results obtained from principal component analysis. The eigenvalues indicate that the first principal component explains about 49.2 per cent of the standardized variance, the second principal component explains another 20.3 per cent and so on. The first principal component is computed as a linear combination of the nine financial policy measures with weights given by the first eigenvector. In this case, the six largest principal components are extracted, and they are able to capture 95.7 per cent of the information from the original data set. The remaining principal components

*Table 4.1* Principal component analysis for the financial liberalization index

| | *Principal component* | | | | | | | | |
|---|---|---|---|---|---|---|---|---|---|
| | *1* | *2* | *3* | *4* | *5* | *6* | *7* | *8* | *9* |
| Eigenvalues | 4.430 | 1.826 | 0.929 | 0.622 | 0.534 | 0.268 | 0.192 | 0.135 | 0.065 |
| % of variance | 0.492 | 0.203 | 0.103 | 0.069 | 0.059 | 0.030 | 0.021 | 0.015 | 0.007 |
| Cumulative % | 0.492 | 0.695 | 0.798 | 0.867 | 0.927 | 0.957 | 0.978 | 0.993 | 1.000 |
| *Variable* | *Eigenvector* | | | | | | | | |
| | *1* | *2* | *3* | *4* | *5* | *6* | *7* | *8* | *9* |
| *PSR* | –0.401 | 0.072 | 0.237 | –0.381 | 0.358 | –0.410 | –0.011 | –0.083 | –0.574 |
| *PIR* | –0.341 | –0.357 | –0.323 | 0.259 | –0.292 | 0.159 | 0.465 | 0.238 | –0.450 |
| *MIL* | 0.373 | –0.123 | 0.515 | 0.094 | –0.276 | 0.262 | 0.075 | –0.499 | –0.415 |
| *MAL* | –0.264 | –0.345 | 0.625 | –0.035 | –0.360 | –0.276 | 0.053 | 0.296 | 0.352 |
| *MID* | 0.236 | –0.396 | –0.243 | –0.794 | –0.108 | 0.046 | 0.237 | –0.112 | 0.125 |
| *MAD* | 0.388 | –0.305 | –0.161 | 0.042 | –0.186 | –0.302 | –0.606 | 0.344 | –0.342 |
| *PSL* | –0.416 | 0.014 | 0.070 | –0.274 | –0.126 | 0.672 | –0.514 | 0.103 | –0.061 |
| *SRR* | –0.094 | 0.585 | –0.166 | –0.181 | –0.715 | –0.252 | –0.002 | –0.105 | –0.061 |
| *CLR* | 0.355 | 0.377 | 0.258 | –0.193 | 0.086 | 0.230 | 0.296 | 0.669 | –0.179 |

*Notes:* PSR = maximum lending rate for priority sector, PIR = policy intervention rate, MIL = minimum lending rate, MAL = maximum lending rate, MID = minimum deposit rate, MAD = maximum deposit rate, PSL = priority sector (native Malays community) lending target rate, SRR = statutory reserve ratio, and CLR = commercial bank liquidity ratio.

are not considered since their marginal information content is relatively small. The percentages of variance are adjusted to make sure that their absolute values sum up to one. These adjusted values are then used as the weights to compute the index. In this connection, the first principal component, which accounts for 49.2 per cent of the total variation of the policy variables, has a weight of 49.2/95.7, and so on. The reciprocal of this index represents the extent of financial liberalization.

### *(d) Savings series*

Malaysia does not have directly estimated savings data. Gross national savings ($GNS_t$) is defined as the sum of gross capital formation and balance on current account (including goods, services and transfers) (BNM, 1994). Public savings ($PUS_t$) refers to total public sector current surpluses or deficits. That is, it is defined as government revenue minus operating expenditure plus non-financial public enterprise surpluses. Private savings ($PRS_t$) is derived by taking $GNS_t$ minus $PUS_t$. These savings variables are measured in real terms using the GDP deflator. Ideally, a consumption deflator should be used to obtain real savings. However, sufficiently long time series data on a consumption deflator is not available for Malaysia.

### *(e) Private income*

Real private income is measured by gross private income ($GPI_t$), deflated by the GDP deflator. $GPI_t$ is the difference between gross national product ($GNP_t$) and government revenue ($GR_t$). The former equals GDP plus net factor income payments from abroad ($NFI_t$), while the latter refers to the sum of public savings ($PUS_t$) and public consumption ($PUC_t$).

$$\begin{aligned} GPI_t &= GNP_t - GR_t \\ &= (GDP_t + NFI_t) - (PUS_t + PUC_t) \end{aligned} \tag{4}$$

### *(f) Young and old age dependency*

Young age dependency ($YAG_t$) is population with ages 0–14 to working-age population with ages 15–64, whereas old age dependency ($OAG_t$) is defined as population with ages 65 and above, i.e. over the working population age. Although the common retirement age in Malaysia is 55, data constraints limit following this definition, which has been widely adopted in many past studies on this subject.[3]

$$YAG_t = \frac{Population\ ages\ 0\text{–}14}{Population\ ages\ 15\text{–}65} \tag{5}$$

$$OAG_t = \frac{Population\ ages > 65}{Population\ ages\ 15\text{–}65} \tag{6}$$

*(g) Expected benefits of pension savings*

The cumulative contributions of employee provident funds relative to private income are used to measure the expected benefit of pension savings ($PEN_t$). Hence, it is a stock variable of provident funds with adjustment for withdrawals. This ratio is lagged by one period since individuals are likely to base savings decisions on the amount of accumulated EPF savings available at the beginning of the year.

$$PEN_t = \frac{Cumulative\ EPF\ saving_{t-1}}{GPI_{t-1}} \tag{7}$$

*(h) Investment*

Private investment ($PRI_t$) is measured by gross fixed private capital formation ($GPRI_t$), public investment ($PUB_t$) is measured by gross fixed public capital formation ($GPUB_t$), and private domestic investment ($PDI_t$) is measured by private investment minus $FDI_t$. However, it must be highlighted that the estimation for domestic investment may be subject to some measurement issues, since the data sources for private investment are not compatible with those obtained for $FDI_t$. In Malaysia, like many other countries, data on private investment are obtained directly from the national account statistics. Data on $FDI_t$ are taken from the balance of payments accounts, which are estimated by BNM using capital flow data from commercial bank records, and supplemented by information directly obtained from a company survey on reinvested earnings of foreign-invested firms (multinational enterprise subsidiaries). Although the incompatibility of data sources may be a concern, it is unlikely to distort the estimation results significantly. All investment series are expressed in real terms using the gross capital formation deflator.

*(i) User cost of capital*

It is well known that user cost of capital ($COC_t$) is difficult to estimate, especially for developing countries. A commonly used proxy for the user cost of capital is the real domestic interest rate. However, this measure ignores other important factors, i.e. tax rate, investment credit, capital stock depreciation and the price of capital stock, which may have a significant impact on investment decision making. An analytical expression for the user cost of capital has been developed by Hall and Jorgenson (1969). It refers to the cost of using one unit of capital relative to the cost of purchasing that unit of capital during a particular period, which can be formulated as:

$$COC_t = PK_t\left(\frac{(i_t - \pi_t + \delta_t)(1 - k_t)(1 - \tau_t z_t)}{1 - \tau_t}\right) \tag{8}$$

where $PK_t$ is the price of a unit of capital input, $i_t$ is the financing cost of capital good, $\pi_t$ is the inflation rate, $\delta_t$ is the rate of depreciation, $k_t$ is the rate of investment tax credit, $z_t$ is the present value of tax depreciation allowances, and $\tau_t$ is the rate of corporate income taxes. For the case of Malaysia, it is difficult to estimate the rate of investment tax credit ($k_t$) and the present value of tax depreciation allowances ($z_t$). Hence, both $k_t$ and $z_t$ are assumed to be zero. Therefore, Equation (8) reduces to:

$$COC_t = PK_t\left(\frac{i_t - \pi_t + \delta_t}{1 - \tau_t}\right) \tag{9}$$

The price of capital ($PK_t$) is measured by the deflator of gross capital formation. Commercial banks' average lending rates ($CAL_t$) are used to measure the financing cost ($i_t$). Ideally, the weighted average costs of financing should be used, since firms in Malaysia were not restricted from borrowing overseas prior to 1995. However, data constraints limit consideration to only the domestic cost of financing in the computation of the user cost of capital. The rate of inflation ($\pi_t$) is constructed from the GDP deflator. The depreciation rate ($\delta_t$) is assumed to be constant at 5 per cent. This implies that capital stocks in Malaysia have an average life of 20 years. The assumption that capital stocks depreciate at the rate of 5 per cent per annum is consistent with Sarel (1997) and Gan and Soon (2000) in their analyses of productivity growth for ASEAN countries and Malaysia, respectively.

The corporate tax rate ($\tau_t$) is measured by the statutory company tax rate ($CTR_t$). In reality, tax structures across different industries are complex due to different treatments of tax credits and tax exemptions during different periods, and the statutory tax rate is just an approximation, with shortcomings. For instance, the provision of generous depreciation allowances may result in a lower effective tax rate although the statutory tax rates appear high. Hence, caveats must be borne in mind that the assumptions of zero investment tax credit and no tax depreciation allowances may over-estimate the effective tax rate and therefore the user cost of capital.

### *(j) Bank credit*

As highlighted previously, bank credit to the private sector is often used in the finance and development literature to measure how efficiently funds are utilized in financial systems, given that the private sector is able to utilize funds in a more efficient and productive manner compared with the public sector. The availability of bank credit ($BC_t$) is measured by changes in commercial bank lending to the private sector in real terms (e.g. see Tun Wai and Wong, 1982; van Wijnbergen, 1982; Blejer and Khan, 1984),[4] and this is a flow variable rather than a stock variable. An increase in the value of this variable indicates greater relaxation of financial constraints.

$$BC_t = \Delta \ln \left( \frac{Bank\ credit\ to\ the\ private\ sector_t}{GDP\ deflator_t} \right) \tag{10}$$

In this research, macroeconomic uncertainty ($UNC_t$) refers to a situation when there are severe fluctuations in output levels, which induce greater variance in returns on investment activities. To obtain a proxy for macroeconomic uncertainty ($UNC_t$), the approach of Athukorala and Sen (2002) is followed by taking the three-year moving average deviation of the change in output between period $t$ and $t$-1, defined as:

$$UNC_t = \left[ (1/3) \sum_{i=1}^{3} (\ln GDP_{t+i-1} - \ln GDP_{t+i-2})^2 \right]^{1/2} \tag{11}$$

*(k) Capital stocks*

Department of Statistics (1965, p.16) estimated capital stocks in 1954 were in the range of RM 6,000–7,000 million. Since no estimate is available for 1960, the upper limit of RM 7,000 million is taken to be the initial level of capital stocks for Malaysia in 1960. It is assumed that capital stocks in Malaysia have an average life of 20 years and therefore depreciate at the rate 5 per cent per annum. This is consistent with the assumption used in the computation of the user cost of capital ($COC_t$). Capital stocks ($K_t$) can be computed using the standard perpetual inventory model as:

$$K_t = (1 - \delta)K_{t-1} + GCF_t \tag{12}$$

where the depreciation rate ($\delta$) is assumed to be 5 per cent, and $GCF_t$ refers to gross capital formation.

The computation of real private capital stocks ($PRK_t$) and real public capital stocks ($PUK_t$) deserves some explanation. First of all, the initial level of physical stocks of RM 7,000 million in 1960 needs to be split. The share of private and public fixed capital formation in total fixed capital formation over the period 1960–2005 is used as the basis of segregation in this study. The computation shows that private fixed capital formation contributes an average of 60 per cent to the total fixed gross capital formation. Thus, $PRK_t$ and $PUK_t$ in 1960 are obtained to be RM 4,200 million and RM 2,800 million, respectively. These two series are deflated by the gross capital formation deflator to express them in real terms.

*(l) Labour force*

Following the definition of World Development Indicators (2005), total labour force ($LF_t$) refers to all individuals willing to supply labour for the production of goods and services during a specified period. It comprises both the employed and the unemployed. Labour force includes the armed forces, unemployed individuals, and first-time job-seekers, but excludes housewives and other unpaid workers in the informal sector.

## 4.4 Econometric methodology

### *4.4.1 General issues in modelling time series data*

The main objective of this empirical study is to estimate the long-run relationships involving financial development, private savings, private investment and aggregate output. The estimation of a long-run relationship often begins with unit root tests. If the mean, variance or autocovariance at various lags of a process change over time, the series is said to be non-stationary. Such series either contains a deterministic trend or a unit root. In contrast, if a time series is stationary, its mean, variance and autocovariance at various lags are constant over time. A non-stationary series is said to be integrated of order $d$, or $I(d)$, if it needs to be differenced $d$ times to achieve stationarity.

Most 'classical' econometric theory is built on the assumption of stationarity (Hendry and Juselius, 2000). Regressing a non-stationary variable on another non-stationary variable may result in a 'spurious' regression, in which the estimates and test statistics are misleading. However, if a particular linear combination of a set of non-stationary variables can be found such that the linear relationship is stationary, a long-run relationship between these variables is said to exist, and the variables are cointegrated (Engle and Granger, 1987). Evidence of cointegration between variables can be viewed as evidence against the possibility of the estimated relationship being 'spurious' or nonsense (see Granger and Newbold, 1974).

Recent developments in non-stationarity and cointegration theory have contributed to a better understanding of the short-run and long-run dynamics in economics, and the equilibrium behaviour of economic variables. Cointegration testing provides evidence on the existence of a stable long-run linear relationship between the variables under consideration. The existence of such a long-run equilibrium relationship has an important implication for the short-run behaviour of the underlying variables, given that there must be a mechanism that drives the variables to their long-run relationship. This adjustment process is modelled by an error-correction mechanism, which leads to the formulation of an error-correction model (ECM).

To sum up, the three important aspects to consider while estimating relationships between variables are unit root (integration) properties, the multivariate aspect and the dynamics. An ideal econometric estimation technique should be able to: 1) incorporate all prior knowledge about the presence of unit roots; 2) account for the simultaneous determination of several variables (so as to avoid endogeneity bias); and 3) adequately capture both short and long run dynamics.

### 4.4.2 Traditional cointegration tests and their limitations

The two most widely adopted cointegrated techniques are the two-step residual-based procedure of Engle and Granger (1987) and the system-based reduced rank approach of Johansen (1991, 1995). The former assumes that there is only one unique cointegrating vector whereas the latter allows for the estimation of multiple cointegrating vectors when the test involves more than two variables.[5]

Although the residual-based approach can be implemented easily, it is subject to some shortcomings. Firstly, the estimation of the long-run equilibrium relationship involves a simple OLS regression on levels of the variables. This method is appealing due to computational convenience. However, as pointed out by Banerjee, Dolado, Hendry and Smith (1986), the omission of dynamics can generate substantial bias in finite samples, and this severely undermines the performance of the estimator. Also, endogeneity bias can affect small sample estimates, even though endogeneity has negligible effects asymptotically. Secondly, the two-step procedure uses the generated residual in the first step to form a new regression model in the second stage. Hence, the errors introduced in the first step are carried into the second step (Enders, 2004). Thirdly, Park and Phillips (1988) have pointed out the OLS estimator in the first step has a non-normal asymptotic distribution that depends on nuisance parameters. Hence, the reported *t*-statistics on the long-run parameters are misleading.

Similarly, the Johansen approach is not free from criticism. While the inclusion of lags ameliorates the omitted lagged variable bias that affects the two-step approach, and the system approach removes endogeneity bias, insufficient degrees of freedom to choose the optimal number of lags appears to be the most serious drawback of Johansen's method (see Gonzalo, 1994). The small sample properties of these approaches are also unknown. Another remark concerns the number of cointegrating vectors found. When more than one cointegrating vectors is found, it is often hard to interpret each implied economic relationship.

Both the residual-based and the system-based approach are criticized on the grounds that the number of lags is unknown and the residuals are assumed to be Gaussian. Furthermore, the test results may be sensitive to the inclusion of intercepts and trends in the specification. In addition, both approaches focus on cases in which the underlying variables are integrated of order one, i.e., $I(1)$. In the presence of a mixture of $I(0)$ and $I(1)$ variables, the implementation of these techniques become more onerous. Furthermore, the presence of $I(2)$ variables can introduce further complications.[6]

### *4.4.3 Alternative cointegration test and its advantages*

These issues prompt consideration of an alternative cointegration technique. The autoregressive distributed lag (ARDL) bounds test of Pesaran *et al.* (2001) proposed in this study is able to address all the above concerns. This procedure has several desirable features:

- It is common for macroeconomic variables to be affected by their own past values and hence their relationship should be viewed in the context of a multivariate autoregressive process. The bounds tests are performed based on an ARDL framework, which contains a rich set of dynamics and therefore addresses the concern about omitted lagged variable bias.
- The approach has several desirable statistical properties, such as precise estimates of long-run parameters and valid *t*-statistics, even in the presence of endogenous explanatory variables. Using Monte Carlo experiments, Inder (1993) demonstrates that the problems of endogeneity bias are minimal and relatively unimportant in many situations.[7] Similarly, Pesaran and Shin (1998) show that appropriate modification of the orders of the ARDL model, together with an IV estimation approach, is adequate to correct for both the omitted lagged variables bias and the problems of endogeneity bias. They also show that the OLS estimators of the short-run parameters are consistent and the ARDL-based estimators of the long-run coefficients are super-consistent in small sample sizes. Hence, valid inferences on the long-run parameters can be made using standard normal asymptotic theory, once standard errors have been appropriately adjusted.
- The method allows for the specification of a combination of stationary, i.e. $I(0)$, and non-stationary variables, i.e. $I(1)$, in the model. The problems of having a mixture of $I(0)$ and $I(1)$ variables in cointegration analysis have been highlighted in a survey article by Pagan and Wickens (1989). Pesaran *et al.* (2001) show that the ARDL approach yields consistent and asymptotically normal estimates for the long-run coefficients regardless of whether the underlying variables are $I(0)$ or $I(1)$.
- Under an ARDL framework, the proposed bounds procedure provides a convenient step to adopt the general-to-specific modelling technique of Hendry (1995) in order to obtain a parsimonious representation of the data generation process.

The relative attractiveness of this approach has been assessed in several recent studies. In Pesaran and Shin (1998), the small sample performance of the ARDL procedure and the fully modified OLS approach of Phillips and Hansen (1990) are compared using Monte Carlo experiments. The results provide strong evidence in favour of the ARDL approach. In another study that evaluates the forecasting performance of three single equation time series estimation techniques, i.e. Engle–Granger's ECM, the fully modified OLS and the ARDL approach, Fatai *et al.* (2003) find that the ARDL approach yields the best forecasting performance. One shortcoming of the approach is that it only allows for single long-run relationship between the variables, but in many applications, multiple long-run relationships are not expected.

### *4.4.4 The testing procedure*

The testing procedure involves four steps:

1. The first is to examine the integration properties of each variable. In order to apply the cointegration tests, it is important to ensure the variables under consideration are not integrated at an order higher than one. In the presence of $I(2)$ variables, the critical values provided by Pesaran *et al.* (2001) are no longer valid.
2. The second step is to test for cointegration using the ARDL bounds test, which consists of both a $t$-test and an $F$-test. It is worth noting that the $t$-test was first developed by Banerjee *et al.* (1998), known as the ECM test.
3. If cointegration is detected, the third step is to obtain a long-run model using an unrestricted ECM as proposed by Inder (1993). An instrumental technique is employed to correct the standard errors so that valid inference can be drawn (Bewley, 1979).
4. Finally, to obtain a parsimonious ECM, the general-to-specific modelling technique of Hendry (1995) is used.

### *4.4.5 Unit root tests*

Three unit root tests – augmented Dickey–Fuller (ADF) test, Phillips–Perron (PP) test and the Kwiatkowiski–Phillips–Schmidt–Shin (KPSS) test – are used to assess the degree of integration of the variables under investigation. The first two tests account for the structure of the data in different ways whereas the choice of the KPSS test is motivated by the argument that tests designed on the basis of the null that a series is $I(1)$ have low power for rejecting the null. Since most economic time series are not very informative about whether or not there is a unit root, it would be useful to perform tests of the null hypothesis of stationarity as well as tests of the null hypothesis of a unit root (Kwiatkowski *et al.*, 1992). These unit root tests are briefly described in the following.

#### *(a) Augmented Dickey–Fuller (ADF) test*

One commonly used method to test for the existence of unit roots is the augmented Dickey–Fuller test (see Dickey and Fuller, 1979). This involves running the following univariate regression:

$$\Delta y_t = \alpha + \beta y_{t-1} + \sum_{i=1}^{p} \gamma_i \Delta y_{t-i} + u_t \tag{13}$$

The above specification can be appended with a deterministic trend term if appropriate. The null hypothesis is that $\beta = 0$ (there is a unit root) against the alternative hypothesis $\beta \neq 0$ (stationary). The test statistic is given as:

$$DF = \hat{\beta} / \hat{\sigma}_{\beta} \tag{14}$$

where $\hat{\sigma}_{\beta}$ is the least squares standard error of $\hat{\beta}$. However, given that the distribution of ADF does not follow the standard student's $t$-distribution, the computed $t$-statistic is compared with the critical values provided by MacKinnon (1996). Highly negative test statistics reject the null hypothesis.

### *(b) Phillips–Perron (PP) test*

The ADF test assumes the errors are statistically independent and have a constant variance. Hence, in applying this technique it must be ensured that the error terms are uncorrelated and have constant variance. The alternative approach suggested by Phillips and Perron (1988) requires little attention to be paid to the assumptions of the error terms. The PP test can be viewed as a generalization of the ADF test, which accounts for the heteroskedasticity and serially correlated error terms. A non-parametric correction to the $t$-test statistic is undertaken to account for the serial correlation that might be present, so that serial correlation does not affect the asymptotic distribution of the test statistic.

An asymptotically valid unit root test for Equation (14) is given by the Phillips $Z$-test:

$$Z(\tau_{\mu}) = (S_u / S_{Tl})\tau_{\mu} - \frac{1}{2}(S_{Tl}^2 - S_u^2)\left\{S_{Tl}\left[T^2 \sum_{t=2}^{T} (y_{t-1} - \bar{y})^2\right]^{1/2}\right\}^{-1} \tag{15}$$

where $\tau_{\mu}$ is the $t$-statistic associated with testing the null hypothesis $\beta = 0$ in Equation (14), $S_u^2 = T^{-1}\Sigma_I^T (u_t^2)$ and $S_{Tl}^2 = T^{-1}\Sigma_I^T (u_t^2) + 2T^{-1}\Sigma_1^l \Sigma_{I=J+I}^T u_t u_{t-j}$, which are consistent estimators of $\sigma_u^2$ and $\sigma^2$, respectively, and $T$ is the number of observations. The critical values are the same as those for the ADF test.

### *(c) Kwiatkowski–Phillips–Schmidt–Shin (KPSS) test*

The Kwiatkowski, Phillips, Schmidt, and Shin (KPSS) test is different from the above unit root tests in that the series is assumed to be stationary under the null. The KPSS test assumes a time series can be decomposed into three components: a deterministic time trend term ($\delta t$), a random walk process ($r_t$), and a stationary error term ($\varepsilon_t$), as given in Equation (16).

$$y_t = \delta t + r_t + \varepsilon_t \tag{16}$$

where $r_t$ is a random walk process given as $r_t = r_{t-1} + u_t$, and $u_t$ is assumed to follow $i.i.d.(0,\sigma_u^2)$. Given that $\varepsilon_t$ is stationary, the stationary hypothesis implies $\sigma_u^2 = 0$. Under this hypothesis, $y_t$ is trend stationary. The KPSS test statistic tests the null hypothesis of stationary against the alternative of non-stationary, and can be computed as:

$$LM = T^{-2}\sum_{t=1}^{T} S_t^2/\sigma^2(p) \tag{17}$$

where $S_t^2$ is the partial sum process of the residuals from a regression of $y_t$ on an intercept and time, $\sigma^2(p)$ is a consistent estimate of the error variance from the same regression, $p$ is the lag truncation parameter, and $T$ is the number of observations. The distribution for the LM test statistic is non-standard. The critical values are provided by Kwiatkowski *et al.* (1992) based on Monte Carlo simulation.

### *4.4.6 The data generation process*

An important concept here is the data generation process (DGP), which refers to the probability mechanism in the space of those variables under analysis. In other words, it is the joint distribution of the subset of variables under analysis or the process of generating the sample of data.

To describe the ARDL bounds procedure and the ECM test, it is assumed the data generating process for the relationship of interest is a log-linear vector autoregressive (VAR) model in levels, which can be augmented with deterministics, such as intercepts and time trends. The idea here is to specify a set of useful information to provide an adequate approximation for the DGP. Such a general model captures the key features of the underlying data set, and its formulation is often guided by economic theory. The VAR model is given as:

$$\boldsymbol{x}_t = \boldsymbol{\mu} + \sum_{i=1}^{p} \phi_i \boldsymbol{x}_{t-i} + \varepsilon_t \tag{18}$$

where $\boldsymbol{x}_t$ is a vector of $k$ endogenous variables, $\boldsymbol{\mu}$ is a vector of deterministic terms, and $\phi_j$ is a matrix of VAR parameters for lag $i$. The vector of error terms is, $\varepsilon_t \sim \mathrm{IN}(\mathbf{0},\boldsymbol{\Omega})$, where $\Omega$ is the residual covariance matrix. It is well established by Engle and Granger (1987) that cointegrated variables must have an error correction representation in which an error correction term

(ECT) is incorporated into the model. Accordingly, a vector error correction model (VECM) is formulated to reintroduce the information lost in the differencing process, thereby allowing for long-run equilibrium as well as short-run dynamics. The VAR model in Equation (18) can be transformed into a vector error correction model (VECM) after some mathematical manipulations. This leads to:

$$\Delta \boldsymbol{x}_t = \boldsymbol{\mu} + \pi\, \boldsymbol{x}_{t-1} + \sum_{i=1}^{p-1} \gamma_i \Delta \boldsymbol{x}_{t-i} + \varepsilon_t \tag{19}$$

By construction, $\pi$ has rank $r$ (with $r < k$) and can be decomposed into $\pi = \alpha\beta'$. The elements of $\alpha$ are known as the speed of adjustment parameters, it is a $(k \times r)$ matrix where a larger $\alpha$ suggests a faster convergence towards the long-run equilibrium when there are short-run deviations from its equilibrium. $\beta'$ is a $(k \times r)'$ matrix of cointegrating vectors, i.e. the long-run coefficients in the VECM.

Hendry *et al.* (1984) propose that expectations formation by economic agents and non-instantaneous adjustment leads to the theoretical consideration of dynamics. Empirically, dynamics can be adequately represented by ARDL models. By breaking Equation (19) into $k$ individual equations, $k$ unrestricted ARDL models are obtained, and they can be estimated using OLS. Stock (1987) proves that OLS regression yields super-consistent estimators of the cointegrating parameters such that the OLS estimates converge faster to their true parameter values than in other OLS model with stationary variables.

For illustration purposes, consider the special case of $r = 1$, the conditional ECM of the first variable, $X_{1t}$, can be expressed as:

$$\Delta X_{1t} = \beta_0 + \beta_1 X_{1t-1} + \beta_2 X_{2t-1} + \ldots + \beta_k X_{kt-1} + \sum_{i=1}^{p} \gamma_{1i} \Delta X_{1t-i} + \sum_{i=0}^{p} \gamma_{2i} \Delta X_{2t-i} + \ldots + \sum_{i=0}^{p} \gamma_{ki} \Delta X_{kt-i} + \varepsilon_t \tag{20}$$

The above econometric specification is based upon the assumption that the disturbance term $\varepsilon_t$ is serially uncorrelated. Hence, in empirical implementation, it is critical to ensure that an optimal lag order $p$ of the underlying model is chosen appropriately in order to strike a satisfactory balance between the two competing concerns, in which the lag order is high enough to ameliorate the residual serial correlation problems and low enough that the conditional ECM is not subject to over-parameterization problems. This is particularly important in this study given that a small sample is used. Augmenting the specification with an adequate number of lagged changes in the regressors also mitigates the problems of bias due to omitted lags.

### *4.4.7 Cointegration tests*

The ARDL bounds procedure and the ECM test are performed based on the conditional ECM in Equation (20). To test for the existence of a long-run relationship, the former involves using an *F*-test for the joint significance on the coefficients of the lagged level terms ($H_0$: $\beta_1 = \beta_2 = \ldots = \beta_k = 0$) whereas the latter involves a *t*-test for the significance of the coefficient associated with $X_{1t}$ ($H_0$: $\beta_1 = 0$). Two asymptotic critical value bounds provide a test for cointegration when the independent variables are $I(d)$ (where $0 \leq d \leq 1$). The lower bound assumes all the independent variables are $I(0)$, and the upper bound assumes they are $I(1)$. If the test statistics exceed their respective upper critical values, the null is rejected and it can be concluded that a long-run relationship exists. If the test statistics fall below the lower critical values, the null hypothesis of no cointegration cannot be rejected. If the statistics fall within the band, the statistical inference is inconclusive.

The critical values are provided by Pesaran *et al.* (2001). An excerpt of these critical values is given in Appendix 5. Following the results of the cointegration tests, the long-run relationship can first be estimated and then Hendry's (1995) general-to-specific modelling technique can be employed to obtain a parsimonious specification.

### *4.4.8 The long-run model*

Traditionally, long-run equilibrium relationships have been obtained by using the Engle and Granger (1987) two-step procedure, which involves a simple OLS regression on the levels of the variables. This method is appealing due to the benefit of computational convenience. However, as pointed out by Banerjee *et al.* (1986), the omission of dynamics in this levels regression can generate substantial bias in finite samples, severely undermining the performance of the estimator. In view of this, the unrestricted ECM estimator proposed by Inder (1993) is adopted. This involves estimating the long-run parameters by incorporating adequate dynamics into the specification, as given in Equation (23).[8] Once this is done, estimation of the long-run parameters can be carried out using the standard OLS method.

$$X_{1t} = \delta_0 + \delta_1 X_{2t} + \delta_2 X_{3t} + \ldots + \delta_k X_{kt} + \sum_{i=0}^{p} \gamma_{1i} \Delta X_{1t-i} + \sum_{i=0}^{p} \gamma_{2i} \Delta X_{2t-i} + \ldots + \sum_{i=0}^{p} \gamma_{ki} \Delta X_{kt-i} + u_t \qquad (21)$$

When the above long-run relationship is estimated, it will generally give less biased estimates compared with that obtained from a 'potentially cointegrating regression'.[9] However, as pointed out by Phillips (1988), this approach is not asymptotically optimal, given that it takes no account of the possible endogeneity of the explanatory variables. Hence, proper inference cannot be made without adjusting for this problem. Two approaches are available to obtain valid estimates and standard errors: the delta method and the instrumental variable (IV) approach of Bewley (1979). The choice between these two approaches is only a matter of computational convenience, given that they yield identical results (Pesaran and Shin, 1998). Thus, for simplicity, to obtain valid standard errors the latter approach is followed. Bewley (1979) suggests using the first lag of $X_{1t}$, $X_{2t}$, . . ., and $X_{kt}$ as instruments for the current differenced $X_{1t}$, $X_{2t}$, . . ., and $X_{kt}$. The Monte Carlo evidence of Inder (1993) shows that this technique yields precise estimates and valid *t*-statistics, even in the presence of endogenous explanatory variables. Therefore, valid inference can be drawn from the estimated results.

The long-run model for $X_{1t}$ can be obtained from the reduced form solution of Equation (21), when all differenced terms of the regressors are set to zero, i.e. $\gamma_{1i} = \gamma_{2i} = \ldots = \gamma_{ki} = 0$ for $i = 0, 1, \ldots, p$. Thus, the following steady-state solution is obtained:

$$X_{1t} = \delta_0 + \delta_1 X_{2t} + \delta_2 X_{3t} + \ldots + \delta_k X_{kt} \tag{22}$$

### *4.4.9 Short-run dynamic model*

Having obtained this long-run relationship, the error-correction term (ECT) can be obtained by taking $X_{1t-1} - \delta_0 - \delta_1 X_{2t} - \delta_2 X_{3t} - \ldots - \delta_k X_{kt}$ to formulate an ECM. In the hypothesis testing of the presence of a long-run level equation for $\Delta X_{1t}$, it is important to ensure no restrictions are imposed on the coefficients of the lagged terms. Otherwise, the test results are subject to a pre-testing problem (Pesaran *et al.*, 2001). However, to estimate both the level effects and short-run dynamics of the adjustment in, $X_{1t}$, the use of a parsimonious specification is more desirable. To this end, Hendry's (1995) general-to-specific modelling approach is adopted to derive a satisfactory model for equation $\Delta X_{1t}$, as discussed below.

### *4.4.10 General-to-specific modelling technique*

In Hendry's approach, econometric models are formulated based on statistical data and economic theory. Statistical data are realizations from the DGP whereas economic theory guides the econometric specification. As Hendry (1983) argues, every empirical model is a reduction of the underlying DGP, and it is nested in the DGP. In sum, Hendry's approach is a simplification of the unknown DGP.

Pagan (1987) summarizes Hendry's methodology as the following four steps:

1 The first step formulates an initial general model, based on economic theory, to suggest which variables might enter the equilibrium specification. Such a general unrestricted model provides an approximation of the

DGP. At this stage, the lag length for each variable is chosen to be as large as econometrically feasible.

2 The next step involves reparameterizing the model into an error-correction representation so that it is easier to understand and interpret in terms of the final equilibrium.
3 Next, the complexity of the general model can be reduced by deleting statistically insignificant variables, or, equally, imposing acceptable restrictions, to obtain a 'congruent' model, i.e. the final parsimonious model should be able to adequately characterize the empirical evidence within the proposed theoretical framework.
4 The resulting model is subject to a series of diagnostic checks through an extensive analysis of the residuals and predictive performance in order to identify any weakness obtained in the preceding step, and restrictions are accepted only if they pass diagnostic checks.[10]

These include satisfying evidence against non-normality, serial correlation, autoregressive conditional heteroskedasticity, heteroskedasticity and model misspecification.

The performance of this modelling technique has recently been assessed for its ability to recover the DGP through a Monte Carlo study by Hoover and Perez (1999). They find that the technique is able to recover the correct specification, or a closely related specification, most of the time. Extending their investigations to cross-section data sets, Hoover and Perez (2004) find an equally impressive performance for this technique.

## 4.5 Conclusions

This chapter discusses the data sources and the construction of variables that will be used in this study in order to set the stage for the ensuing empirical analyses in Chapters 5 to 9. The autoregressive distributed lag (ARDL) bounds procedure and the error-correction model (ECM) test are proposed as the cointegration tests. The unrestricted error-correction model is adopted, which accounts for omitted lagged variable bias. To estimate the long-run relationship, an instrumental variable technique is used so that reliable inference can be drawn from the estimates. The general-to-specific modelling technique is used to simplify the conditional error-correction model. In order to test the robustness of the results and to facilitate their interpretation, all estimations are subject to various diagnostic tests.

# 5 Financial deepening and its determinants*

## 5.1 Introduction

This chapter seeks to examine the determinants of financial deepening in Malaysia, with a focus on how real output and financial policies affect financial deepening. Financial deepening is measured by the ratios of private credit to GDP and M2 to GDP. To measure the effects of financial sector policies, two different measures are proposed: real interest rates and an index of financial liberalization.

As part of the emergence of the new theories of endogenous economic growth over the past two decades, there has been a surge of interest in the potential role played by financial deepening in economic development. As discussed in the literature review of Chapter 2, the finance–growth empirical literature is dominated by cross-country analyses. With few exceptions, these studies have consistently shown that financial deepening has a beneficial impact on economic growth. Importantly, most studies have ignored the possibility of reverse causation in the finance–growth nexus. When financial deepening is specified as the dependent variable instead, the country case studies evidence of Demetriades and Luintel (1997, 2001) show that economic development has a positive impact on financial deepening. Hence, although the positive correlation between financial deepening and economic growth is already a stylized fact, as verified by many empirical studies, an important and yet somewhat under-researched issue is what determines financial deepening?

Development of the financial system is shaped by financial sector policies. Despite liberalizing interest rates in 1978, the Malaysian financial system continues to operate within the context of repressionist policies through the provision of subsidized credit to certain priority sectors.[1] This chapter addresses the important question of how the effects of government intervention in the financial system have affected development of the financial sector. This question is of significant relevance for the formulation of financial sector policies.[2]

* Parts of this chapter were previously printed in Ang (2008b).

Empirical studies of the effects of financial sector policies on financial deepening have typically used real interest rates as the proxy for financial liberalization, where a rise in this measure implies greater liberalization in the financial sector.[3] However, real interest rates may be affected by a number of factors other than changes of policy environment in the financial system, rendering it an inadequate measure of financial liberalization. In a cross-country analysis, where real interest rates are averaged over a long period of time, this problem may not be severe. However, for a country case study in which the time dimension is important, the use of real interest rates as the sole proxy for the level of financial liberalization can be misleading. As De Gregorio and Guidotti (1995) put forward, higher interest rates may reflect a lack of confidence in economic policy and the banking system, or the adoption of a more risky behaviour in investment undertakings, rather than greater financial liberalization. Furthermore, financial liberalization is not restricted to changes in interest rate policies. In the light of these concerns, an index is constructed using the method of principal component analysis to provide a summary of the joint influence of financial policies. This index captures information on various types of financial restraint imposed on Malaysia's financial system, including interest rate controls, reserve and liquidity requirements and directed credit programmes, to measure the extent of financial liberalization.

The chapter proceeds as follows:

- Section 5.2 provides the motivation of this analysis;
- Section 5.3 discusses the analytical framework; Section 5.4 describes the data;
- section 5.5 presents and analyses the estimated results; and
- Section 5.5 summarizes the results.

## 5.2 Analytical framework

### *5.2.1 Financial deepening and economic development*

As seen in Chapter 2, expansion in the financial system may be induced by higher per capita income due to higher demand for financial services. This is based on Robinson's (1952) hypothesis that more financial institutions, financial products and services will emerge in response to greater demand for financial services when an economy expands. The cost of financial services involves a significant fixed component so average costs will fall if the volume of transactions increases. As such, wealthier economies have a greater demand for financial services and are more able to afford a costly financial system. This implies that the level of real economy activity crucially affects financial deepening.

### *5.2.2 Financial sector policies*

#### *(a) Interest rate restrictions*

The McKinnon–Shaw framework suggests that interest rate controls, particularly interest rate ceilings, may distort the economy in several ways:

- It may discourage entrepreneurs from investing in high risk but potentially high-yielding investment projects.
- Financial intermediaries may become more risk averse and offer preferential lending to established borrowers.
- Borrowers who obtain their funds at relatively low cost may prefer to invest only in capital intensive projects.

McKinnon (1973) and Shaw (1973) argue in favour of liberalizing the financial sector by way of removing interest rate controls and allowing the market to determine its own credit allocation in order to deepen the financial system.

However, some counter arguments suggest that liberalizing interest rates may not necessarily lead to higher financial deepening. For instance, in the presence of deposit insurance or implicit government guarantee for rescuing troubled banks, the absence of interest rate control may result in overly risky lending behaviour among banks due to moral hazard problems (Villanueva and Mirakhor, 1990; McKinnon and Pill, 1997). Using a dynamic model of moral hazard, Hellmann *et al.* (2000) show that an increase in banking competition following liberalization of the financial sector (including removing interest rate restraints) may result in a weaker banking system. Studies have also shown that a significant increase in interest rates, which often follows from interest rate liberalization, is systematically related to financial crises (see Demirguc-Kunt and Detragiache, 1998a, b). In fact, Stiglitz (1994) argues that interest rate restraints may lead to higher financial saving in the presence of good governance in the financial system. When depositors perceive restrictions as policies aimed at enhancing the stability of the financial system, they may well be more willing to keep their savings in the form of bank deposits, thereby increasing the depth of the financial system. Hence, the theoretical impact of a change in interest rates on financial deepening is unclear.

#### *(b) Financial liberalization*

It is widely recognized that financial liberalization is an integral part of financial deepening. According to the McKinnon–Shaw school of thought, government restrictions on the operation of the financial system, such as an interest rate ceiling, directed credit programmes and high reserve requirements (dubbed ‘financial repression’), may hinder financial deepening. This may in turn affect the quality and quantity of investments and retard development in the financial system. In the simple AK model that involves financial factors presented by Pagano (1993), financial restraints (which may include interest rate controls and reserve requirements) reduce the amount of resources available for financial intermediating activities. Similarly, the endogenous finance and growth model developed by King and Levine (1993b) also shows that financial repression may negatively impact on financial deepening.

However, there is empirical evidence that financial liberalization can induce destabilization in the financial system and trigger financial crises in the absence of appropriate accompanying policies, in particular sound macroeconomic policies (see Diaz-Alejandro, 1985; Villanueva and Mirakhor, 1990). For example, the implementation of financial liberalization programmes by Latin American countries in the 1970s resulted in a number of bank failures and other bankruptcies. Interest rates soared and the financial systems in these countries were severely undermined. As Arestis and Demetriades (1999) point out, the financial liberalization hypothesis is based on a set of unrealistic assumptions, including perfect competition, perfect information, and a sound institutional framework. The fact that these assumptions are unlikely to hold in practice may explain the failure of the financial liberalization programmes undertaken by many developing countries. It appears, in principle, therefore, that financial liberalization can either induce financial fragility or deepen the financial systems.

### *5.2.3 Model specification*

The empirical specification of the steady-state equation for financial deepening draws upon the theoretical considerations discussed above. Given that real interest rates and the level of financial liberalization may have different impacts on evolution of the financial sector, both variables are included in the financial deepening specification to capture the effects of financial sector policies. The standard approach used in the literature is followed by taking the ratio of private credit to GDP and the ratio of M2 to GDP, denoted as $BCY_t$ and $M2Y_t$, respectively, as the measures of financial deepening. The model that uses $BCY_t$ as the dependent variable is known as Model A whereas the one that estimates for $M2Y_t$ is referred to as Model B. The same set of regressors is used in each model.

$$\text{Model A}: BCY_t = f_A(PGDP_t, FL_t, RI_t, D_{85\text{–}86}, D_{97\text{–}98}) \quad (1)$$

$$\text{Model B}: M2Y_t = f_B(PGDP_t, FL_t, RI_t, D_{85\text{–}86}, D_{97\text{–}98}) \quad (2)$$

The independent variables, with the expected signs in the parentheses, are given as:

$PGDP_t$ = real per capita GDP (+)
$RI_t$ = real interest rates (?)
$FL_t$ = financial liberalization (?)

Except for $RI_t$, all variables are measured in natural logarithms in the estimation. The above financial deepening specifications include two dummy variables to account for the impacts of the global economic recession in 1985–86 and the 1997–98 Asian financial crisis, defined as:

$$D_{85\text{–}86} = \begin{cases} 1 & \text{if } t = 1985\text{–}86 \\ 0 & \text{otherwise} \end{cases} \qquad \text{and}$$

$$D_{97\text{–}98} = \begin{cases} 1 & \text{if } t = 1997\text{–}98 \\ 0 & \text{otherwise} \end{cases}$$

## 5.3 Data

Figure 5.1 presents the series in their original forms (before taking logarithms). It is evident that both financial deepening (indicated by $BCY_t$ and $M2Y_t$) and the levels of per capita real GDP ($PGDP_t$) have increased significantly over time. All three series are affected by the Asian financial crisis.

Real interest rates ($RI_t$) have been stable in most periods except for the plunge that took place in the period 1973–74. This was the outcome of the first oil crisis that hit Malaysia in 1973 and subsequently led to a hike in price levels. However, the series rebounded within a short period and has remained fairly stable since. Hence, it appears that Malaysia did not experience any sharp fluctuations in real interest rates following interest rate liberalization in 1978. During the Asian financial crisis period, $RI_t$ increased initially when BNM raised the interbank interest rates to prevent the ringgit from falling, but it declined sharply following a change of the interest rate policy adopted by BNM.

The construction of the financial liberalization index has been explained in Chapter 4. A rise in the financial liberalization index indicates an increase in financial liberalization whereas the reverse implies a greater extent of financial repression. Interestingly, the index coincides rather well with the policy changes that took place in Malaysia during the sample period. It is evident that the extent of financial liberalization from 1960 to 1970 appears to be quite moderate. However, the index begins to move downwards from 1971 mainly due to an increase in the statutory reserve ratio and 1975 saw a plunge in the index, coinciding with the implementation of directed credit programmes. During that year, at least 50 per cent of the total lending made by banks had to be advanced to the *bumiputra* (native Malay) community. The extent of financial repression was subsequently mitigated when the target rate was reduced to only 20 per cent in 1976 and was not implemented in 1977. The decline in 1978 primarily reflects the reintroduction of this policy. A major reform in interest rate policy occurred in late 1978 when the central bank allowed banks to determine their own interest rates. 1985 saw another small reduction in the level of financial liberalization when the liquidity ratio was raised and banks were required to peg their interest rates with the two leading domestic banks. The pegged interest rate regime was later abolished in 1987. The index was fairly stable before the onset of the Asian financial crisis. In 1997, several interventions on interest rates were introduced to mitigate the impact of the crisis. After the crisis, there were signs that liquidity controls were loosened through a significant reduction in the statutory reserve ratio.

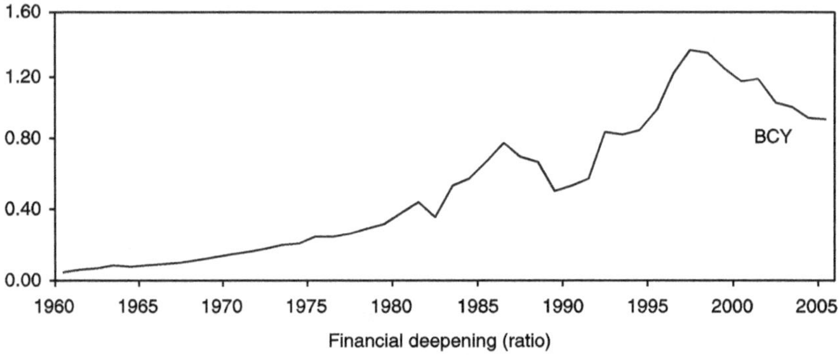


*Notes: BCY = bank credit to the private sector/GDP.*

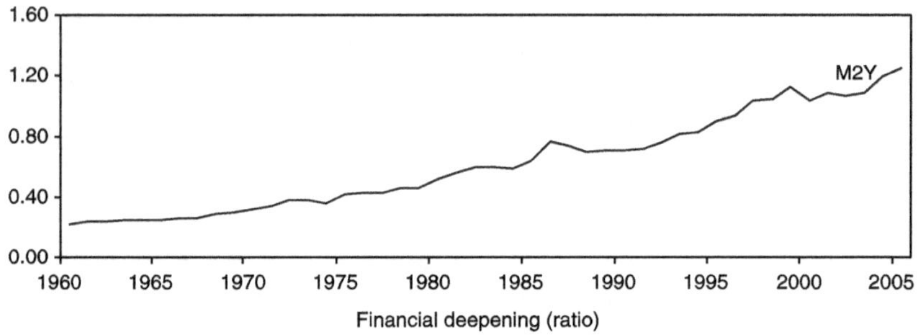


*Notes: M2Y = broad money M2/GDP.*

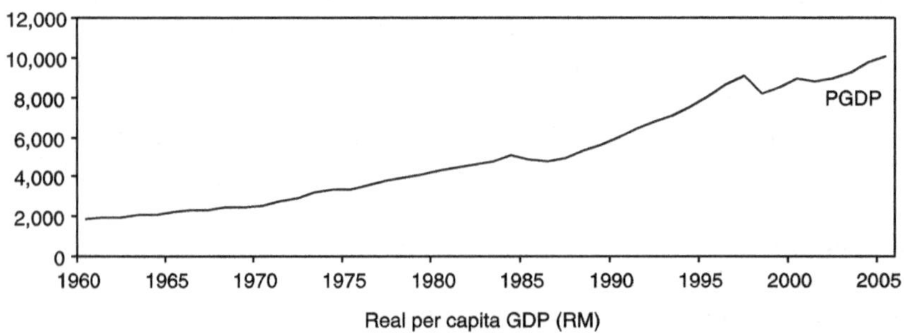


*Notes: PGDP = per capita gross domestic product measured in 1987 constant prices.*

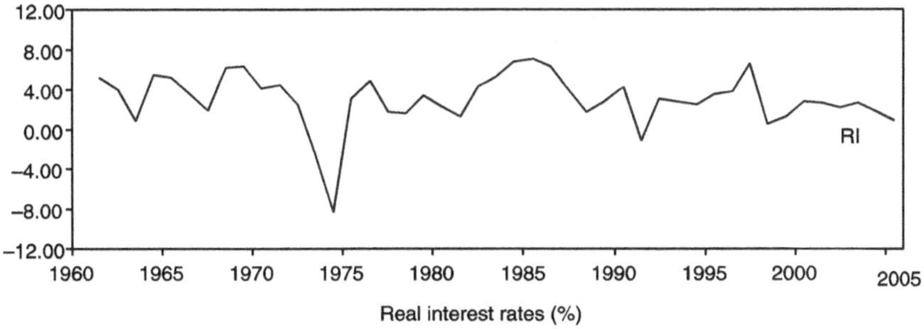


*Notes: RI = 12-month commercial banks deposit interest rate - inflation rate (constructed by CPI).*

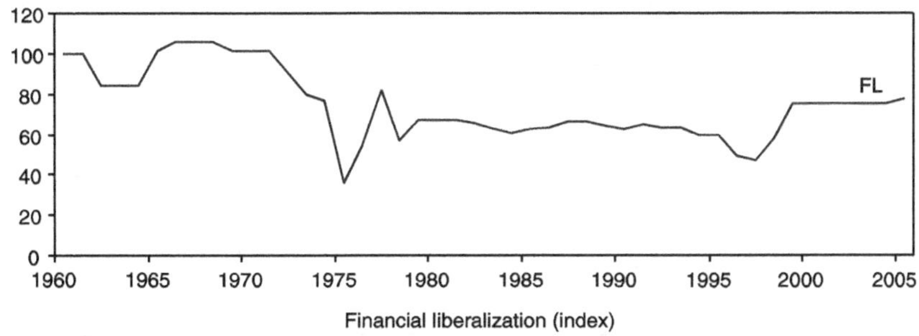


*Notes: FL is constructed by taking the joint influence of interest rate policies, statutory reserve and liquidity requirements, and directed credit programs into consideration using the technique of principal component analysis. See Chapter 4 for more details.*

*Figure 5.1* Time series plots of variables.

## 5.4 Results

The unit tests provided in Appendix 3 show that all variables used in the estimation are either $I(0)$ or $I(1)$. Given that none of the variables appears to be integrated at an order higher than one, this allows legitimate use of the ARDL bounds procedure of Pesaran *et al.* (2001) and the ECM test of Banerjee *et al.* (1998). To test for the presence of a cointegrated relationship, a conditional ECM is estimated with one and two lags for each model. Table B.1 in Appendix 4 gives the $F$- and $t$-statistics for the ARDL bounds and ECM tests, respectively, as well as the Akaike's and Schwarz's Bayesian Information Criteria (denoted by AIC and SBC, respectively). Ascertaining the existence of a level relationship between the variables requires satisfying both the $F$-tests and the $t$-tests. The results indicate that the null hypothesis, that there exists no level financial deepening equation, is rejected at the 10 per cent significance level for both models when only one lag is chosen. In line with the results of the cointegration tests, both AIC and SBC prefer a simpler dynamic specification of one lag.

Panel A of Table 5.1 provides estimates of the long-run equilibrium

*Table 5.1* Long-run and short-run results of the financial deepening equations

| | *A. The long-run equilibrium level relationship* | | | |
|---|---|---|---|---|
| | *Model A (Dep. = lnBCY$_t$)* | | *Model B (Dep. = lnM2Y$_t$)* | |
| | *Coefficient* | *p-value* | *Coefficient* | *p-value* |
| *Intercept* | −10.389*** | 0.000 | −8.281*** | 0.000 |
| ln$PGDP_t$ | 1.529*** | 0.000 | 0.974*** | 0.000 |
| ln$FL_t$ | −0.784*** | 0.000 | −0.125** | 0.034 |
| $RI_t$ | 0.060*** | 0.000 | 0.017*** | 0.005 |
| | *B. The short-run dynamic model* | | | |
| | *Model A (Dep. = ΔlnBCY$_t$)* | | *Model B (Dep. = ΔlnM2Y$_t$)* | |
| | *Coefficient* | *p-value* | *Coefficient* | *p-value* |
| *Intercept* | 0.040** | 0.027 | 0.042*** | 0.000 |
| $ECT_{t-1}$ | −0.407*** | 0.000 | −0.385*** | 0.000 |
| Δln$FL_t$ | −0.394*** | 0.001 | −0.127*** | 0.010 |
| Δ$RI_t$ | | | 0.004 | 0.135 |
| Δ$RI_{t-1}$ | −0.010 | 0.185 | | |
| Δln$PGDP_{t-1}$ | | | −0.545** | 0.024 |
| *Diagnostic checks* | *Test-statistic* | *p-value* | *Test-statistic* | *p-value* |
| $\chi^2_{NORMAL}(2)$ | 3.395 | 0.183 | 2.564 | 0.277 |
| $\chi^2_{SERIAL}(1)$ | 0.024 | 0.874 | 0.159 | 0.689 |
| $\chi^2_{SERIAL}(2)$ | 1.545 | 0.461 | 1.212 | 0.545 |
| $\chi^2_{ARCH}(1)$ | 0.001 | 0.973 | 1.162 | 0.281 |
| $\chi^2_{WHITE}$ | 5.610 | 0.468 | 7.453 | 0.488 |
| $\chi^2_{RESET}(1)$ | 1.269 | 0.259 | 0.061 | 0.804 |

*Notes:* The regressions for the long-run model are based on an unrestricted ECM, and corrected for both omitted lagged variable bias and endogeneity bias. The regressions for the short-run dynamic model are based on a conditional ECM. *, ** and *** indicate 10%, 5% and 1% level of significance, respectively. $\chi^2_{NORMAL}(2)$ refers to the Jarque–Bera statistic of the test for normal residuals, $\chi^2_{SERIAL}(1)$ and $\chi^2_{SERIAL}(2)$ are the Breusch–Godfrey LM test statistics for no first and second order serial correlation, respectively, $\chi^2_{WHITE}$ denotes the White's test statistic to test for homoskedastic errors, with degrees of freedom equal to the number of slope coefficients, $\chi^2_{ARCH}(1)$ is the Engle's test statistic for no autoregressive conditional heteroskedasticity, and $\chi^2_{RESET}(1)$ is the Ramsey's test statistic for no functional misspecification.

relationships, whereas panel B gives the results of the short-run dynamic models. To obtain the long-run model, an unrestricted ECM is estimated by an IV estimator. Based on the results reported in Table 5.1, the estimation begins with one lag and the insignificant terms are systematically dropped. The first lags of the variables have been used as the instruments for the current differenced terms in order to obtain valid standard errors in the presence of endogenous explanatory variables. The conditional ECM associated with the above long-run level relationship is estimated by OLS and reported as the short-run dynamic model in panel B of Table 5.1. The error-correction term was obtained by rearranging the terms in the long-run relationships and lagging by one period. In other words, it is the residuals from the levels regressions reported in panel A lagging by one period, designed to capture the financial deepening evolution process by which agents adjust for prediction errors made in the last period.

As is evident, all variables enter the long-run equations in panel A significantly at the 5 per cent level. The signs and magnitudes of the coefficients appear reasonable. Although the magnitudes of all estimated coefficients are smaller in Model B, the qualitative aspect of the results remains largely unchanged. While increases in real GDP and real interest rates have a positive impact on financial deepening, an increase in the extent of financial liberalization does the opposite. The results highlight the following points:

- The long-run elasticity of financial deepening with respect to output is found to be 1.529 in Model A and 0.974 in Model B. The results imply that the process of financial deepening in Malaysia has been shaped by a higher level of economic activity, which results in higher demand for financial services. Such a finding corroborates the empirical evidence of several studies, including Demetriades and Luintel (1997, 2001) and Arestis *et al.* (2002). Since higher output serves to deepen the financial system, greater efforts by the government are necessary to ensure sustained development in the economy.
- The long-run elasticities of financial deepening with respect to financial liberalization are found to be –0.784 and –0.125 for Model A and Model B, respectively. The results corroborate those of Arestis and Demetriades (1997) and Demetriades and Luintel (2001) for the Korean experience, and Arestis *et al.* (2002) for both Egypt and the Philippines. The results imply that the financial constraints imposed on the Malaysian financial system seem to have helped to deepen the financial system. This finding is plausible and accords well with the market structure of the banking system in Malaysia. Compared with other more advanced financial systems, the market concentration ratio in Malaysia is rather high since market capitalization is highly concentrated in the hands of the ten largest banks. This implies that banks in Malaysia may act like a cartel and behave as a monopolist, as suggested by Stiglitz (1994). Using a simple monopoly bank model, Demetriades and Luintel (2001) have shown that financial repression, which may occur through imposing interest rate ceilings, will deepen the financial systems in this situation. As conjectured by Demetriades and Luintel (1997, 2001), the success of financial sector policies may depend on the effectiveness of the institutions that implement them. In the case of Malaysia, this positive impact may also be due to the presence of a sound central bank, which has enabled the repressionist policies to be carried out effectively and resulted in a favourable

effect on the financial system. It is important to note that while a positive effect of financial repression on financial deepening is found, the results do not necessarily recommend repressing the financial system. Nevertheless, the results imply that some form of financial repressionist policies may be conducive to financial deepening in Malaysia.[4]

- The results show a positive real interest rates long-run semi-elasticity of 0.060 for Model A and 0.017 for Model B. These effects are small but statistically significant at the 1 per cent level. Our findings of a small positive real interest rates effect are consistent with Demetriades and Luintel (1997, 2001), who find the magnitudes of the coefficients to be in the range 0.002–0.003 for India and Korea. The evidence implies that interest rate liberalization, through removing interest rate controls, has a favourable effect on stimulating financial deepening. Thus, BNM's success in changing the real interest rates from negative to positive levels after the first oil shock in 1973–74 may have mobilized the funds available in the financial system. The results seem to suggest that allowing interest rates to operate in a free market environment has provided greater incentives to save and invest. Since real interest rates appear to have a separate effect on financial deepening, this highlights the importance of treating this variable separately from financial liberalization.

The dummy variables that capture the effects of the global economic recession, i.e. $D_{85\text{–}86}$, and the Asian financial crisis, i.e., $D_{97\text{–}98}$, are found to be statistically insignificant. Therefore, they are dropped from the estimation.

The regression results for the short-run models of $\Delta$ ln $BCY_t$ and $\Delta$ ln $M2Y_t$, reported in panel B of Table 5.1, show several desirable features. Except for real interest rate variables, all coefficients are statistically significant at the 5 per cent level. The results imply that changes in real deposit rates do not have any short-run impact on financial deepening. This is probably because deposit interest rates in Malaysia are subject to much regulation, and are therefore less likely to have an impact on financial deepening in the short-run. The results are consistent with Demetriades and Luintel (1997) for the Indian experience. In first-differenced form, $\Delta \ln FL_t$ has the appropriate signs, consistent with the results reported in the long-run models.

The coefficients on $ECT_{t-1}$, which measure the speed of adjustment back to the long-run equilibrium value, are statistically significant at the 1 per cent level and correctly signed, i.e. negative. This implies an error correction mechanism exists. The speed of adjustment at 38.5 to 40.7 per cent a year is considered relatively high. It takes only about 2.5 years to achieve long-run equilibrium whenever there is a deviation from the long-run steady state. Finally, all regression specifications fit remarkably well and pass the diagnostic tests against non-normal residuals, serial correlation, autoregressive conditional heteroskedasticity, heteroskedasticity and the regression specification error test (or Ramsey's RESET test), at the 5 per cent level of significance.

## 5.5 Conclusion

This chapter examines the determinants of financial deepening in Malaysia by taking real GDP, real interest rates, and a set of financial sector policies into account. Principal component analysis is used to construct a summary measure of financial sector policies to address the difficult problem of measuring the extent of financial liberalization. The results suggest that financial deepening in Malaysia depends on the level of output and the financial sector policies formulated by the government. The evidence provides some support for the efficacy of interest rate liberalization as a device for deepening the financial sector. Financial repressionist policies (including interest rate controls, reserve and liquidity requirements, and directed credit programmes) appear to have contributed to the development of the Malaysian financial system. Hence, financial liberalization seems to have a direct negative effect on financial deepening, separate from the influence through real interest rates.

# 6 The patterns and determinants of private saving*

## 6.1 Introduction

The objective of this chapter is to examine the determinants of private saving in Malaysia. As was outlined in Chapter 3, the saving record in Malaysia has been very impressive over the past few decades. Hence, the focus in this chapter is on what key macroeconomic and financial determinants are driving the high saving record in Malaysia. Understanding saving behaviour will allow a critical insight into how financial development is linked to economic growth, the central issue examined in this book.

This study uses the life cycle theory as the cornerstone in constructing the analytical framework while taking into consideration other important aspects, including EPF saving contribution, financial development, and fiscal policy to account for the structural and institutional features of the Malaysian economy. Forced savings in the form of compulsory contribution by employees to a broad-based EPF scheme makes up a significant proportion of total private savings in Malaysia (see Chapter 3 for more details). As such, it is important to study private saving with and without EPF contributions to avoid aggregation bias. Focusing on the component of voluntary private saving enables a closer look at the behaviour of private saving, since the proportion of forced saving in private saving is determined by government policy. Notwithstanding the increasing importance of EPF in Malaysia, no known study has been conducted to analyse how the presence of EPF saving affects the evolution of private saving and voluntary private saving. The analysis provided in this chapter is an attempt to fill this gap in the literature.

The chapter is arranged as follows:

- Section 6.2 sets out the analytical framework, drawing upon the life cycle hypothesis. Appropriate modifications and extensions to the life cycle model are introduced;
- Section 6.3 describes the data;

* Parts of this chapter were previously printed in Ang (2008b).

- Section 6.4 presents and analyses the empirical results;
- Section 6.5 summarizes the findings.

## 6.2 Analytical framework

In an empirical study of this nature, there is always a trade-off between estimating a specification derived directly from theoretical consumption/saving optimization models and a reduced-formed specification obtained by incorporating many saving determinants (Agenor and Montiel, 1999; Loayza *et al.*, 2000). In this study, an approach is taken to strike a balance between these two considerations, i.e. in order to encompass a sound theoretical underpinning on the determinants of saving while taking into account the structural characteristics of Malaysia, the empirical specification is derived using the life cycle model (henceforth LCM) augmented with certain key macroeconomic features of Malaysia, rather than adhering to any narrow model of consumption/saving. The LCM, which is the model most frequently used in the studies of saving determinants, can be extended to consider many other aspects, such as financial deepening, social security programmes, and government saving. The LCM has the flexibility of incorporating these additional features without changing its basic insight (Deaton, 2005; Jappelli, 2005).

### *6.2.1 The 'stripped down' LCM*

In the LCM, the primary motive for saving is to accumulate financial resources for retirement. Individuals tend to smooth out consumption over their lifetime by saving more during good times and less during bad times. The basic model is based on two key assumptions: the utility function is homogenous with respect to consumption at different moments, and the individual neither expects to receive nor desires to leave any inheritance (Ando and Modigliani, 1963; Modigliani, 1986). These two assumptions together imply that in any given year $t$, total consumption ($c_t^T$) of an individual at age $T$ will be proportional to the present value of total resources ($v_t^T$) accruing to him over his lifetime, or:

$$c_t^T = \delta_t^T v_t^T \tag{1}$$

In this equation, $\delta_t^T$ is a proportional factor that depends on the functional form of the utility function, the rate of return of assets, and the present age of the individual. The present value of resources at age $T$ is the sum of present income ($y_t^T$), plus income the individual expects to earn over his remaining earning life ($ey_t^T$), and his net worth carried over from the previous period ($a_{t-1}^T$).

$$v_t^T = y_t^T + \sum_{i=t+1}^{t+(N-T)} \frac{ey_i^T}{(1+r)^{i-t}} + a_{t-1}^T \tag{2}$$

where $N$ is retirement age and $r$ is the rate of return on assets. The average annual expected income can be expressed as:

$$ey_t^T = \frac{1}{N-T}\left(\sum_{i=t+1}^{t+(N-T)} \frac{ey_i^T}{(1+r)^{i-t}}\right) \tag{3}$$

Using Equation (1) to Equation (3), the following expression of total consumption is obtained:

$$c_t^T = \delta_t^T y_t^T + \delta_t^T (N-T)\, ey_t^T + \delta_t^T a_{t-1}^T \tag{4}$$

If the value of the proportional factor ($\delta_t^T$) is identical across all individuals in a given age group $T$, it is easy to aggregate Equation (4) over an age group to obtain:

$$C_t^T = \delta_t^T Y_t^T + \delta_t^T (N-T)\, EY_t^T + \delta_t^T A_{t-1}^T \tag{5}$$

where $C_t^T$, $Y_t^T$, $EY_t^T$ and $A_{t-1}^T$ are the corresponding aggregates for the age group $T$ of $c_t^T$, $y_t^T$, $ey_t^T$ and $a_{t-1}^T$. Finally, aggregating all age groups, the consumption function for the whole community is obtained:

$$C_t = \alpha_1 Y_t + \alpha_2 EY_t + \alpha_3 A_{t-1} \tag{6}$$

where $C_t$, $Y_t$, $EY_t$ and $A_{t-1}$ are obtained by summing respective $C_t^T$, $Y_t^T$, $EY_t^T$ and $A_{t-1}^T$ over all age groups $T$. Since expected income is not directly observable, it is convenient to assume $EY_t = \beta Y_t$ and $\beta \approx 1$ so that:

$$C_t = \alpha' Y_t + \alpha_3 A_{t-1} \tag{7}$$

where $\alpha' = \alpha_1 + \beta\alpha_2 \approx \alpha_1 + \alpha_2$. The saving function is, therefore, given as:

$$S_t = (1-\alpha')\, Y_t - \alpha_3 A_{t-1} \tag{8}$$

According to this model, one of the key determinants of saving is the growth rate of per capita income (Modigliani, 1966, 1970, 1986; Modigliani and Brumberg, 1954). As income grows, the life earnings and consumption of each successive age group will be larger than for the preceding group. If each successive age group is aiming for a higher level of consumption in retirement, the aggregate saving of those working relative to those not earning income would increase. Therefore, saving will tend to rise with income growth, given that the higher the growth rate of income, the greater the gap between the targeted levels of consumption of the workers in the current generation and the dissaving of retirees from a less well-off generation.

The LCM focuses on income growth, with little attention paid to the role of income level. This is based on the assumption that households are forward looking, and therefore base their savings decision on lifetime income rather than current income. However, this assumption may not be applicable to a developing country like Malaysia. As Modigliani (1993) notes, the portion of population that lives at subsistence level may find it too burdensome to set aside additional resources now for future consumption. Therefore, for countries with low per capita income, saving tends to rise with the level of income. For this reason, both income growth and income level are taken into consideration in this analysis of saving behaviour in Malaysia.

In the life cycle setting, the age structure of the population has a direct impact on saving behaviour. Individuals will have negative saving when they are young and when they are old, whereas positive saving occurs during their productive years, i.e. saving follows a hump-shaped pattern over an individual's lifetime. At an aggregate level, aggregate saving might be expected to be lower when there are more dependants in an economy. Hence, higher age dependency in the population tends to reduce saving.

Another important determinant of saving implied by the LCM is real interest rates. How real interest rates affect saving is unclear in the model. Whether saving responds positively or negatively to real interest rates depends on the relative magnitude of the substitution and income effects. Higher interest rates may induce more saving due to the higher price of present consumption relative to the future price (substitution effects), but it may also reduce saving if the individual is a net lender (income effects). These two effects may offset each other. Furthermore, as postulated by Ogaki *et al.* (1996), a change in real interest rates may not have any impact on saving if household income levels in poor countries are close to the subsistence level. Hence, the impact of real interest rates on saving is theoretically ambiguous.

### 6.2.2 Modifications and extensions

The empirical implementation of the basic model described above raises several issues, which are discussed in the following.

#### *(a) Pension saving*

A key limitation of the LCM is the assumption that individuals are able to make rational decisions in developing a lifetime plan of consumption and saving. However, in practice, many workers are unable to enter retirement with sufficient financial resources (Lesnoy and Leimer, 1985). In fact, this was the main reason for the introduction of the social security programme in Malaysia. The analysis provided in Chapter 3 clearly highlights the need to capture the effects of pension saving, given that it is a key driver in the Malaysian financial system which mobilizes a lot of saving.

The importance of social security on the behaviour of saving has been highlighted in an early study by Friedman (1957), and later formally incorporated into the analysis of the LCM by Feldstein (1974) and Munnell (1976).[1]

This new LCM proposes that the presence of a sound social security framework effectively reduces the amount of saving during the working years. This is because if savers perceive they will receive high pension benefits at the point of retirement, they will tend to reduce the amount saved during their working lives, weakening the precautionary motive for saving. Hence, in principle, an increase in the perceived benefits of pension saving reduces the desire to accumulate financial assets and may therefore discourage household saving (Feldstein, 1980; Evans, 1983).

Given this consideration, the model set out in Section 6.2.1 is modified to capture the effects of pension coverage. Expected pension benefits after retirement ($pen_t^T$) are considered as part of the total resources of the individual. Thus, Equation (2) can be rewritten as:

$$v_t^T = y_t^T + \sum_{i=t+1}^{t+(N-T)} \frac{ey_i^T}{(1+r)^{i-t}} + a_{t-1}^T + \sum_{i=t+1}^{t+(D-N)} \frac{pen_i^T}{(1+r)^{i-t}} \tag{9}$$

where $D$ is age of death. Average annual expected pension benefits can be written as:

$$pen_t^T = \frac{1}{D-N}\left( \sum_{i=t+1}^{t+(D-N)} \frac{pen_i^T}{(1+r)^{i-t}} \right) \tag{10}$$

It follows that the consumption function for the whole community in Equation (6) can then be expressed as:

$$C_t = \alpha_1 Y_t + \alpha_2 EY_t + \alpha_3 A_{t-1} + \alpha_4 PEN_t \tag{11}$$

and, finally, the modified saving function is given as:

$$S_t = (1 - \alpha')Y_t - \alpha_3 A_{t-1} - \alpha_4 PEN_t \tag{12}$$

Although the rationale that higher social security benefits tend to lower the savings rate is clear from the modified LCM, some counter-arguments have been proposed in the literature. As Pechman, Aaron and Taussig (1968) postulate, to the extent that savers are not rational, they may ignore the benefits of social security. Cagan (1965) argues that participation in a social security programme has an educational effect, which increases the awareness of savers about the importance of saving for their old age. Similarly, Feldstein (1974) postulates that social security can increase saving by inducing early retirement. This expands the span of retirement years and therefore increases the need for more saving during the working life in order to achieve a targeted level of retirement income. In line with these, Barro (1978) and Barro and MacDonald (1979) argue that individual savers may save more in response to an increase in social security benefits. This is because they may increase bequests to their children in order to compensate for the higher social security taxes borne by future generations.

In sum, social security has dual effects on saving: it lowers saving because it substitutes for household assets, but it also increases saving due to irrational behaviour, educational effects, induced retirements, and inter-generational transfers. Thus, it appears that economic theory provides no a priori argument for or against the effects of social security on saving. The net effect depends on the relative strengths of these opposing forces. Hence, the expected sign of this variable is indeterminate and the issue is an empirical one.

### *(b) Age structure*

As highlighted in an important study by Horioka (1997), age dependency should be segregated into young and old age dependency, since they each may have a different bearing on the behaviour of saving. This point has been further developed by Athukorala and Tsai (2003) who argue that with economies of scale in family consumption, large families are able to provide a child with the same amount of welfare with a less than proportionate increase in household expenditures compared with a small family. In addition, when parents intend to increase the family size, they may reduce consumption and save more in anticipation of higher expenditures after births. Thus, young and old age dependency may have different effects on saving and they should be treated separately in the analysis.

### *(c) Financial deepening*

Financial deepening may induce more saving through two channels. Firstly, the incentives to save may increase with the proliferation of financial instruments, which can satisfy the diverse needs and portfolio preference of various savers, i.e. a greater variety of financial tools can induce individuals to save more since it becomes more convenient to save. Therefore, willingness to save may depend on the degree of sophistication of the financial systems (Goldsmith, 1969; Park, 1994). The second argument is based on Shaw's (1973) financial intermediation view. Shaw argues that the existence of a sophisticated financial system facilitates the intermediation between savers and investors. More intermediation between savers and investors enhances the incentives to save since an efficient financial system effectively reduces risk and information costs, which can increase net real returns of savers and positively affect saving.

However, financial deepening is also likely to impact negatively on saving. The LCM depends on the ability to borrow when young to smooth out consumption throughout a lifetime. The model assumes a world of perfect capital markets in which credit is easily available. In reality, imperfections in credit markets may prevent households from borrowing as much as they would wish. This may reduce consumption and increase saving (Modigliani, 1986). Financial development takes place when there is an increase in financial intermediating activities, which follows from the removal of credit constraints. Therefore, this implies that the relaxation of credit constraints, which may lead to expanded consumer lending and increased financial development, is likely to result in lower saving. As Liu and Woo (1994) postulate, an insufficient level of financial deepening induces individuals to save more in order to undertake self-financed investment projects. In sum, financial deepening appears to be a double-edged sword with regard to saving.

*(d) Public saving*

The government can finance fiscal expenditure by issuing bonds. However, it must eventually repay this borrowing by increasing taxes in future. Using an overlapping generations model, Barro (1974) shows that there would be no marginal net-wealth effect of government bonds so long as individuals from one generation can transfer resources to the next generation. This is because households would save more to compensate for the higher taxes they have to pay in future, despite having more disposable income in the present. The model implies that an increase in government debt does not lead to an increase in household wealth, given that tax liabilities can be shifted from one generation to another.

In the analysis of saving behaviour, this hypothesis implies that an increase in government saving will have no effect on total saving, since it will be met by an equal reduction in private saving, i.e. when the government runs a budget deficit, the private sector will respond by saving more to offset this undesirable effect on future generations. Hence, any change in public saving will be fully offset by an equal change in private saving. This text is based on the assumption of a perfect capital market where households can borrow as much as they want, widely known as the Ricardian equivalence hypothesis.[2]

### 6.2.3 The model

The above theoretical considerations lead to formulation of the empirical specification of the saving equations given in Equation (13) and Equation (14).[3] Both real private saving ($PRS_t$) and real voluntary private saving ($VPRS_t$) are estimated using the same set of regressors as follows:

$$\text{Model A}: PRS_t = f_A(PPI_t, RI_t, YAG_t, OAG_t, FD_t, PEN_t, PUS_t, D_{85-86}, D_{97-98}) \tag{13}$$

$$\text{Model B}: VPRS_t = f_B(PPI_t, RI_t, YAG_t, OAG_t, FD_t, PEN_t, PUS_t, D_{85-86}, D_{97-98}) \tag{14}$$

where $PRS_t$ is real private saving and $VPRS_t$ is real voluntary private saving, defined as real private saving net of annual EPF contributions. Notice that the growth rate of per capita real private income ($\Delta \ln PPI_t$) is not included in the long-run specification, but is captured in the short-run conditional error-correction model. The independent variables, with the expected signs in the parentheses, are given as:

$PPI_t$ = per capita real private income (+)
$RI_t$ = real interest rates (?)
$YAG_t$ = young age dependency (–)
$OAG_t$ = old age dependency (–)
$FD_t$ = financial deepening (?)[4]
$PEN_t$ = expected benefits of EPF saving (?)
$PUS_t$ = real public saving (–)

The variables $PRS_t$, $VPRS_t$, $PPI_t$, $FD_t$, $PEN_t$ and $PUS_t$ are measured in natural logarithms. The above saving specifications include two dummy variables to account for the impacts of the global economic recession in 1985–86 and the 1997–98 Asian financial crisis, defined as:

$$D_{85\text{–}86} = \begin{cases} 1 & \text{if } t = 1985\text{–}86 \\ 0 & \text{otherwise} \end{cases} \qquad \text{and}$$

$$D_{97\text{–}98} = \begin{cases} 1 & \text{if } t = 1997\text{–}98 \\ 0 & \text{otherwise} \end{cases}$$

## 6.3 Results

Table B.2 in Appendix 4 gives the $F$- and $t$-statistics for the ARDL bounds and ECM tests, respectively, as well as the lag length selection criteria. The results indicate that the null hypothesis, that there exists no long-run level private saving equation, is rejected at the 5 per cent significance level for both Model A and Model B when only one lag is chosen. In terms of lag length selection, both AIC and SBC suggest a simpler dynamic specification of one lag. This is consistent with the results of cointegration tests.

The results reported in panel A of Table 6.1 represent the long-run equilibrium relationships whereas those in panel B show the short-run dynamic models. While some changes are observed in the magnitudes of the estimated coefficients, the qualitative aspect of the results in these two models remains largely unaltered. Except for $YAG_t$ and $OAG_t$, all variables enter the long-run equations in panel A significantly.

Consistent with the predictions made in the LCM, the results show that private saving rises with per capita real private income, with a long-run elasticity of 1.649 for Model A and 2.040 for Model B. This finding is consistent with the results of Yaakop (1988), Modigliani (1993), Edwards (1996),

*Table 6.1* Long-run and short-run results of the private saving equations

| | *A. The long-run equilibrium level relationship* | | | |
|---|---|---|---|---|
| | *Model A (Dep. = lnPRS$_t$)* | | *Model B (Dep. = lnVPRS$_t$)* | |
| | *Coefficient* | *p-value* | *Coefficient* | *p-value* |
| *Intercept* | −2.620 | 0.300 | −8.725** | 0.014 |
| ln$PPI_t$ | 1.649*** | 0.000 | 2.040*** | 0.000 |
| $RI_t$ | 0.019** | 0.025 | 0.019* | 0.060 |
| $YAG_t$ | −0.880 | 0.386 | 1.501 | 0.237 |
| $OAG_t$ | 0.187 | 0.984 | 17.418 | 0.237 |
| ln$FD_t$ | 0.407*** | 0.002 | 0.458*** | 0.004 |
| ln$PEN_t$ | −0.360*** | 0.003 | −0.366** | 0.024 |
| ln$PUS_t$ | −0.096** | 0.046 | −0.101* | 0.075 |
| | *B. The short-run dynamic model* | | | |
| | *Model A (Dep. = ΔlnPRS$_t$)* | | *Model B (Dep. = ΔlnVPRS$_t$)* | |
| | *Coefficient* | *p-value* | *Coefficient* | *p-value* |
| *Intercept* | 0.032 | 0.304 | −0.255** | 0.042 |
| $ECT_{t-1}$ | −0.767*** | 0.000 | −0.463*** | 0.000 |
| $\Delta RI_t$ | 0.011** | 0.028 | | |
| $\Delta YAG_t$ | −8.575*** | 0.010 | −13.220** | 0.039 |
| $\Delta OAG_t$ | −30.938* | 0.073 | −81.113** | 0.014 |
| Δln$PEN_t$ | −1.929*** | 0.000 | −1.776*** | 0.000 |
| Δln $PUS_t$ | −0.087*** | 0.003 | | |
| Δln $PPI_{t-1}$ | | | | |
| $\Delta YAG_{t-1}$ | 8.910*** | 0.005 | 14.362** | 0.018 |
| $\Delta OAG_{t-1}$ | −36.939** | 0.046 | −77.028** | 0.032 |
| *Diagnostic checks* | *Test-statistic* | *p-value* | *Test-statistic* | *p-value* |
| $\chi^2_{NORMAL}(2)$ | 1.563 | 0.457 | 2.299 | 0.316 |
| $\chi^2_{SERIAL}(1)$ | 0.001 | 0.987 | 1.998 | 0.157 |
| $\chi^2_{SERIAL}(2)$ | 2.973 | 0.226 | 1.997 | 0.368 |
| $\chi^2_{ARCH}(1)$ | 0.014 | 0.905 | 0.922 | 0.336 |
| $\chi^2_{WHITE}$ | 20.645 | 0.192 | 9.930 | 0.622 |
| $\chi^2_{RESET}(1)$ | 0.712 | 0.398 | 4.829 | 0.027** |

*Notes:* The regressions for the long-run model are based on an unrestricted ECM, and corrected for both omitted lagged variable bias and endogeneity bias. The regressions for the short-run dynamic model are based on a conditional ECM. *, ** and *** indicate 10%, 5% and 1% level of significance, respectively. $\chi^2_{NORMAL}(2)$ refers to the Jarque-Bera statistic of the test for normal residuals, $\chi^2_{SERIAL}(1)$ and $\chi^2_{SERIAL}(2)$ are the Breusch-Godfrey LM test statistics for no first and second order serial correlation, respectively, $\chi^2_{WHITE}$ denotes the White's test statistic to test for homoskedastic errors, with degrees of freedom equal to the number of slope coefficients, $\chi^2_{ARCH}(1)$ is the Engle's test statistic for no autoregressive conditional heteroskedasticity, and $\chi^2_{RESET}(1)$ is the Ramsey's test statistic for no functional misspecification.

Hussein and Thirlwall (1999), Loayza *et al.* (2000), Athukorala and Sen (2002) and Athukorala and Tsai (2003).

A one percentage point increase in the real interest rates leads to only a 0.019 percentage point increase in both private saving and voluntary private saving. The finding of a positive role for real interest rates corroborates the empirical results of Warman and Thirlwall (1994), Masson *et al.* (1998) and Athukorala and Tsai (2003). This positive impact on saving implies that substitution effects outweigh income effects. These results are not surprising given that the Malaysian financial system consists of a large number of small depositors with relatively few large lenders. As such, substitution effects are likely to dominate the direction of change following a rise in real interest rates. The evidence seems to suggest that the interest rate reforms adopted in Malaysia have encouraged more saving.[5] However, given that private saving has a low degree of responsiveness with respect to real rates of interest, this implies that liberalizing the interest rates is only a moderately effective tool to spur private saving.

The coefficients of the young age dependency ratio and the old age dependency ratio are found to be statistically insignificant. The results seem to suggest that demographic factors do not have an impact on the behaviour of private saving in the long-run. The finding that demographic variables have no role to play in the determination of private saving in the long run is consistent with the results of Agrawal (2001) for the Indian experience. Several previous studies have also found evidence that demographic factors have no significant impact on saving. These include Dayal-Ghulati and Thinmann (1997) for the ASEAN and Latin American experience, Masson *et al.* (1998) in their cross-sectional estimation for 40 developing countries, Bonser-Neal and Dewenter (1999) for 16 emerging markets, Kraay (2000) for the Chinese experience, and Ozcan *et al.* (2003) for the Turkish experience. Hence, this finding is not inconsistent with the literature.[6]

Financial deepening is found to have played a beneficial role in the accumulation of saving in the private sector. This coincides with the empirical findings of a number of studies, including Gupta (1987), Fry (1991), Edwards (1996), Hussein and Thirlwall (1999) and Athukorala and Sen (2002). The long-run elasticity derived from the coefficients on financial deepening suggests a 1 per cent increase in financial deepening yields about a 0.403 to 0.442 per cent increase in private saving. Insofar as the estimated coefficient represents the private saving effects of a change in the level of financial deepening, the positive sign is consistent with the view that saving rises with a proliferation of financial tools and an improvement in the financial system.

The expected benefits of EPF saving are found to have a negative influence on private saving, with a long-run elasticity of –0.360 for Model A and –0.366 for Model B. The results are compatible with the view that a social security system discourages saving and corroborates the empirical findings of Munnell (1976), Feldstein and Pellechio (1979), Feldstein (1980), Modigliani and Sterling (1983), Lee and Chao (1988) and Edwards (1996). The results are also in line with Shome and Saito (1980) for the Malaysian experience during the 1970s and Dayal-Ghulati and Thinmann (1997) for the experience of ASEAN countries (including Malaysia) during the period 1975–95.

The results seem to suggest that development of the pension system in Malaysia, through a higher accumulation of EPF saving, tends to discourage private saving. The results are not surprising given the operation of the EPF in Malaysia. Traditionally, the EPF is only permitted to invest in highly rated financial assets and contributors are not allowed to withdraw their entire pension saving until retirement. Hence, it is likely that the anticipation of receiving secured high pension benefits at the point of retirement reduces the desire to save. This interpretation is consistent with the predictions of the modified LCM.

The results show that a rise in government saving leads to a reduction in private sector saving, suggesting that changes in the government fiscal position have some impacts on private saving. However, public saving seems to crowd out private saving only partially, providing no full support for the Ricardian equivalence hypothesis. The results are in line with a number of empirical studies, including Edwards (1996), Hussein and Thirlwall (1999), Loayza *et al.* (2000) and Athukorala and Sen (2002), which consistently show that the Ricardian hypothesis does not hold strictly although some offsetting exists.

The rejection of this hypothesis may be partly due to the presence of an imperfect financial market in Malaysia, which invalidates one of the key assumptions in the Ricardian equivalence text of Barro (1974). Specifically, an increase in public saving by one percentage point will result in a 0.125 percentage point decline in private saving and a 0.180 percentage point decline in voluntary private saving. The crowding out effect is found to be slightly larger in Model B that excludes EPF contributions in the analysis.

The coefficients on $D_{85\text{–}86}$ and $D_{97\text{–}98}$ are found to be statistically insignificant, implying that neither the world economic recession in 1985–86 nor the 1997–98 Asian financial crisis had an impact on saving. Therefore, they are dropped from the estimation.

With regard to short-run dynamics, the regression results for the conditional ECM of $\Delta \ln PRS_t$ and $\Delta \ln VPRS_t$ reported in panel B of Table 6.1 show that, except for the intercepts, all coefficients are statistically significant at the 10 per cent level. In first-differenced form, all variables have the appropriate signs, consistent with the results obtained in the long-run models. The coefficient on $\Delta \ln PPI_t$ is not reported since it is found to be statistically insignificant, suggesting that income growth has no impact on the evolution of private saving behaviour in Malaysia. The result that private saving is dominated by the influence of income is in line with the Keynesian absolute income hypothesis.

Interestingly, in contrast with the long-run results, the coefficients of $YAG_t$ and $OAG_t$ are found to be statistically significant and have the expected (negative) signs in the short-run models. This suggests that the private sector tends to save less in the short term with the increase of dependent population relative to working population, which is consistent with the prediction of the LCM. The evidence also highlights that the proportion of elderly population relative to persons of working age has a much larger negative impact on the behaviour of saving in the private sector, compared with the proportion of young age population, supporting the argument of treating young and old age dependency as two separate demographic factors in the analysis. The results provide some support for the view that demographic factors are crucial in explaining the variations in private saving across time, as suggested by previous studies, including Edwards (1996), Horioka (1997), Masson *et al.* (1998), Loayza *et al.* (2000) and Athukorala and Tsai (2003).

The coefficients on $ECT_{t-1}$, which measure the speed of adjustment back to the long-run equilibrium value, are statistically significant at the 1 per cent level and have the right sign, i.e. negative, suggesting that an error correction mechanism exists. The speed of adjustment at 46.3 to 76.7 per cent a year is considered quite high. It takes between 1.3 to 2.2 years to achieve long-run equilibrium whenever there is a deviation from the long-run steady state. The adjustment towards equilibrium is found to faster in Model B since voluntary private saving is less subject to government policy. Finally, all regression specifications fit remarkably well and pass the diagnostic tests against non-normality, serial correlation, autoregressive conditional heteroskedasticity and heteroskedasticity, at the 5 per cent level of significance. However, only Model A passes the Ramsey's RESET test at the conventional levels.

## 6.5 Conclusion

This chapter examines the determinants of private saving in Malaysia. Drawing on the life cycle theory, the saving function is estimated by incorporating other relevant structural features of Malaysia into the specification. Particular emphasis has been placed on the effect of mandated retirement saving schemes on private saving behaviour, since EPF saving constitutes a large proportion of private saving in Malaysia. The predictions of the life cycle hypothesis are supported by the finding of a positive impact from real income. A negative effect of the age dependency ratio on private saving is found in the short-run but not the long-run. From a policy point of view, the evidence suggests that an increase in financial deepening and real interest rates contribute positively to private saving. Compulsory saving, in the form of EPF, seems to exert a negative influence on private saving. Hence, pension saving appears to be a substitute for private saving. The Ricardian equivalence hypothesis does not seem to hold strictly in Malaysia, given that public saving only partially crowds out private saving.

# 7 The determinants of private investment*

## 7.1 Introduction

This chapter examines the determinants of private investment, with an emphasis on the role of financial sectors. Given that capital formation in the private sector is the key engine for long-term growth in Malaysia, the understanding of investment behaviour in the private sector provides an important insight into how development in the Malaysian financial system impacts on economic growth.

The analytical framework is derived from the neoclassical investment model, with appropriate modifications to account for the structural features observed in the Malaysian economy. The investment function is disaggregated into private and public investment, with the focus specifically on the former. Private investment comprises private domestic investment and FDI. As highlighted in Chapter 3, FDI constitutes a significant proportion of total investment in Malaysia. Since FDI depends on a set of determinants which is quite different from that of private domestic investment, a private domestic investment function (private investment excludes FDI) is estimated separately to avoid aggregation bias.

This chapter proceeds as follows:

- Section 7.2 derives the investment function from the neoclassical framework. This simple framework is inadequate to characterize the unique structural features of Malaysia, and therefore it is modified to provide an alternative specification of the investment equation. A cost-minimization problem is adopted to introduce dynamics into the model by assuming that firms optimize their investment levels with respect to a quadratic loss function. The dynamic investment function is then estimated using an ECM.
- Section 7.3 describes the data;
- Section 7.4 tests the private investment and private domestic investment models, and the results are presented and analysed.
- Section 7.5 summarizes the findings.

* Parts of this chapter were previously printed in Ang (2008b).

## 7.2 A model of private investment

In an empirical study of this nature, there is always a trade-off between estimating a specification derived directly from theoretical investment optimization models, and an *atheoretical* reduced-formed specification obtained by incorporating many investment determinants. In view of this, an approach is taken to strike a balance between these two considerations. The empirical specification is first derived using the neoclassical model, which is a widely adopted specification for investment analysis (Blejer and Khan, 1984; Chirinko, 1993). This basic model is then modified accordingly to take into account both the new developments in the literature and the structural features observed in the Malaysian economy.[1] This involves the consideration of income level, user cost of capital, bank credit, macroeconomic uncertainty and public investment as the relevant determinants of private investment. By doing so, the specification encompasses a sound theoretical underpinning on the determinants of investment while taking into account the unique structural features of Malaysia.

### *7.2.1 Neoclassical model*

The neoclassical model of investment, pioneered by Jorgenson (1963, 1967, 1971), postulates that output levels and user cost of capital are the two key determinants of investment. Consider a firm which produces an output ($Q_t$) by using only capital ($K_t$) and labour ($L_t$). The firm's objective is to maximize its market value ($V_t$):

$$\max V_t = \int_0^\infty e^{-R_t}\left[p_t Q_t - w_t L_t - q_t I_t^N\right] dt \tag{1}$$

where $R_t$ is the discount rate, and $I_t$ is the net purchase of capital at time $t$. The product $Q_t$ is sold at $p_t$ and the inputs are bought at $w_t$ and $q_t$. The firm has to choose $K_t$, $L_t$, and $I_t$ to maximize its net present value, which depends on the future stream of profits generated by the firm. Assuming certainty, Nickell (1978) shows that Equation (1) can be reduced to a one-period static profit maximization problem:

$$\text{Max } \Pi_t = p_t Q_t - w_t L_t - C_t K_t \tag{2}$$

where $C_t$ is the user cost of capital. Suppose the technology adopted to produce the output can be represented by a simple Cobb–Douglas production function:

$$Q_t = AK_t^\lambda L_t^\gamma \tag{3}$$

Under the assumption of a perfectly competitive market, profit maximization requires:

$$\frac{\partial \Pi_t}{\partial K_t} = \lambda p_t A K_t^{\lambda - 1} L_t^{\gamma} - C_t = 0$$

$$\Rightarrow C_t = \lambda \frac{p_t Q_t}{K_t} = \lambda \frac{Y_t}{K_t} \tag{4}$$

where $\lambda$ is the share of capital in output and $Y_t$ is nominal output (the product of $p_t$ and $Q_t$). Hence, the optimal level of capital stock ($K_t^*$) is given as:

$$K_t^* = \lambda \frac{Y_t}{C_t}. \tag{5}$$

Net investment ($I_t^N$) can be represented by a distributed lag on the past changes in desired capital stock:

$$I_t^N = \sum_{j=0}^{n} b_j (\Delta K_{t-j}^*) = \lambda \sum_{j=0}^{n} b_j \Delta(Y_{t-j} / C_{t-j}). \tag{6}$$

Assuming that replacement investment ($I_t^R$) is linearly related to capital stock lagged by one period:

$$I_t^R = dK_{t-1}, \tag{7}$$

where $d$ is the rate of depreciation of capital stock, which is usually assumed to be constant. Hence, the gross investment function is:

$$I_t = I_t^N + I_t^R = \lambda \sum_{j=0}^{n} b_j \Delta(Y_{t-j} / C_{t-j}) + dK_{t-1}. \tag{8}$$

### *7.2.2 Modified neoclassical model*

This basic neoclassical investment framework is modified drawing upon Bischoff (1967, 1970, 1971). Bischoff's modification of the model is based on the observation that most changes in the capital–output ratio (or the relative prices of input) depend on *new* equipment and structures, rather than on existing capital stocks. Hence, the changes in relative prices of input should be different from changes in output. Accordingly, demand for investment should depend on the *levels* of output, instead of the *changes* of output as predicted by the standard neoclassical model:

$$I_t = \lambda \sum_{j=0}^{n} b_j (Y_{t-j} / C_{t-j}) + dK_{t-1}. \tag{9}$$

Adopting the strict version of Jorgenson's neoclassical model may pose some problems. For example, it is unlikely the expression of $K_t^* = \lambda Y_t / C_t$ will hold strictly as the demand function for desired level of capital stock. Similarly, not all entities share the ultimate objective of maximizing market values or profits. For example, educational institutions, welfare organizations, and religious bodies do not belong to this category (Bischoff, 1970). For these reasons, a simple linear specification is preferred:

$$K_t^* = f(Y_t, C_t) \tag{10}$$

Given the perpetual inventory model, $I_t = K_t - (1 - \delta)K_{t-1}$, steady state equilibrium condition gives $K_t^* = K_t = K_{t-1}$. Hence, $I_t^* = \delta K_t^*$ so that Equation (10) also determines equilibrium investment:

$$I_t^* = f(Y_t, C_t) \tag{11}$$

where $I_t^*$ is the steady state of investment. Such a linear specification is consistent with the empirical strategy adopted by the modern empirical literature on investment demand functions.[2] Next, the specification for investment in Equation (10) is modified to account for the institutional and structural features of a developing country.

### *(a) Bank credit*

The neoclassical model of investment is based upon the restrictive assumption that financial markets are frictionless and there is unlimited supply of credit. However, developing countries are often characterized by credit constraints due to market imperfections such as problems of asymmetric and contract enforcement (Ganesh-Kumar *et al.*, 2003). Imperfections in credit markets may prevent firms from borrowing as much as they would wish. Such a constraint will in general discourage the undertaking of investment projects. The McKinnon–Shaw thesis of financial liberalization postulates a complementary relationship between the accumulation of financial assets and physical capital. In this connection, the removal of financial constraints may mitigate the liquidity constraints faced by entrepreneurs, and significantly increase the amount of funds available for investment. Furthermore, development of financial systems can help overcome these market frictions by exploiting economies of scale in the evaluation and monitoring of borrowers, and thus facilitating the flow of funds between savers and investors. This largely ameliorates credit constraints faced by firms lacking an easy access to bank credit (Cornelli *et al.*, 1996).

*(b) Macroeconomic uncertainty*

Investment may be adversely affected by economic uncertainty (Villanueva and Mirakhor, 1990). Macroeconomic uncertainty in this study refers to a situation when there are severe fluctuations in output levels, which induce greater variance in returns on investment projects. If investments are irreversible, firms are more prone to delay or abandon investment projects in an uncertain economic environment.[3] Postponing investment until the future becomes more certain may generate opportunity costs whereas forgoing an investment project results in a loss of initial outlays. Furthermore, in an uncertain economic environment, firms will be encouraged to maintain a highly liquid asset position. Productive activities requiring commitments in long-term fixed investments will be discouraged. As such, less capital accumulation will occur in a highly uncertain economic environment. In this way, a negative link between investment and macroeconomic uncertainty is established.

*(c) Public investment*

It is a widely accepted view that public investment may be complementary to, rather than competing with, private investment in developing countries. Public investment may facilitate and stimulate private investment through the provision of infrastructural support (Sundararajan and Thakur, 1980; Blejer and Khan, 1984; Greene and Villanueva, 1991). This can raise the productivity of capital and expand the overall resource availability by increasing output. On the other hand, public investment may also crowd out private investment. This occurs when additional public investment requires raising future tax and domestic interest rates, or if the public sector produces investment goods that directly compete with private goods. In addition, the utilization of additional physical and financial resources, which would otherwise be available to the private sector, may also depress private investment (Blejer and Khan 1984; Aschauer 1989a).

### 7.2.3 FDI flows and domestic investment

FDI can have both positive and negative effects on private domestic investment. It can stimulate domestic investment by providing new investment opportunities for local firms through the provision of machinery and technology which cannot otherwise be produced domestically (Sun, 1998). Local firms can emulate the new technology introduced by foreign firms, which may stimulate domestic investment (Noorzoy, 1979). Besides, an increase in domestic investment is likely to be accompanied by an increase in FDI inflows when there are more joint venture activities between local firms and foreign firms (Jansen, 1995). FDI may also contribute to higher domestic investment through introducing new export industries to the host country. These new industries are integrated into worldwide networks of production, enabling them to grow rapidly (Lipsey, 2004). In this way, FDI and private domestic investment are complementary to each other.

On the other hand, FDI may crowd out domestic investment if foreign firms compete with local firms for the use of domestic scarce resources, such as skilled labour, financial resources, etc. (Jansen, 1995). FDI may also disrupt backward linkages in domestic manufacturing through the substitution of imports for domestic goods. Furthermore, FDI may substitute for domestic investment if foreign firms have an edge in technological or managerial expertise, or tax benefits provided by the host country (Noorzoy, 1979). These new technologies embodied in FDI may accelerate technological obsolescence of traditional technologies used in developing countries and therefore crowd out domestic investment (Kim and Seo, 2003; Lipsey, 2004).

The above discussion suggests that the effects of FDI on private domestic investment may vary from country to country, depending on the types of FDI, the trade policies adopted in the host country, and the strengths of the domestic firms. Therefore, the impact of FDI inflows on private domestic investment is ultimately an empirical matter.

### 7.2.4 Model specification

Renaming the variables as $Y_t = GDP_t$ and $C_t = COC_t$, and augmenting Equation (11) with the above theoretical considerations leads to formulation of the following empirical specifications of the long-run private investment and private domestic investment equations:

$$\text{Model A}: \bar{I}_t^* = f_A(GDP_t, COC_t, BC_t, UNC_t, PUB_t, D_{69}, D_{85\text{–}86}, D_{97\text{–}98}) \quad (12a)$$

$$\text{Model B}: \tilde{I}_t^* = f_B(GDP_t, COC_t, BC_t, UNC_t, PUB_t, D_{69}, D_{85\text{–}86}, D_{97\text{–}98}) \quad (12b)$$

$$\text{Model C}: \tilde{I}_t^* = f_C(GDP_t, COC_t, BC_t, UNC_t, PUB_t, FDI_t, D_{69}, D_{85\text{–}86}, D_{97\text{–}98}) \quad (12c)$$

where $\bar{I}_t^*$ is the steady-state real private investment ($PRI_t$) and $\tilde{I}_t^*$ is the steady state real private domestic investment ($PDI_t$). Although the main objective is to estimate a private domestic investment function, a private investment function is also estimated in Model A to allow for comparison of the results with other studies, which have largely focused on analysing the behaviour of private investment. The same set of regressors is used in both Model B and Model C except that FDI is included as an additional variable in the latter. The specification in Model C allows examination of whether FDI crowds in or crowds out private domestic investment in Malaysia. The independent variables, with the expected signs in the parentheses, are defined as follows:

$GDP_t$ = real output (+)
$COC_t$ = real user cost of capital (–)
$BC_t$ = real bank credit flow to the private sector (+)
$UNC_t$ = macroeconomic uncertainty (–)
$PUB_t$ = real public investment (?)
$FDI_t$ = real foreign direct investment (?)

$PRI_t$, $PDI_t$, $GDP_t$, $PUB_t$ and $FDI_t$ are converted into natural logarithms. The above specification includes three dummy variables to account for the racial riots in 1969, the global economic recession that hit Malaysia in 1985–86, and the 1997–98 Asian financial crisis, defined as:

$$D_{69} = \begin{cases} 1 \text{ if } t = 1969 \\ 0 \text{ otherwise} \end{cases}; \qquad D_{85\text{–}86} = \begin{cases} 1 \text{ if } t = 1985\text{–}86 \\ 0 \text{ otherwise} \end{cases} \text{ and}$$

$$D_{97\text{–}98} = \begin{cases} 1 \text{ if } t = 1997-98 \\ 0 \text{ otherwise} \end{cases}$$

### 7.2.5 Dynamic specification

Having established the steady-static (long-run) specification of the investment function, dynamics are now introduced. To derive a dynamic investment model suitable for econometric estimation, Sims' (1974) approach is followed by postulating a dynamic cost optimization problem that imposes costs on 'mistakes' made by agents. Suppose that every year, each firm in the economy has a desired level of investment $I^*_t$. This ideal level of investment depends on a number of factors stated in Equation (12a, b, c). The actual level of investment ($I_t$) differs from that of the desired level ($I^*_t$) due to the costs associated with adjusting $I_t$. To illustrate how this would lead to a dynamic investment model, consider that in any period $t$, the representative firm's objective is to minimize the following penalty function by optimizing the level of investment:[4]

$$\underset{I_t}{\text{Min}}\ E_t \left\{ \sum_{t=1}^{\infty} \delta^t \left[ a(I_t - I^*_t)^2 + b(I_t - I_{t-1})^2 - 2c(I_t - I_{t-1})(I^*_t - I^*_{t-1}) \right] \mid \Omega_t \right\} \tag{13}$$

where $\delta^t$ is the discount factor which takes a value between 0 and 1, and $\Omega_t$ is the firm's information set at time $t$. The first term in the square bracket represents the cost of deviation from the desired level of investment. The second term is the cost of rapidly changing the level of investment. The last term is included due to Hendry and von Ungern-Sternberg (1981), who argue that the penalty is reduced if firms move in the correct direction, i.e. towards the equilibrium level of investment. The last term will converge to zero if the desired level of investment remains unchanged.

The firm seeks to minimize the expectation of the future stream of costs associated with investment decision making, conditional upon all available information $\Omega_t$ at time $t$. Since it is difficult to estimate the discount factor, the approach of Callen *et al.* (1990) is taken by setting it to unity for simplicity. This does not affect the general form of the solution to the model. Invoking the certainty equivalence theorem and the rational expectation hypothesis so that expectation is replaced by future realization, and choosing $I_t$ at time $t$ to minimize expected costs leads to the following Euler condition:

$$(a + 2b)I_t - b(I_{t-1} + I_{t+1}) = (a + 2c)I_t^* - c(I_{t-1}^* + I_{t+1}^*) \tag{14}$$

Next,

$$\text{Let } x_t = I_t - \frac{c}{b} I_t^* \tag{15}$$

Equation (14) can be written as:

$$[(a + 2b) - bL - bL^{-1}]x_t = \frac{a(b-c)}{b} I_t^* \tag{16}$$

or

$$A(L)x_t = \frac{a(b-c)}{b} I_t^* \tag{17}$$

A solution for Equation (17) may be defined as:

$$A(L) = \lambda(1 - \theta L)(1 - \phi\theta L^{-1}) \tag{18}$$

and so Equation (17) may be written as:

$$\lambda(1 - \theta L)(1 - \phi\theta L^{-1})x_t = \frac{a(b-c)}{b} I_t^*$$

$$\Rightarrow x_t = \theta x_{t-1} + \frac{a(b-c)}{\delta b} \sum_{i=0}^{\infty} (\theta\phi)^i I_{t+i}^*. \tag{19}$$

Using Equation (15) and some manipulation obtain:

$$\Delta I_t = (\theta - 1)I_{t-1} + \frac{c}{b} \Delta I_t^* + \frac{c(1-\beta)}{b} I_{t-1}^* + \frac{a(b-c)}{\lambda b} \sum_{i=0}^{\infty} (\theta\phi)^i I_{t+i}^*. \tag{20}$$

Nickell (1985) shows that the use of a standard ECM is consistent with the optimizing behaviour of economic agents. The simplest case demonstrated by Nickell is followed by assuming $I^*_{t+i}$ follows a random walk with drift:

$$I^*_{t+i} = I^*_t + gi \tag{21}$$

where $g$ is the drift term. Then substituting Equation (21) into Equation (20), and rearranging the terms gives the familiar error correction representation of the dynamic investment demand model:

$$\Delta I_t = a_0 + a_1 \Delta I^*_t - a_2(I_{t-1} - I^*_{t-1}) \tag{22}$$

The error-correction term $(I_{t-1} - I^*_{t-1})$ captures the long-run equilibrium relationship between variables whereas the differenced terms $(\Delta I^*_t)$ capture the short-run dynamics. The use of an ECM is appropriate in this context since investment decisions are likely to be gradual and subject to revision in a developing country. Although equilibrium investment $I^*_t$ is unobservable, Equation (22) can be estimated by using the long-run steady state investment functions in Equation (12a, b, c).

## 7.3 Results

To perform cointegration tests, the conditional ECM is estimated with one and two lags for each model. The results summarized in Table B.3 of Appendix 4 indicate that the null hypothesis that there exists no level private investment equation is rejected at the 1 per cent significance level for all models when two lags are chosen. Some weak evidence is found to support the existence of a long-run relationship when one lag is chosen for Model B. In line with the results of cointegration tests, both AIC and SBC suggest a richer dynamic specification of two lags.

Based on the cointegration results, the estimation begins with two lags and systematically drops the insignificant terms. The estimated long-run and short-run results of the private investment equations are summarized in Table 7.1. All variables except $COC_t$ enter the long-run equations with the predicted signs, and the coefficients are quite significant (see Table 7.1, panel A).

On the whole, the findings are consistent with the theoretical predictions of a neoclassical model that private investment varies positively with output. A one per cent increase in output will result in a 1.195 to 1.365 per cent increase in private investment. The finding that $\ln GDP_t$ is an important determinant of private investment is consistent with the empirical evidence of Blejer and Khan (1984) and Greene and Villanueva (1991). However, $COC_t$ is found to be statistically insignificant and has the wrong (positive) sign. Hence, there is no evidence to suggest that user cost of capital is an important variable in explaining private investment behaviour in Malaysia.[5]

In countries with directed credit programs and rationing financial systems,

*Table 7.1* Long-run and short-run results of the private investment equations

| | Model A (Dep. = $lnPRI_t$) | | Model B (Dep. = $lnPDI_t$) | | Model C (Dep. = $lnPDI_t$) | |
|---|---|---|---|---|---|---|
| | *A. The long-run equilibrium level relationship* | | | | | |
| | *Coefficient* | *p-value* | *Coefficient* | *p-value* | *Coefficient* | *p-value* |
| *Intercept* | −6.759*** | 0.000 | −6.445*** | 0.000 | −5.718*** | 0.000 |
| $\ln GDP_t$ | 1.365*** | 0.000 | 1.280*** | 0.000 | 1.195*** | 0.000 |
| $COC_t$ | 0.078 | 0.880 | 0.566 | 0.425 | −0.289 | 0.561 |
| $BC_t$ | 1.232*** | 0.001 | 0.916* | 0.061 | 1.018** | 0.013 |
| $UNC_t$ | −0.003*** | 0.000 | −0.004*** | 0.000 | −0.004*** | 0.000 |
| $\ln PUB_t$ | 0.045 | 0.747 | 0.046 | 0.826 | 0.017 | 0.913 |
| $\ln FDI_t$ | | | | | 0.160** | 0.024 |
| $D_{69}$ | −0.394** | 0.041 | −0.826*** | 0.004 | −0.548*** | 0.008 |
| | *B. The short-run dynamic model* | | | | | |
| | *Model A (Dep. = $\Delta lnPRI_t$)* | | *Model B (Dep. = $\Delta lnPDI_t$)* | | *Model C (Dep. = $\Delta lnPDI_t$)* | |
| | *Coefficient* | *p-value* | *Coefficient* | *p-value* | *Coefficient* | *p-value* |
| *Intercept* | −0.212*** | 0.000 | −0.006 | 0.947 | −0.323*** | 0.000 |
| $ECT_{t-1}$ | −0.309*** | 0.001 | −0.575*** | 0.000 | −0.584*** | 0.000 |
| $\Delta \ln GDP_t$ | 4.163*** | 0.000 | 3.656*** | 0.000 | 3.616*** | 0.000 |
| $\Delta BC_t$ | 0.252** | 0.013 | | | | |
| $\Delta UNC_t$ | −0.001** | 0.031 | −0.003*** | 0.000 | −0.003*** | 0.002 |
| $\Delta \ln PDI_{t-1}$ | | | 0.316** | 0.021 | 0.290** | 0.029 |
| $\Delta \ln GDP_{t-1}$ | 1.727*** | 0.002 | 3.078*** | 0.002 | 2.290** | 0.019 |
| $\Delta BC_{t-1}$ | | | −0.510*** | 0.009 | −0.516*** | 0.010 |
| $\Delta UNC_{t-1}$ | | | 0.002** | 0.034 | | |
| $\Delta COC_{t-2}$ | −0.553*** | 0.006 | | | | |
| $\Delta BC_{t-2}$ | | | −0.377** | 0.034 | −0.369** | 0.041 |
| *Diagnostic checks* | *Test-statistic* | *p-value* | *Test-statistic* | *p-value* | *Test-statistic* | *p-value* |
| $\chi^2_{NORMAL}(2)$ | 3.753 | 0.153 | 2.533 | 0.281 | 0.188 | 0.909 |
| $\chi^2_{SERIAL}(1)$ | 2.751* | 0.097 | 0.006 | 0.935 | 0.741 | 0.389 |
| $\chi^2_{SERIAL}(2)$ | 3.755 | 0.152 | 0.630 | 0.729 | 0.908 | 0.634 |
| $\chi^2_{ARCH}(1)$ | 1.305 | 0.253 | 0.031 | 0.859 | 0.150 | 0.698 |
| $\chi^2_{WHITE}$ | 10.125 | 0.604 | 11.270 | 0.792 | 24.329 | 0.051* |
| $\chi^2_{RESET}(1)$ | 4.629** | 0.031 | 5.978** | 0.014 | 3.750 | 0.053* |

*Notes:* The regressions for the long-run model are based on an unrestricted ECM, and corrected for both omitted lagged variable bias and endogeneity bias. The regressions for the short-run dynamic model are based on a conditional ECM. *, ** and *** indicate 10%, 5% and 1% level of significance, respectively. $\chi^2_{NORMAL}(2)$ refers to the Jarque-Bera statistic of the test for normal residuals, $\chi^2_{SERIAL}(1)$ and $\chi^2_{SERIAL}(2)$ are the Breusch-Godfrey LM test statistics for no first and second order serial correlation, respectively, $\chi^2_{WHITE}$ denotes the White's test statistic to test for homoskedastic errors, with degrees of freedom equal to the number of slope coefficients, $\chi^2_{ARCH}(1)$ is the Engle's test statistic for no autoregressive conditional heteroskedasticity, and $\chi^2_{RESET}(1)$ is the Ramsey's test statistic for no functional misspecification.

the quantity rather than the cost of financing is more likely to be the main determinant of investment (see Chibber and Shafik, 1992; Schmidt-Hebbel and Muller, 1992; Agrawal, 2004). In Malaysia, bank credit is found to have a strong positive and statistically significant impact on private investment, with a long-run elasticity in the range of 0.916 to 1.232. This implies that the shortage of credit during the crisis period dampened private capital formation.[6] The size of the coefficient is found to be largest in Model B which does not consider FDI. The results are not surprising given that foreign investors are likely to bring in their own financial resources whereas domestic investors are more likely to obtain funding in the domestic financial sector. The finding of a significant positive impact of bank credit on investment corroborates the empirical evidence of Yaakop (1988), Shafik (1992), Voridis (1993), Guncavdi *et al.* (1998), Ndikumana (2000) and Ganesh-Kumar *et al.* (2001, 2003).

Consistent with the argument of Villanueva and Mirakhor (1990), an increase in macroeconomic uncertainty exerts a negative effect on private investment. The long-run elasticity derived from the coefficient on $UNC_t$ suggests a 1 per cent increase in macroeconomic uncertainty yields a 0.003 to 0.004 per cent reduction in private investment. The results tend to support the empirical findings of Greene and Villanueva (1991) and Ozler and Rodrik (1992) and seem to suggest that in order to provide a favourable investment climate for entrepreneurs, it is crucial for the government to maintain a sound political and economic environment. Macroeconomic policies designed to stabilize the economic environment could have the potential for boosting private investment especially in times of rapid output changes.

There is no evidence that public investment crowds in or crowds out private investment, given that the coefficients on $\ln PUB_t$ are found to be insignificant at the conventional levels. Public investment expenditure has been used in Malaysia as a key policy tool to stimulate economic growth, particularly after the Asian financial crisis. However, the evidence obtained in this study seems to suggest that public investment has no effect on private sector investment. Hence, the ongoing pump-priming efforts made by the Malaysian government to revive total investment appear to be ineffective in stimulating private investment. This is likely to be the case when additional government investment competes with private investment and results in a higher cost of financing. Similarly, more public investment may have led to an increase in anticipated future tax, which tends to discourage private investment. These two opposing forces may offset each other and result in no overall effect on private investment.

The coefficient on $\ln FDI_t$ in Model C is statistically significant with a positive sign. A 1 per cent increase in FDI inflows will lead to a 0.160 per cent increase in private domestic investment. Even if a positive relationship between FDI and domestic investment can be established, the impact of FDI on a host country can be small if FDI inflows are a minor part of the country's capital formation (Lipsey, 2000). In Malaysia, the average share of FDI in total gross domestic capital formation was only 13 per cent per year over the period 1960–2005 (see Chapter 3). Hence, it is not surprising FDI exerts a small effect on private domestic investment.

The result that FDI has a complementary role to play in domestic capital formation is consistent with the findings of Van Loo (1977) and Noorzoy (1979) for the Canadian experience, Jansen (1995) for the Thai experience, Sun (1998) for the Chinese experience, Bosworth and Collins (1999) for 58 developing countries over the period 1978–95, and Agosin and Machado (2005) in panel regressions of five Asian countries (including Malaysia). The crowding-in effect observed in Malaysia may imply that the domestic financial markets are not too tight. In cases where there are difficulties in raising funds in the domestic market, a crowding-out effect is likely to be observed (Jansen, 1995).

Finally, the coefficient on $D_{69}$ is found to be negative, implying that the racial riots of 1969 had a negative impact on private investment. The dummy variables which capture the effect of the global economic recession, i.e. $D_{85-86}$, and the Asian financial crisis, i.e. $D_{97-98}$, are found to be statistically insignificant and therefore excluded from the estimation.

The results suggest that the sharp decline in private investment during the post-crisis period is largely attributable to the above-mentioned factors. To revive private investment, the government should consider adopting policies that boost economic development, easing credit constraints by developing a more efficient financial system, reducing macroeconomic uncertainties, restraining public investment expenditure, and encouraging FDI inflows. Among these, expanding the economy and improving the financial system seem to be the most effective mechanisms to boost private investment.

With regard to short-run dynamics, the regression results for the conditional ECM of $\Delta \ln PRI_t$ and $\Delta \ln PDI_t$, reported in panel B of Table 7.1, show several desirable features. Except for the intercept terms in Model A and Model B, all coefficients are statistically significant at the 10 per cent level. In first-differenced form, all the variables have expected signs, consistent with the results reported in the long-run models.

The coefficients on $ECT_{t-1}$ are statistically significant at the 1 per cent level and have the correct sign, providing further evidence for the use of an ECM framework. In Model A, private investment adjusts at the speed of 30.9 per cent every year, or it takes about 3.2 years, to restore equilibrium when there is a shock on the steady-state relationship. The speed of adjustment for Model B and Model C, ranging from 57.5 to 58.4 per cent a year, implies that it takes less than two years to achieve long-run equilibrium whenever there is a deviation from the long-run steady state. The results are not surprising given that there is little government control on private domestic investment.

All the regression specifications fit remarkably well, satisfying normality, no serial correlation, absence of autoregressive conditional heteroskedasticity and homoskedastic residuals (see Table 7.1). However, Model A and Model B fail the regression specification error test (or Ramsey's RESET test) at the 5 per cent level of significance. This is probably due to the presence of some non-linear effects in the adjustment process of private investment which the linear specification adopted here is unable to take into account.

## 7.5 Conclusion

This chapter examines the determinants of real private investment in Malaysia in an autoregressive distributed lag (ARDL) framework, paying particular attention to the testing for a long-run cointegrating relationship between the variables under consideration. Most previous empirical studies have simply bypassed the theoretical considerations by adopting an encompassing approach which incorporates a large number of potential determinants of private investment in the model specification. The analysis in this chapter makes use of a private investment model, drawing on the neoclassical framework while incorporating relevant institutional and structural features of Malaysia into the specification.

The estimated results suggest that the predictions of the neoclassical model are supported by the findings of a large positive impact of aggregate output on private investment. However, user cost of capital appears to be unimportant in private capital formation. Macroeconomic uncertainty exerts a negative influence on private investment. While there is also evidence that FDI crowds in private domestic investment, public investment partially crowds out private investment. More importantly, the evidence indicates that increased bank credit contributes positively to private investment, suggesting that financial development is crucial for the undertaking of investment projects in the private sector.

# 8 The saving and investment nexus*

## 8.1 Introduction

This chapter examines the relationship between the domestic saving and investment rates in Malaysia. Given that these two variables are cointegrated, the relationship is estimated using an ECM with a cointegrating framework to allow for an analysis on both the short-run and long-run dynamics of the saving–investment relationship.

The last two chapters have shown that financial factors affect both saving and investment decisions. The quantification of the link between saving and investment is crucial since higher capital accumulation necessitates more saving, which can be mobilized domestically or obtained from foreign countries. However, the link between domestic saving and investment may be significantly weakened by international capital mobility as saving accumulated in one country can be easily transferred to and invested in another country. Thus, it is important to examine the extent to which domestic saving has been used to facilitate the undertaking of investment projects. An important aspect of this relationship is the adoption of capital controls by the Malaysian government in the aftermath of the Asian financial crisis. This policy choice may have important implications in the dynamic relationship between saving and investment.

The chapter is organized as follows:

- Section 8.2 discusses the conceptual issues;
- Section 8.3 derives the empirical specification for the dynamic saving–investment relationship, based on an intertemporal current account model;
- Section 8.4 sets out the empirical model and describes the data;
- Section 8.5 presents and analyses the results. Policy implications of the results are briefly discussed;
- Section 8.6 provides the conclusion.

* Parts of this chapter were previously printed in Ang (2008b).

## 8.2 Conceptual issues

In a seminal study, Feldstein and Horioka (1980) examine the extent of correlation between saving and investment across 16 OECD countries. They argue that there should be no relationship between a country's domestic saving and domestic investment in the presence of perfect capital mobility. Extra saving in any country will be channelled to the world capital market to fund other countries with favourable investment climates. Using cross-sectional analysis, they show that 85 to 95 per cent of domestic savings are transformed into investment in the domestic economies. They find that the regression coefficient of saving on domestic investment is statistically different from zero but not different from one, suggesting that international capital mobility is rather low. This observed phenomenon is widely known as the 'Feldstein–Horioka puzzle'.

Following this controversial finding, the relationship between saving and investment has been the subject of intense research over the past two decades. The Feldstein–Horioka puzzle has been examined by a large number of authors, using both cross-country and time series data for individual countries. Many of these studies have confirmed the Feldstein–Horioka results of a high saving–investment correlation. Using a cross-sectional framework, the findings of Feldstein (1983), Penati and Dooley (1984), Dooley *et al.* (1987), Vos (1988) and Feldstein and Bacchetta (1989), among others, suggest a close relationship between domestic saving and investment rates. In line with these, time series studies in this strand of literature examine the dynamic saving–investment nexus over time and across different exchange rate and capital control regimes, and report similar findings (see Jansen and Schulze, 1996; Hussein, 1998; Taylor, 1998; De Vita and Abbott, 2002; Pelagidis and Mastroyiannis, 2003; Hoffmann, 2004; Payne, 2005).

However, whether the results provide an indication of the degree of capital immobility remains debatable. Many economists disagree with the interpretation of the Feldstein–Horioka results due to one thing: the increased integration of the global financial markets observed today is inconsistent with the argument of declining capital mobility. Using alternative measures of capital mobility, such as purchasing power and interest rate differentials, the results of Sachs (1981), Obstfeld (1986), Frankel and MacArthur (1990) and Baxter and Crucini (1993), among others, show that the long-run capital mobility is increasing over time.

Based on these findings, a number of authors argue that the Feldstein–Horioka finding is simply due to various methodological problems, such as endogeneity problems (Dooley *et al.*, 1987), and failure to appropriately allow for differences in country size (Ho, 2003; Bahmani-Oskooee and Chakrabarti, 2005), financial structure (Kasuga, 2004), non-traded goods (Wong, 1990), productivity shocks (Obstfeld, 1986; Cardia, 1991), fiscal policy (Bayoumi, 1990), and intertemporal budget constraints (Coakley *et al.*, 1996; Moreno,

1997). After accounting for these differences, the link between domestic saving and investment is found to be significantly weaker.

## 8.3 An intertemporal model of current account

In this chapter, the model developed by Sheffrin and Woo (1990) is used to derive a current account dynamic model based on intertemporal optimization. This model originates from the seminal work of Sachs (1981), and has been widely adopted in many studies of current account dynamics. The current account intertemporal model embodies an important econometric feature of the saving–investment relationship, i.e. these two variables are cointegrated. This cointegrating feature can be demonstrated using the approach of Campbell (1987) and Campbell and Shiller (1987).

To begin with, consider the international borrowing and lending model of Sachs (1981), which assumes a small open economy. Such an assumption is particularly pertinent to the case of Malaysia. The economy faces a given world interest rate ($r$) and the stock of foreign assets ($F_t$) evolves according to the following equation:

$$F_{t+1} = (1 + r)F_t + (Y_t - C_t - I_t - G_t) \tag{1}$$

where $Y_t$ refers to GDP, $C_t$ denotes consumption, $I_t$ is investment, and $G_t$ is government spending. The solvency condition requires satisfying the no Ponzi scheme, with a full repayment of lending in infinity.[1]

$$\lim_{i \to \infty} \frac{F_{t+i}}{(1 + r)} = 0 \tag{2}$$

Let $Z_t = Y_t - C_t - I_t - G_t$, assuming agents are forward looking, solving Equation (1) iteratively yields:

$$F_{t+1} = (1 + r)F_t + Z_t$$

$$F_{t+2} = (1 + r)F_{t+1} + Z_{t+1} = (1 + r)^2 F_t + (1 + r)Z_t + Z_{t+1}$$

$$F_{t+3} = (1 + r)F_{t+2} + Z_{t+2} = (1 + r)^3 F_t + (1 + r)^2 Z_t + (1 + r)Z_{t+1} + Z_{t+2}$$

$$\vdots$$

$$F_{t+i} = (1 + r)F_{t+i-1} + Z_{t+i-1} = (1 + r)^i F_t + (1 + r)^{i-1} Z_t + (1 + r)^{i-2} Z_{t+1} + \ldots + Z_{t+i-1}$$

$$\Rightarrow \frac{F_{t+i}}{(1 + r)^i} = F_t + \sum_{i=1}^{i} \frac{Z_{t+i-1}}{(1 + r)^i}$$

When, $i \to \infty$, applying the no Ponzi condition in Equation (2) yields:

$$F_t = -\sum_{i=1}^{\infty}\left[\frac{Y_{t+i-1} - C_{t+i-1} - I_{t+i-1} - G_{t+i-1}}{(1+r)^i}\right] \quad (3)$$

Equation (3) can be rearranged as:

$$\sum_{i=1}^{\infty}\frac{C_{t+i-1}}{(1+r)^i} = F_t + \sum_{i=1}^{\infty}\frac{(Y_{t+i-1} - I_{t+i-1} - G_{t+i-1})}{(1+r)^i} \quad (4)$$

Equation (4) states that the discounted future stream of consumption is equal to claims on foreign assets plus the discounted future stream of output, net of investment expenditure and government expenditure.

The economy is assumed to be populated by an infinitely lived representative agent, who maximizes an intertemporal utility function of the form:

$$\sum_{i=0}^{\infty}(1+r)^{-i}E_t\,[u(C_t)] \quad (5)$$

Assuming that the utility function follows a quadratic form, and maximizing Equation (5) subject to the constraint in Equation (4) leads to:

$$C_t = r\left[F_t + \left(\frac{1}{1+r}\right)\sum_{i=0}^{\infty}(1+r)^{-i}E_t\,(Y_{t+i} - I_{t+i} - G_{t+i})\right] \quad (6)$$

Define the current account ($CA_t$) as:

$$CA_t = (Y_t - I_t - G_t) - C_t + rF_t \quad (7)$$

Substituting Equation (6) into Equation (7) gives:

$$CA_t = -\sum_{i=1}^{\infty}\left[(1+r)^{-i}E_t\Delta(Y_{t+i} - I_{t+i} - G_{t+i})\right] \quad (8)$$

Equation (8) gives an intertemporal model of current account. Accordingly, the current account is represented as the discounted sum of expected changes in $(Y_t - I_t - G_t)$.[2] The interpretation of Equation (8) is straightforward: foreign saving increases if output net of investment and government spending is expected to fall in future. This interpretation is analogous to the saving model of Campbell (1987) in which people save more in anticipation of a fall in future income. Equation (8) has an important econometric implication: if

$(Y_t - I_t - G_t)$ can be characterized as an $I(1)$ process, then $\Delta(Y_t - I_t - G_t)$ will be $I(0)$, and therefore $CA_t$ will be stationary.

According to national account identity, GNP is defined as the sum of consumption $(C_t)$, investment $(I_t)$, government spending $(G_t)$, exports $(X_t)$ minus imports $(M_t)$, and net factor income from abroad $(NFIA_t)$:

$$GNP_t = C_t + I_t + G_t + (X_t - M_t) + NFIA_t \tag{9}$$

Given that $CA_t$ is defined as $(X_t - M_t) + NFIA_t$, and saving $(S_t)$ is defined as $GNP_t - C_t - G_t$, it follows that the current account can be expressed as saving minus investment:

$$CA_t = S_t - I_t \tag{10}$$

Since the current account balance is obtained by subtracting investment from saving, these two variables should be cointegrated with a vector [1 −1], irrespective of the degree of capital mobility. Thus, the theory here implies that saving and investment should be cointegrated, even if capital is perfectly immobile.[3]

## 8.4 Model and data

### *8.4.1 Model specification*

Feldstein and Horioka (1980) adopt the following simple static specification to examine the saving–investment link:

$$(I / Y)_t = \alpha + \beta(S / Y)_t + \varepsilon_t \tag{11}$$

where $(I/Y)_t$ and $(S/Y)_t$ are the shares of gross domestic investment and gross domestic saving in output. However, such a simple econometric specification is subject to the problems of omitted lagged variable bias since no dynamics are included in the specification (Banerjee *et al.*, 1986). Furthermore, if $(I/Y)_t$ and $(S/Y)_t$ contain unit roots, then regressing Equation (11) in levels may produce 'spurious' regression results (Granger and Newbold, 1974).

In view of these, a dynamic specification in the form of an unrestricted ECM is adopted to estimate the long-run relationship between domestic saving and investment rates:

$$(I/Y)_t = \alpha_0 + \beta_1 D_{98\text{-}05} + \beta_2 (S/Y)_t + \sum_{i=0}^{p} \gamma_{1i} \Delta(I/Y)_{t-i}$$

$$+ \sum_{i=0}^{p} \gamma_{2i} \Delta(S/Y)_{t-i} + \sum_{i=0}^{p} \gamma_{2i} \Delta D_{98\text{-}05} \mathrm{x}\, (S/Y)_{t-i} + u_t \tag{12}$$

A step dummy and a slope dummy are included in the specification to account for the adoption of the capital control regime for the period 1998–2005. Incidentally, this period coincides with the structural break observed in the investment series due to the catastrophic effects of the Asian financial crisis. The dynamic specification in Equation (12) allows for a possible shift in the function and a change in the coefficients due to these specific events.

### *8.4.2 Time series plots of variables*

Figure 8.1 presents the time series plots of gross domestic saving rate $(S/Y)_t$ and gross domestic investment rate $(I/Y)_t$. Gross domestic investment refers to the sum of private fixed capital formation, public fixed capital formation and change in stocks. Gross domestic saving is defined as the total saving of the private and public sector.

It is clear that both series have increased significantly over time. The share of gross domestic saving to GDP rose from just 26 per cent in 1960 to 43 per cent in 1996, before the onset of the Asian financial crisis. Gross domestic investment increased from 14 per cent of GDP to 42 per cent of GDP during the same period. Both $(S/Y)_t$ and $(I/Y)_t$ have declined during the post-crisis

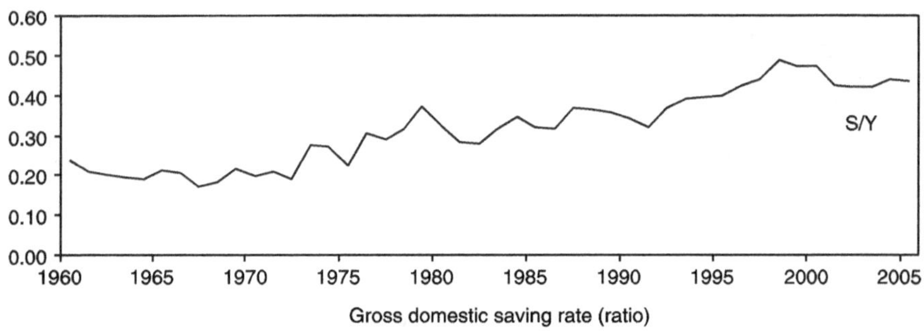


*Notes: S/Y* = gross domestic saving/GDP.

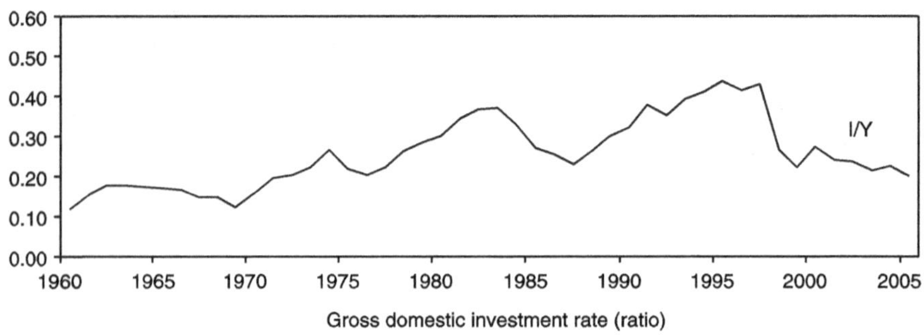


*Figure 8.1* Time series plots of variables.

*Notes: I/Y* = gross domestic investment/GDP.

period of 1998–2005, but a more substantial decline is observed in $(I/Y)_t$, as highlighted in Chapters 3 and 7 previously.

## 8.5 Empirical findings

The results of cointegration tests reported in Table B.4 of Appendix 4 indicate that the null hypothesis that there is no cointegration between $\ln(S/Y)_t$ and $\ln(I/Y)_t$ is rejected at the 10 per cent significance level. The evidence of cointegration is found to be stronger when two lags are chosen. With regard to the choice of lag length, the results are ambiguous since AIC prefers two lags whereas SBC suggests a simpler dynamic specification of one lag.

Panel A of Table 8.1 shows both $\ln(S/Y)_t$ and $D_{98\text{-}05}$ enter the long-run equation significantly at the 1 per cent level. The elasticity of investment rate with respect to saving rate is found to be around 1.21 in the long run, suggesting a positive long-run relationship between the saving and investment rates. The findings of a robust long-run cointegrated relationship suggest that any change in domestic saving will be closely associated with a change in domestic investment. Hence, financial sector policies targeted at mobilizing domestic saving are critical for capital accumulation. However, it should also be noted that over-reliance on domestic saving may limit an economy's growth opportunity. As such, policy makers should also focus on attracting foreign capital as part of the development policy while mobilizing resources in the domestic economy. Policy makers should ensure that these additional foreign resources are channelled to productive sectors and utilized efficiently for sustained development.

The dummy variable used to capture the effect of the capital control regime is found to have a negative effect on the investment rate. The results are not surprising given that the investment rate plunged after the Asian financial crisis, coinciding with the adoption of a capital control regime. The regression results for the short-run model, reported in panel B of Table 8.1, show that, except for the intercept, all coefficients are statistically significant at the 10 per cent level. In first-differenced form, both $\Delta\ln(S/Y)_t$ and $\Delta D_{98\text{-}05}\text{x}\ln(S/Y)_t$ have the appropriate signs. The coefficient on $ECT_{t-1}$, which measures the speed of adjustment back to the long-run equilibrium value, is statistically significant at the 1 per cent level and correctly signed, i.e. negative, implying that an error correction mechanism exists. The speed of adjustment at 46.5 per cent a year suggests that it takes only about two years to achieve long-run equilibrium whenever there is a deviation from the long-run steady state.

Contrary to the findings of Jansen and Schulze (1996) and Payne (2005), who have reported a negative relationship between domestic saving and investment rates, the contemporaneous saving variable enters the equation with a positive sign. Specifically, a one percentage point increase in $\Delta\ln(S/Y)_t$ leads to a 0.269 percentage point increase in $\Delta\ln(I/Y)_t$. As the standard intertemporal open economy model implies, saving and investment should be cointegrated irrespective of the degree of capital mobility, given that current

*Table 8.1* Long-run and short-run results of the investment rate equation

| | *A. The long-run equilibrium level relationship* | |
|---|---|---|
| | *Coefficient* | *p-value* |
| *Intercept* | 0.142 | 0.186 |
| $\ln(S/Y)_t$ | 1.210*** | 0.000 |
| $D_{98\text{-}05}$ | –0.522*** | 0.000 |
| | *B. The short-run dynamic model* | |
| | *Coefficient* | *p-value* |
| *Intercept* | –0.006 | 0.728 |
| $ECT_{t-1}$ | –0.465*** | 0.000 |
| $\Delta\ln(S/Y)_t$ | 0.269* | 0.076 |
| $\Delta D_{98\text{-}05}\text{x}\ln(S/Y)_t$ | 0.696*** | 0.000 |
| $\Delta\ln(I/Y)_{t-1}$ | 0.337*** | 0.007 |
| $\Delta\ln(I/Y)_{t-2}$ | 0.319** | 0.031 |
| $\Delta D_{98\text{-}05}\text{x}\ln(S/Y)_{t-2}$ | –0.419** | 0.017 |
| *Diagnostic checks* | *Test-statistic* | *p-value* |
| $\chi^2_{NORMAL}(2)$ | 0.573 | 0.750 |
| $\chi^2_{SERIAL}(1)$ | 0.331 | 0.565 |
| $\chi^2_{SERIAL}(2)$ | 1.087 | 0.580 |
| $\chi^2_{ARCH}(1)$ | 4.274** | 0.038 |
| $\chi^2_{WHITE}$ | 10.129 | 0.604 |
| $\chi^2_{RESET}(1)$ | 0.295 | 0.586 |

*Notes:* The regressions for the long-run model are based on an unrestricted ECM, and corrected for both omitted lagged variable bias and endogeneity bias. The regressions for the short-run dynamic model are based on a conditional ECM. *, ** and *** indicate 10%, 5% and 1% level of significance, respectively. $\chi^2_{NORMAL}(2)$ refers to the Jarque-Bera statistic of the test for normal residuals, $\chi^2_{SERIAL}(1)$ and $\chi^2_{SERIAL}(2)$ are the Breusch-Godfrey LM test statistics for no first and second order serial correlation, respectively, $\chi_{WHITE}$ denotes the White's test statistic to test for homoskedastic errors, with degrees of freedom equal to the number of slope coefficients, $\chi^2_{ARCH}(1)$ is the Engle's test statistic for no autoregressive conditional heteroskedasticity, and $\chi^2_{RESET}(1)$ is the Ramsey's test statistic for no functional misspecification.

account imbalances are unsustainable. Consequently, the short-run correlation is more indicative about the degree of capital immobility. The positive coefficient on $\Delta D_{98\text{-}05}\text{x}\ln(S/Y)_t$ suggests that the correlation greatly strengthens during the increased capital immobility period, providing some evidence that the Feldstein–Horioka approach is partially informative about the level of capital mobility. Another interesting finding is that the long-run saving–investment relationship is stronger than that of the short-run, consistent with the results of Levy (2000).

Thus, the results suggest that the 'Feldstein–Horioka puzzle' is not applicable to the Malaysian experience since the adoption of a capital control regime from 1998 onwards coincides with an increased value of the saving–investment correlation. On the whole, these results are consistent with the time series findings of Jansen and Schulze (1996), Moreno (1997) and De Vita and Abbott (2002), who have found little support for the 'Feldstein–Horioka puzzle'.[4]

The regression specifications reported in Table 8.1 pass the diagnostic tests against non-normal residuals, serial correlation, heteroskedasticity and the regression specification error test, at the 5 per cent level of significance, but not the autoregressive conditional heteroskedasticity test.

## 8.6 Conclusion

This chapter examines the relationship between the domestic saving and investment rates in a cointegration framework. Cointegration tests using the ARDL procedure and the ECM approach indicate a fairly robust long-run relationship between the domestic saving and investment rates, with a cointegrating vector [1 –1.21]. The findings suggest that the degree of association between these two variables found in the time series data is consistent with the degree of capital mobility. The results show that the saving–investment relationship is stronger when capital controls are present in Malaysia, implying an increasing isolation from international capital markets. Thus, the close relationship between saving and investment observed in Malaysia does not represent a 'puzzle'. It can be inferred from the results that capital accumulation channel through which financial development can impact on economic growth is present for the Malaysian experience.

# 9 Financial intermediation and economic growth*

## 9.1 Introduction

The neoclassical growth model of Solow (1956) and Swan (1956) postulates two major sources that contribute to economic growth: accumulation of factors of production and productivity growth (technological progress). In principle, an improvement in the financial systems can affect economic growth via these two channels: the capital accumulation channel and the total factor productivity (TFP) channel. In this book, these two channels are examined separately in the context of Malaysia.

The first channel, also known as the quantitative channel, is rather straightforward. Economic growth depends on capital accumulation through both domestic and foreign capital investment. To mobilize savings and channel them to capital accumulation, an efficient financial system is essential. In this way, financial development and economic growth are linked. The empirical evidence presented in Chapters 6 and 7 shows that financial development positively affects both saving behaviour and investment activities in Malaysia. Given that saving and investment are strongly connected, as shown in Chapter 8, it can be inferred that financial development leads to higher economic growth via the capital accumulation channel.

The TFP channel, which is referred to as the qualitative channel, suggests that an efficient financial system facilitates the adoption of modern technology to boost development of the knowledge- and technology-intensive industries through the provision of efficient credit facilities and other financial services. Testing whether this channel exists in the Malaysian economy is the central focus of this chapter. The standard augmented neoclassical growth model is used to examine to what extent financial development contributes to output expansion in Malaysia.

The chapter is divided into five sections:

- Section 9.2 performs a growth accounting exercise for Malaysia;
- Section 9.3 sets out the empirical model and describes the data;

* This chapter was previously printed in Ang (2007a).

- Section 9.4 provides and discusses the empirical results;
- Section 9.5 provides the conclusion.

## 9.2 Growth accounting

An efficient financial system performs the task of screening investment projects. With an effective risk evaluation on different investment opportunities, the selection of the most promising investment projects could improve the quality of investments, reduce business failures, and effectively raise productivity (Greenwood and Jovanovic, 1990). To assess the impact of financial intermediation via the productivity channel, this study assumes that the effect of financial intermediation on the economy operates through TFP. That is, TFP $= f$(financial intermediation). Thus, examining the contribution of TFP to growth provides some indication of the influence of financial intermediation in the process of economic development, via the productivity channel.

Growth accounting is the standard approach used to segregate the growth in real output into the growth in productivity and the growth in factor inputs. Deriving the growth accounting equation begins with a Cobb-Douglas production function in the form:

$$Y_t = A_t K_t^{\alpha} L_t^{\beta} \tag{1}$$

where $Y_t$ is the aggregate level of output, $A_t$ indicates the level of technology, $K_t$ refers to physical capital, $L_t$ is the labour force, and $\alpha$ and $\beta$ are the shares of factor inputs in production. Taking logarithms and first differencing gives the following growth accounting equation:

$$\Delta \ln Y_t = \Delta \ln A_t + \alpha \Delta \ln K_t + \beta \Delta \ln L_t \tag{2}$$

or

$$\hat{Y}_t = \hat{A}_t + \alpha \hat{K}_t + \beta \hat{L}_t \tag{3}$$

where the 'hat' sign represents growth rates. The production function is assumed to display constant returns to scale so that $\alpha$ and $\beta$ sum to one. With the assumption of perfect competition in the factor markets, each factor is paid the value of its marginal product so that $\alpha$ and $\beta$ can be approximated by the shares of capital and labour in total output, respectively. From Equation (3), $\hat{A}_t$ or TFP growth can be obtained by:

$$\hat{A}_t = \hat{Y}_t - \alpha \hat{K}_t - \beta \hat{L}_t \tag{4}$$

Equation (4) shows that TFP growth is calculated as a residual, which is the portion of output growth not accounted for by inputs growth. This is also known as the 'Solow residual'. It is important to highlight that this conventional approach does not take into consideration any changes in the quality of physical capital and work force due to the lack of appropriate data. Human capital stocks are not accounted for due to the same reason.

Next, an estimate of $a$ is needed. As mentioned earlier, in a competitive economy, $a$ can be given by the share of income earned by capital, and it should vary across time. However, as in most developing countries and even some developed countries, reliable measures of factor income are not available. In a growth accounting exercise, Young (1995) estimates a capital share of 0.37 for Hong Kong, 0.49 for Singapore, 0.3 for Korea, and 0.26 for Taiwan. Ghani and Suri (1999) assume a capital share 0.33 in their analysis of productivity growth in Malaysia for the period 1970–97. Sarel (1997) estimates the value of capital share for Malaysia to be around 0.32 for the period 1978–96. In the analysis of Collins and Bosworth (1996), a uniform capital share of 0.35 is used in their entire analysis for selected Asian economies. Using the results of Collins and Bosworth (1996) and Sarel (1997) as the benchmark, Nazrin (2000) assumes the capital share for Malaysia to be 0.3. This estimate is also in line with the assumption of King and Levine (1993a) in their seminal study of the broad relationship between financial development and economic growth. Based on these studies, the capital share estimates ($a$) in this analysis are assumed to be in the range of 0.25–0.35. As a sensitivity check, the value of $a$ is varied with an increment of 0.05.

The period under study is broken into four sub-periods: 1961–70, 1971–84, 1985–97 and 1998–2005:

- The period 1961–70 can be characterized as a highly uncertain period. The economy faced several challenges: an unstable export sector, the confrontation with Indonesia in the early 1960s, the separation of Singapore in 1965, and the racial riots in 1969 (Hasan, 1980).
- The next period 1971–84 marked the inception of the NEP. The economy underwent a rapid industrialization process before it went into recession in 1985.
- The period 1985–97 marked another rapid growth phase, after the economy recovered from the economic setback in 1985. Growth in this period was mainly driven by a boom in the export sector.
- The economy continued to perform very well before it was hit by the 1997–98 Asian financial crisis.
- Finally, the post-crisis period 1997–2005 saw a recovery of the economy from the crisis.[1]

The results of the growth accounting exercise are presented in Table 9.1. Except for the post-crisis period, capital stocks grew at a rapid rate of higher than 9 per cent on average per year in each period. Growth rates of the labour force remained quite stable at around 3 per cent. Consistent with the declines in GDP growth rates, both factors of production and productivity grew at a much lower rate during the period 1998–2005 due to the effects of the crisis. Productivity growth increased strongly over the past four decades, but it slowed significantly and recorded zero growth during the post-crisis period. For the entire period, TFP growth averaged between 1.37 and 1.91 per cent, depending on the assumption about the capital share in income ($a$). These TFP growth estimates seem reasonable compared to the findings of other studies (see Table 9.2). Overall, it appears that the patterns of change of the growth rates of productivity and factor inputs are not very sensitive to the value of $a$.

Estimates of the contribution of growth of factor inputs and TFP to output expansion in the four sub-periods are given in Table 9.3. It is evident that the contribution from labour has remained quite stable, except for the period 1998–2005. On the other hand, the contribution from capital shows a declining trend over the years. In particular, the ratio in the post-crisis period 1998–2005 is significantly lower than the previous periods. In contrast, TFP has become increasingly important in contributing to output growth over the years. This pattern of development has not been affected by the Asian financial crisis. The estimates suggest that the contribution of capital accumulation has been substituted by the contribution from productivity. For the entire period, growth does not seem to have been driven solely by capital and labour inputs. The results are in line with Sarel (1997) and Nazrin (2000), who find a very impressive growth rate of TFP for Malaysia. Consequently, financial development may have played a critical role in driving economic growth in Malaysia through enhancing productivity gains.

*Table 9.1* Average annual rate of growth (%)

| *Period* | *Output* | *Capital* | *Labour* | *TFP* | | |
|---|---|---|---|---|---|---|
| | | | | $a = 0.25$ | $a = 0.30$ | $a = 0.35$ |
| 1961–1970 | 6.28 | 9.60 | 2.83 | 1.76 | 1.42 | 1.08 |
| 1971–1984 | 7.25 | 9.82 | 3.39 | 2.26 | 1.93 | 1.61 |
| 1985–1997 | 7.22 | 9.24 | 3.15 | 2.55 | 2.24 | 1.94 |
| 1998–2005 | 3.59 | 1.75 | 2.78 | 1.07 | 1.12 | 1.17 |
| 1961–2005 | 6.38 | 8.17 | 3.09 | 2.02 | 1.76 | 1.51 |

*Table 9.2* Estimates of TFP growth in Malaysia

| *Author(s)* | *Period* | *Annual rate of TFP growth* |
|---|---|---|
| Collins and Bosworth (1996) | 1960–94 | 0.4–1.4% |
| Dowling and Summers (1998) | 1961–95 | 1.5–2.5% |
| Klenow and Rodriguez-Clare (1997) | 1960–85 | 2.0% |
| Nazrin (2000) | 1975–97 | 1.9% |
| Sarel (1997) | 1978–96 | 2.0% |
| WorldBank (1993) | 1960–89 | 1.5–1.6% |
| Young (1994a) | 1970–85 | 1.1% |

*Table 9.3* Contribution to GDP growth (%)

| *Sources of growth* | *1961–1970* | *1971–1984* | *1985–1997* | *1998–2005* | *1961–2005* |
|---|---|---|---|---|---|
| $a = 0.25$ | | | | | |
| Capital | 34.7 | 33.1 | 28.9 | 11.2 | 31.2 |
| Labour | 33.8 | 34.2 | 29.7 | 39.8 | 36.4 |
| TFP | 31.5 | 32.8 | 41.4 | 49.0 | 32.5 |
| $a = 0.3$ | | | | | |
| Capital | 41.6 | 39.7 | 34.7 | 13.4 | 37.4 |
| Labour | 31.5 | 31.9 | 27.7 | 37.1 | 33.9 |
| TFP | 26.8 | 28.4 | 37.6 | 49.5 | 28.6 |
| $a = 0.35$ | | | | | |
| Capital | 48.6 | 46.3 | 40.4 | 15.7 | 43.6 |
| Labour | 29.3 | 29.6 | 25.8 | 34.5 | 31.5 |
| TFP | 22.2 | 24.1 | 33.8 | 49.9 | 24.8 |

## 9.3 Empirical specification

As highlighted in the preceding section, the effect of financial intermediation on the economy is assumed to operate through TFP. Following an analysis of the sources of growth in Malaysia through a growth-accounting framework, this section describes the model used to test the productivity channel. The growth model draws upon the standard neoclassical model, augmented with financial deepening. In this way, financial development is assumed to affect growth via the productivity channel. The rationale for this specification is simple: if financial deepening affects economic development solely through the factor accumulation channel, financial deepening should not be expected to appear significantly in the augmented neoclassical growth model, since it is already captured in physical capital stocks (Benhabib and Spiegel, 2000).

Capital stock is decomposed into private and public capital stocks. The segregation of total capital stocks is important, given that private and public capital stocks may have different effects on output expansion, as highlighted by a number of authors (see Aschauer, 1989a, b; Baltagi and Pinnoi, 1995; and Holtz-Eakin, 1994, among others). Private capital stocks, which arise from investment in the private sector such as machinery and equipment, are likely to have a positive role to play in enhancing growth through the adoption of new technologies in the production process. Aschauer (1989a) argues that public sector capital, such as infrastructure, may complement private sector capital and therefore contribute positively to output expansion. However, if the public sector is associated with waste and inefficiency, this may affect the quality of public infrastructure, thereby retarding output growth. Hence, how public capital stocks affect real output is ambiguous.

The empirical specifications of the real output equation are given in Equations (5) and (6).

$$GDP_t = f_A(PRK_t, PUK_t, LF_t, PC_t) \tag{5}$$

$$GDP_t = f_B(PRK_t, PUK_t, LF_t, MON_t) \tag{6}$$

where $GDP_t$ is the aggregate output measured at 1987 prices. The independent variables, with the expected signs in the parentheses, are given as:

$PRK_t$ = real private capital stocks (+)
$PUK_t$ = real public capital stocks (?)
$LF_t$ = labour force (+)
$BCY_t$ = financial deepening measured by private credit to GDP (+)
$M2Y_t$ = financial deepening measured by M2 to GDP (+)

All variables are converted into natural logarithms. As in Chapter 5, two different indicators of financial development are used in the estimation to provide a sensitivity check on the results. The specifications include two dummy variables to account for the impacts of the global economic recession in 1985–86 and the 1997–98 Asian financial crisis, defined as:

$$D_{85\text{–}86} = \begin{cases} 1 & \text{if } t = 1985\text{–}86 \\ 0 & \text{otherwise} \end{cases} \quad \text{and}$$

$$D_{97\text{–}98} = \begin{cases} 1 & \text{if } t = 1997\text{–}98 \\ 0 & \text{otherwise} \end{cases}$$

## 9.4 Results

A conditional ECM is estimated with one and two lags for each model to perform cointegration tests. The results in Table B.5 of Appendix 4 indicate that the null hypothesis, that there exists no level output equation, is rejected at the 5 per cent significance level for both models when one lag is chosen. While no cointegration is found based on the ECM test when two lags are chosen, the evidence of cointegration is supported by the ARDL bounds test, at the 5 per cent level of significance. In terms of lag length selection, AIC favours modelling with two lags whereas SBC points to specifying the model with only one lag. The results are not surprising given that SBC always tends to select a model with less dynamics.

The estimated long-run relationships reported in panel A of Table 9.4 show that all variables are statistically significant at the 1 per cent level. Specifically, the results show that capital accumulation has a mixed influence on output expansion. A one percentage point increase in private capital stocks leads to a 0.254 to 0.419 percentage point increase in output, whereas a one percentage point increase in public capital stocks leads to a 0.282 to 0.310 percentage point reduction in output. The finding of a positive effect of private capital stocks provide some support for the view that financial deepening impacts on economic growth through the capital accumulation channel.

The evidence presented here seems to suggest that public sector intervention in the economy appears to be harmful for long-term economic development.[2] This has much to do with the implementation of the NEP. Several arguments have been put forward to support this point of view. State sponsorship for heavy industry has been seen as a way of strengthening the economic position of native-Malays to better achieve the targets set by the NEP. This brings opportunities for *bumiputras* to secure key managerial positions to help achieve ethnic redistributive targets. However, the public sector in Malaysia appears to be associated with waste, inefficiency and corruption. This may distort the decision-making process connected with public investment expenditure and result in a lower quality of public infrastructure (Tanzi and Davoodi, 1997).

Crouch (1996) argues that although the NEP has succeeded in bringing *bumiputras* into business, it is unable to promote the development of an independent *bumiputra* entrepreneur class since they are mainly concerned with maintaining individual links with political patrons. In analysing the effectiveness of the NEP, Mehmet (1988) finds that it has little impact on poverty eradication. Gomez (1990) reports a similar finding, that state involvement in business has not contributed much to the development of productive activities. Instead, it has resulted in the transfer of paper wealth from one company to another in the interests of the politically well-connected few. Searle (1999) concludes that while government intervention by way of the NEP has not created new sources of entrepreneurship that contribute to the economy, these interventions have fostered more rent-seeking activities which are harmful for the development of the economy. Given the above, low-quality government intervention in the economy appears to have resulted in more rent-seeking activities and wasteful resources, and therefore capital formation in the public sector is unlikely to generate long-term growth in Malaysia.

Labour input is found to have a positive impact on real output, with a long-run elasticity of 2.018 for Model A and 1.317 for Model B. The results suggest that a high growth rate in the labour force is conducive to economic growth in Malaysia.

The elasticity of output with respect to financial deepening is 0.087 based on the results of Model A, suggesting that the influence of financial deepening on output is quite small. This impact is found to be much larger in Model B, with a long-run elasticity of 0.277. The finding that financial deepening positively influences economic development via the TFP channel is consistent with the results of Yaakop (1988) for the Malaysian experience during the period 1960–85. The results are also broadly in line with the findings of

*Table 9.4* Long-run and short-run results of the aggregate output equations

| | *A. The long-run equilibrium level relationship* | | | |
|---|---|---|---|---|
| | *Model A (Dep. = lnGDP$_t$)* | | *Model B (Dep. = lnGDP$_t$)* | |
| | *Coefficient* | *p-value* | *Coefficient* | *p-value* |
| *Intercept* | 8.334*** | 0.000 | 7.414*** | 0.000 |
| ln$PRK_t$ | 0.254*** | 0.000 | 0.419*** | 0.000 |
| ln$PUK_t$ | –0.310*** | 0.000 | –0.282*** | 0.000 |
| ln$LF_t$ | 2.018*** | 0.000 | 1.317*** | 0.000 |
| ln$BCY_t$ | 0.087*** | 0.002 | | |
| ln$M2Y_t$ | | | 0.277*** | 0.002 |
| $D_{85–86}$ | –0.083*** | 0.001 | –0.057** | 0.035 |
| | *B. The short-run dynamic model* | | | |
| | *Model A (Dep. = ΔlnGDP$_t$)* | | *Model B (Dep. = ΔlnGDP$_t$)* | |
| | *Coefficient* | *p-value* | *Coefficient* | *p-value* |
| *Intercept* | –0.068*** | 0.005 | 0.000 | 0.983 |
| $ECT_{t-1}$ | –0.578*** | 0.000 | –0.540*** | 0.000 |
| Δln$PRK_t$ | 0.740*** | 0.000 | 0.848*** | 0.000 |
| Δln$PUK_t$ | –0.664*** | 0.000 | –0.618*** | 0.000 |
| Δln$BCY_t$ | 0.043 | 0.189 | | |
| Δln$PRK_{t-1}$ | –0.391*** | 0.002 | –0.443*** | 0.001 |
| Δln$PUK_{t-1}$ | 0.569*** | 0.000 | 0.526*** | 0.000 |
| *Diagnostic checks* | *Test-statistic* | *p-value* | *Test-statistic* | *p-value* |
| $\chi^2_{NORMAL}(2)$ | 4.985* | 0.084 | 2.968 | 0.226 |
| $\chi^2_{SERIAL}(1)$ | 0.765 | 0.381 | 0.005 | 0.939 |
| $\chi^2_{SERIAL}(2)$ | 4.218 | 0.121 | 1.667 | 0.434 |
| $\chi^2_{ARCH}(1)$ | 0.376 | 0.539 | 1.019 | 0.312 |
| $\chi^2_{WHITE}$ | 14.013 | 0.372 | 17.050 | 0.106 |
| $\chi^2_{RESET}(1)$ | 28.797*** | 0.000 | 20.482*** | 0.000 |

*Notes:* The regressions for the long-run model are based on an unrestricted ECM, and corrected for both omitted lagged variable bias and endogeneity bias. The regressions for the short-run dynamic model are based on a conditional ECM. *, ** and *** indicate 10%, 5% and 1% level of significance, respectively. $\chi^2_{NORMAL}(2)$ refers to the Jarque-Bera statistic of the test for normal residuals, $\chi^2_{SERIAL}(1)$ and $\chi^2_{SERIAL}(2)$ are the Breusch-Godfrey LM test statistics for no first and second order serial correlation, respectively, $\chi^2_{WHITE}$ denotes the White's test statistic to test for homoskedastic errors, with degrees of freedom equal to the number of slope coefficients, $\chi^2_{ARCH}(1)$ is the Engle's test statistic for no autoregressive conditional heteroskedasticity, and $\chi^2_{RESET}(1)$ is the Ramsey's test statistic for no functional misspecification.

Benhabib and Spiegel (2000), De Gregorio and Guidotti (1995) and Rioja and Valev (2004).[3]

The results lend some support to the endogenous finance and growth theory, which postulates that financial development acts as a mechanism in facilitating the adoption of new technologies in the domestic economy. Thus, the provision of efficient credit and financial services by the Malaysian financial system appears to have greatly facilitated technological transfer and induced spillover efficiency. Given that evolution of the financial system may affect the speed of technological accumulation and innovations, it is essential to develop a sound financial system in order to reap these efficiency gains and achieve sustained economic growth in the long-run.

The coefficient on $D_{85\text{–}86}$ is found to be negative, implying that the world economic recession in 1985–86 had a negative impact on output. The dummy variable which captures the effect of the Asian financial crisis, i.e. $D_{97\text{–}98}$, is found to be statistically insignificant, and therefore dropped from the estimation.

Interestingly, the short-run impacts of both private and public capital formation are consistent with the long-run results. No short-run inference on labour force and financial deepening can be drawn, since in first-differenced forms these variables are found to be statistically insignificant.

The coefficients associated with $ECT_{t-1}$ are statistically significant at the 1 per cent level and has the right sign. Their magnitudes imply that the economy takes less than two years to achieve long-run equilibrium whenever there is a deviation from equilibrium. The statistical significance of the ECT also provides further evidence against no cointegration between real output and its determinants. The regression results for the conditional ECM of $\Delta \ln GDP_t$ show several desirable statistical features. The regression specifications fit remarkably well and pass the diagnostic tests against non-normal residuals, serial correlation, heteroskedasticity, and autoregressive conditional heteroskedasticity at the 5 per cent level of significance. However, neither model pass the functional form regression specification error test (or Ramsey's RESET test) at the 1 per cent level.

## 9.5 Conclusion

This chapter analyses the role of financial factors in economic growth in Malaysia using the standard growth accounting framework. Malaysia has achieved an exceptional growth record over the past few decades. The evidence presented in this analysis shows that this is mainly due to growth in capital stocks and the labour force. Although the TFP growth has been relatively modest, there is evidence that it has become increasingly important.

In examining the impact of financial deepening on economic development via the productivity channel, a fairly robust long-run relationship is found between output, private and public capital stocks, labour force and financial deepening. The results suggest that financial deepening has a positive impact on economic growth, through both the quantitative and qualitative channels. The operation of the quantitative channel is supported by the finding of a positive impact from private capital stocks. Relating to qualitative effects, there is evidence that an improvement in the financial system leads to higher output growth in the long run, through raising productivity, although its impact is quite small.

# 10 Conclusion

## 10.1 Introduction

This book presents a case study of the role of financial intermediation in the process of economic development in Malaysia for the period 1960–2005. The study begins with a survey of both the theoretical and empirical literature on the relationship between financial development and economic growth. The analysis in Chapter 2 shows that most studies focus on either testing whether financial development plays a positive role in stimulating economic growth or examining the direction of causality between these two variables. Although limitations of the existing econometric techniques do not allow the issue of causality to be satisfactorily addressed, a large body of empirical evidence has overwhelmingly shown that financial development has a positive impact on economic growth. While this positive role of finance has become a stylized fact, little attention has been paid examining the mechanisms that link these two variables.

Theory suggests that financial development can lead to higher economic growth via two channels: the capital accumulation channel and the TFP channel. The capital accumulation channel, often known as the quantitative channel, is developed based on the 'debt-accumulation' hypothesis which focuses on the financial sector's ability to overcome indivisibilities through the mobilization of saving. The mobilized saving is then channelled to productive sectors to fund investment projects, thereby leading to increased capital accumulation and higher output growth. The TFP channel, often known as the qualitative channel, emphasizes the role of innovative financial technologies in reducing informational asymmetries that hinder efficient allocation of financial resources and monitoring of investment projects. An efficient financial system also facilitates the adoption of expensive new technologies, thereby leading to sustained economic development. These two channels are tested separately in this book.

Another gap identified in the literature is that empirical studies in this subject have been dominated by cross-country studies. However, these broad comparative studies serve the limited purpose of providing a generalized picture of the relationship between financial development and economic growth. Given that the finance–growth link is largely determined by the nature and operation of financial institutions, and the policies pursued in each country, it is important to carry out comprehensive country-specific studies in order to relate the findings to appropriate policy designs. Hence, this thesis has conducted an in-depth individual country analysis using Malaysia as the case study.

Before conducting the empirical investigation, an analysis has been provided in Chapter 3 to shed some light on development in the financial and real sectors in Malaysia. The results clearly show that the financial system in Malaysia has deepened significantly over time alongside an increase in the level of economic development. Thus, a positive relationship between financial development and economic growth in Malaysia is observed. Data, variable construction and econometric techniques are described in Chapter 4.

## 10.2 Key findings

The estimated equations in the five empirical chapters are brought together in Figure 10.1. The key inferences of the empirical results are summarized below.

Chapter 5 examines the determinants of financial deepening in Malaysia. The results show that real output positively affects the level of financial deepening, consistent with the general findings of the literature. The effect of real interest rates on financial deepening is found to be positive, providing some support for the effectiveness of interest rate liberalization as a device for deepening the financial sector. Financial repressionist policies, including interest rate controls, reserve and liquidity requirements, and directed credit programmes, seem to have contributed positively to the development of the Malaysian financial system. Hence, financial liberalization appears to have a separate effect on financial deepening, different from that of real interest rates.

The determinants of private saving in Malaysia are examined in Chapter 6. The analytical framework is constructed using the life cycle model with some modifications. The predictions of the life cycle hypothesis are supported by the findings of a positive impact from real income. A negative effect of age dependency on private saving is found in the short run but not the long run. From a policy point of view, the evidence suggests that an increase in financial deepening and real interest rates contribute positively to private saving. Compulsory saving, in the form of EPF, seems to exert a negative influence on private saving. Hence, pension saving appears to be a substitute for private saving. The Ricardian equivalence hypothesis does not seem to hold strictly in Malaysia, given that public saving only partially crowds out private saving.

The estimated results in Chapter 7 suggest that the predictions of the neoclassical model are supported by the finding of a large positive impact of aggregate output on private investment. However, user cost of capital appears to be unimportant in private capital formation. Macroeconomic uncertainty exerts a negative influence on private investment. While there is evidence that FDI crowds in private domestic investment, public investment seems to partially crowd out private investment. More importantly, the evidence indicates that increased bank credit contributes positively to private investment, suggesting that financial development is crucial for the undertaking of investment projects in the private sector.

The results in Chapters 6 and 7 have established that savings behaviour and investment decisions are influenced by the level of financial development. The relationship between domestic saving and investment rates is tested in Chapter 8. The results show that these two variables are indeed moving closely together over time. Thus, it can be inferred that the capital accumulation channel through which financial development can impact on economic growth is present for the Malaysian experience.

Turning to testing the TFP channel, an augmented neoclassical growth model is adopted to shed some light on whether financial development leads to output expansion through raising efficiency gains in Chapter 9. The growth accounting exercise shows that TFP growth is an important driver to boost economic growth in Malaysia, suggesting that financial development may be a key contributor to economic growth through raising productivity gains. This is further supported by the regression results that financial development has an important role to play in stimulating growth by facilitating productivity growth. The results also suggest that private capital stocks and the labour force exert a positive influence on output expansion. In contrast, the accumulation of public capital stocks appears to have a negative effect on output expansion.

The key findings of this study are, by and large, consistent with the existing studies in this subject:

- The results are in line with the arguments put forward by Schumpeter (1911) that financial development leads to higher economic growth by providing entrepreneurs with credit for the adoption of new production techniques. The evidence is also consistent with the view of Gurley and Shaw (1960), Goldsmith (1969) and Hicks (1969) that financial development stimulates economic growth through increasing financial intermediating activities.
- The results also lend some support to Robinson's (1952) view that economic development leads to an improvement in the financial system. These two points suggest that financial development and economic growth in Malaysia show a bidirectional causality pattern, providing some support for the argument of using a system approach, rather than a single equation, to examine the relationship between financial development and economic growth. The results also support the endogenous finance and growth theories which postulate a feedback relationship in the finance–growth nexus.
- The results provide only some qualified support for the McKinnon–Shaw

*Chapter 5* Financial deepening

$$\ln BCY_t = -10.389^{***} + 1.529 \ln PGDP_t^{***} - 0.784 \ln FL_t^{***} + 0.060 RI_t^{***}$$

$$\ln M2Y_t = -8.281^{***} + 0.974 \ln PGDP_t^{***} - 0.125 \ln FL_t^{**} + 0.017 RI_t^{***}$$

*Chapter 6* Private saving

$$\ln PRS_t = -2.620 + 1.649 \ln PPI_t^{***} + 0.019 RI_t^{**} - 0.880 YAG_t + 0.187 OAG_t + 0.407 \ln FD_t^{***} - 0.360 \ln PEN_t^{***} - 0.096 \ln PUS_t^{**}$$

$$\ln VPRS_t = -8.725^{**} + 2.040 \ln PPI_t^{***} + 0.019 RI_t^{*} + 1.501 YAG_t + 17.418 OAG_t + 0.458 \ln FD_t^{***} - 0.366 \ln PEN_t^{**} - 0.101 \ln PUS_t^{*}$$

*Chapter 7* Private investment

$$\ln PRI_t = -6.759^{***} + 1.365 \ln GDP_t^{***} + 0.078 COC_t + 1.232 BC_t^{***} - 0.003 UNC_t^{***} + 0.045 \ln PUB_t - 0.394 D_{69}^{**}$$

$$\ln PDI_t = -6.445^{***} + 1.280 \ln GDP_t^{***} + 0.566 COC_t + 0.916 BC_t^{*} - 0.004 UNC_t^{***} + 0.046 \ln PUB_t - 0.826 D_{69}^{***}$$

$$\ln PDI_t = -5.718^{***} + 1.195 \ln GDP_t^{***} - 0.289 COC_t + 1.018 BC_t^{**} - 0.004 UNC_t^{***} + 0.017 \ln PUB_t + 0.160 \ln FDI_t^{**} - 0.548 D_{69}^{***}$$

*Chapter 8* Investment and saving rates

$$\ln(I/Y)_t = 0.142 + 1.210 \ln(S/Y)_t^{***} - 0.522 D_{98-05}^{***}$$

*Chapter 9* Aggregate output

$$\ln GDP_t = 8.334^{***} + 0.254 \ln PRK_t^{***} - 0.310 \ln PUK_t^{***} + 2.018 \ln LF_t^{***} + 0.087 \ln BCY_t^{***} - 0.083 D_{85-86}^{***}$$

$$\ln GDP_t = 7.414^{***} + 0.419 \ln PRK_t^{***} - 0.282 \ln PUK_t^{***} + 1.317 \ln LF_t^{***} + 0.277 \ln M2Y_t^{***} - 0.057 D_{85-86}^{**}$$

where

| | | |
|---|---|---|
| $BC_t$ | = | real bank credit flow to the private sector |
| $COC_t$ | = | real user cost of capital |
| $D_{69}$ | = | dummy variable for the racial riots |
| $D_{85\text{-}86}$ | = | dummy variable for the global economic recession |
| $D_{97\text{-}98}$ | = | dummy variable for the Asian financial crisis |
| $D_{98\text{-}05}$ | = | dummy variable for the capital control regime |
| $FD_t$ | = | financial deepening (private credit/private income) |
| $FDI_t$ | = | real foreign direct investment |
| $FL_t$ | = | financial liberalization |
| $GDP_t$ | = | real output |
| $LF_t$ | = | labour force |
| $M2Y_t$ | = | financial deepening (M2/GDP) |
| $OAG_t$ | = | old age dependency |
| $BCY_t$ | = | financial deepening (bank credit to private sector/GDP) |
| $PDI_t$ | = | real private domestic investment |
| $PEN_t$ | = | expected pension (EPF) benefits |
| $PGDP_t$ | = | per capita real GDP |
| $PPI_t$ | = | per capita real private income |
| $PRI_t$ | = | real private investment |
| $PRK_t$ | = | real private capital stocks |
| $PRS_t$ | = | real private saving |
| $PUB_t$ | = | real public investment |
| $PUK_t$ | = | real public capital stocks |
| $PUS_t$ | = | real public saving |
| $RI_t$ | = | real interest rates |
| $UNC_t$ | = | macroeconomic uncertainty |
| $VPRS_t$ | = | real voluntary private saving |
| $YAG_t$ | = | young age dependency |
| $(I/Y)_t$ | = | gross domestic investment rate |
| $(S/Y)_t$ | = | gross domestic saving rate |

*Figure 10.1* Summary findings of Chapters 5 to 9.

*Notes:* *, ** and *** indicate 10%, 5% and 1% level of significance, respectively.

financial liberalization thesis. On the one hand, real interest rates have a positive impact on development of the financial system, suggesting that the elimination of interest rate controls may promote financial development. On the other hand, when considering the joint influence of all financial sector policies (including interest rate controls, reserve and liquidity requirements, and directed credit programmes), financial liberalization appears to have a negative effect on financial development. Hence, the improvement in the Malaysian financial sector does not seem to have been retarded by the repressionist policies imposed on the financial system. It is argued that this may be due to the presence of a sound institutional framework, which has enabled the repressionist policies to be carried out effectively, thereby exerting a favourable effect on the financial system.

- Malaysia's saving rate has been very high. This high saving record is partly due to the presence of a forced saving scheme in the form of a broad-based EPF, which constitutes a significant proportion of the total saving. Such a forced saving scheme involves the shifting of a large amount of funds from the private sector to the public sector. Given that the public sector is less efficient, this implies that EPF saving may have an adverse impact on economic growth.
- Contrary to the common view that public sector investment is complementary to private sector investment, the results in Chapter 7 suggest that public investment has no effect on private investment. Related to this, the results in Chapter 9 suggest that public sector capital formation, unlike private sector capital accumulation, is negatively related to long-term growth in the Malaysian economy. This may be partly due to the sweeping affirmative action policy (i.e. the New Economic Policy) introduced in 1970, which has led to resources being allocated to the less efficient sectors that do not generate the most productive gains.
- Finally, the dummy variable used to capture the effect of the Asian financial crisis is found to be statistically insignificant in all estimated equations. This suggests that the Asian financial crisis has no impact on financial development, the saving and investment decision-making process in the private sector or the production of aggregate output.

## 10.3 Policy implications and directions for future research

A key policy implication that emerges from the results is that it is critical for the government to develop the financial sector since financial deepening facilitates mobilization of saving, private capital formation, and long-term economic growth. A sound financial system instils confidence among savers so that resources can be effectively mobilized to increase productivity in the economy. To this end, a credible and reliable support system is indispensable to ensure the smooth-functioning of the financial system. The results also highlight the probability that the financial constraints imposed on the

Malaysian financial system seem to have helped to deepen the financial system. Since the success of financial sector policies may depend on the effectiveness of the institutions that implement them, it is critical to ensure that sound institutional quality is always in place.

The findings in this case study clearly point to the danger involved in generalizing results from multi-country cross-sectional studies. For instance, as opposed to the existing literature, public investment in Malaysia is found to have a crowding out effect, rather than a complementary role, in the capital formation of the private sector. Furthermore, accumulation of public capital stocks appears to be harmful for long-term growth in Malaysia. Thus, there is certainly a need for more country-specific research using appropriate econometric techniques, insight of institution, and the economic histories of each country to address the key issues in financial development in order to inform appropriate analytical as well as policy debate. Although the findings of this analysis may be unique to Malaysia, due to its specific institutional and structural characteristics, the analytical framework employed in this study can be readily extended to include other less-developed countries.

There are several avenues where future research can be directed. The negative effect of public sector capital formation on economic growth appears to be an interesting topic for further study. The results presented in Chapter 9 have only highlighted some plausible causes of these results. A detailed analysis is required to shed more light on this finding. Another useful area for further research would be to examine how the operation of the Employee Provident Fund (EPF) impacts on the Malaysian economy. How the accumulated contributions are invested, with their national gains or losses, may be of significant interest to researchers and policy makers. Furthermore, the analysis carried out in this study is at the macro level. Undertaking an in-depth micro level analysis is desirable to supplement the findings of this study. This book has focused on polices relating to the domestic financial sector liberalization. The impact of capital account opening on domestic saving, investment and growth is an interesting topic that requires more research. Finally, as highlighted in the thesis, Islamic banking has become increasingly important in the Malaysian financial system. Its modalities, operation and development, and their implications on the Malaysian economy, make it another possible candidate for future research.

# Appendices

## Appendix 1: Key events in the financial sector of Malaysia, 1959–2005

| *Date* | *Events* |
|---|---|
| 1959 | The Bank Negara Malaysia (BNM), i.e. the Central Bank of Malaysia, was established. |
| 1960 | Stock trading started in Kuala Lumpur. |
| 1963 | Discount houses were established to facilitate money market and interbank activities. |
| 1965 | Liquid assets requirements for banks were amended so that only Malaysian assets are eligible. |
| 1967 | The authority to issue currency was transferred from the currency board system to BNM. |
| 1970 | Merchant banks were set up. |
| 1971 | Commercial banks were allowed to issue fixed deposits up to 36 months.<br>Foreign banks were prohibited from opening new branches.<br>The second discount house (Malaysian Discount Berhad) was set up. |
| 1972 | Commercial banks were allowed to issue fixed deposits up to 60 months.<br>Credit Guarantee Corporation of Malaysia (CGCM) was set up to facilitate more lending to *bumiputra* economic activities. |
| 1973 | Most restrictions on the exchange rate were uplifted and thus the exchange rate was no longer fixed.<br>Currency convertibility with Brunei and Singapore ended.<br>The last licence to be issued to a foreign banking institution was granted.<br>The combined stock exchange market for Malaysia and Singapore was reconstituted as the Kuala Lumpur Stock Exchange (KLSE) and the Stock Exchange of Singapore (SES), respectively. Listed companies could continue to be traded in both exchange markets if they wished. |

| | |
|---|---|
| 1975 | Directed credit programmes were implemented. Banks were required to meet minimum lending to certain priority sectors, of which the *bumiputra* community was the main target. |
| 1978 | The exchange rate was pegged to a trade-weighted basket of currencies based on the major trading partners. |
| | For the first time commercial banks were allowed to freely determine the deposit and lending rates. Prior to this interest rates were controlled. |
| 1979 | The Industrial Bank of Malaysia was formed to finance loans which exceeded seven years. |
| | Negotiable Certificates of Deposit (NCDs) and Bankers' Acceptances (BA) markets were established. |
| 1983 | Bank Islam Malaysia Berhad (BIMB) was established as the first Islamic bank under the legislation of the Islamic Banking Act 1983. |
| | The base lending rate (BLR) regime was introduced in November, where all banks were required to peg their lending rates to the BLR. |
| 1985 | An economic recession took hold in Malaysia. Interest rate controls were reintroduced (but removed in 1991). |
| | CAGAMAS bonds were introduced to finance the housing credit market. |
| 1985–86 | Monetary control was eased because of the economic recession in order to stimulate investment. |
| 1986 | Greater ownership by foreign companies was granted. |
| | Several cooperative finance companies and banks failed and were bailed out by the central bank. Laws were passed to bring them under closer supervision by BNM. |
| 1987 | New measures were implemented to further liberalize the exchange rate. |
| | Large merchant banks were authorized to issue Negotiable Certificates of Deposit (NCDs). |
| | BNM turned to the use of the BLR to control interest rates (abandoned in 1991). |
| 1988 | The supervision of the insurance industry was brought under the purview of BNM, with the aim of streamlining the supervision of the entire financial system and realizing economies of scale in supervision. |
| 1988–91 | BNM implemented 12 upward revisions of statutory ratios to curb excessive lending to the private sector. |
| 1989 | The double listing of securities in both Malaysia and Singapore ceased following the split of the Stock Exchange of Singapore (SES) from the Kuala Lumpur Stock Exchange (KLSE). The 'over-the-counter' market, Central Limit Order Book (CLOB), was established. |
| | The Banking and Financial Institutions Act placed all banking institutions under the supervision of BNM, aimed at strengthening prudential regulation. |
| | A computerized interbank funds transfer system was introduced. |

(*Continued*)

| *Date* | *Events* |
|---|---|
| 1989–92 | Money market operation ceased. |
| 1990 | Capital market reforms were initiated through easing the entry barriers to broking activities, increasing the number of mutual funds and raising the limit of foreign share-ownership to 49 per cent.<br>The International Offshore Financial Centre was set up in Labuan.<br>A credit rating agency, i.e. the Rating Agency of Malaysia Berhad (RAM), was established. |
| 1991 | The central bank abandoned the use of the BLR as a mechanism to control the interest rates. |
| 1991–92 | Excess funds of the EPF were transferred to BNM. |
| 1993 | Swaps transactions were limited to US$2 million per day per customer. An upper limit of US$5 million on all non-traded foreign exchange transactions was set.<br>A two-tier regulatory system was initiated to improve efficiency of the banking sector. By the end of 1997, 18 banking institutions were qualified and granted incentives. |
| 1994 | The managed float exchange system was abolished.<br>Some temporary capital controls were imposed in January and February.<br>Foreign currency accounts were permitted in selected domestic banks. |
| 1997 | The Malaysian Exchange of Securities Dealing and Automated Quotation (MESDAQ) was established as an avenue for small, high-growth potential and high-technology companies to raise funds.<br>There were massive capital outflows, coupled with rapid decline in equity and real estate values.<br>Ringgit depreciated sharply. BNM intervened aggressively to defend the ringgit. The managed float was abandoned in July.<br>The KLSE banned short selling of stocks in August, but the ban was lifted one week later. |
| 1997–98 | Interbank interest rates were raised from 7.5 per cent in August 1997 to 11 per cent in February 1998 to prevent the ringgit from falling. |
| 1998 | A guarantee for bank depositors by BNM was introduced in January.<br>The required reserve ratios were cut from 13.5 per cent to 10 per cent in February, and further to 4 per cent in September to increase liquidity in the financial system.<br>Mergers and acquisitions among troubled banking institutions were announced in February.<br>Two agencies, i.e. *Danaharta* and *Danamodal*, were created, which were responsible for purchasing non-performing loans at a discount and injecting new capital in selected institutions, respectively. |

| | |
|---|---|
| | The Corporate Debt Restructuring Committee (CDRC) was set up to help large borrowers resolving non-performing loans. |
| | BNM reduced the default period for the classification of non-performing loans from 6 months to 3 months, with the objective of improving prudential supervision. |
| | Overseas trading of Malaysian stocks was banned. The trading of CLOB was discontinued from September. |
| | In September, a wide range of currency and capital controls were introduced. A fixed exchange rate of RM 3.80 per US$ was implemented, effective from October (abandoned in 2005). |
| 1999 | Banking institutions were required to achieve a minimum loan growth of 8 per cent by the end of 1999. |
| | The authorities announced the end of recession as GDP had grown by 4.1 per cent, on a year-on-year basis. |
| 2000 | Several schemes to promote and enhance the regulatory structure of the bond market were introduced. |
| | A set of minimum guidelines on the provision of Internet banking services was laid out. |
| | In December, profits earned from foreign investment were exempted from levy. |
| 2001 | The 10-year Capital Market Master Plan (CMP), with the objectives of improving efficiency and competitiveness of capital markets, was published in February. |
| | The 10-year Financial Sector Master Plan (FSMP), which aimed at transforming the financial sector into a more resilient and competitive system, was launched in March. |
| | A few changes were introduced to the Revision of Corporate Debt Restructuring Committee (CDRC) framework to facilitate and expedite the restructuring efforts. |
| | The Anti-Money Laundering Act 2001 (AMLA) was enacted in July, signifying a concerted effort to combat illegal transfer of financial resources as a means of legitimizing such assets. |
| 2002 | In order to facilitate the restructuring of troubled companies, the relaxation of several conditions for the injection of foreign assets and multinational companies (MNCs) into the local listed companies was announced in May. |
| | A deposit insurance system was introduced to further strengthen the consumer protection framework. It provides an explicit guarantee on insured deposits up to a specified amount in the event that a deposit-taking institution fails to meet its obligations to depositors. |
| | The Islamic Financial Services Board (IFSB) was launched in November with the key objective of establishing standards for regulation of the Islamic financial services industry based on the *Sharia* principles for voluntary adoption by member countries. |

(*Continued*)

| *Date* | *Events* |
|---|---|
| 2003 | The first variable rate financing was developed for the Islamic banking industry under the concept of 'deferred payment sale' to alleviate the mismatching of risks. |
| | The Securities Commission liberalized rules on the use of proceeds from private debt securities (PDS) to allow these funds to be used to fund the development of hypermarkets, which were previously prohibited. |
| | A set of new guidelines was issued in March to liberalize the KLSE listing policies. Large companies were exempted from the three to five profits record requirement. Malaysian businesses abroad and foreign entities with Malaysian operations were allowed to list on the KLSE. |
| | A Special Relief Guarantee Facility was set up in May to assist Severe Acute Respiratory Syndrome (SARs) affected businesses. |
| | The International Centre for Leadership in Finance (ICLIF) was launched in October, with the key objective of developing world class leadership in the finance and business sectors in Malaysia and the region. |
| 2004 | A new interest rate framework was introduced in April. It involved a new policy rate and the abolishment of the ceiling on BLRs and prescribed lending spreads. |
| | Several major foreign exchange administration rules were relaxed to promote the efficiency of business operations in Malaysia |
| | The market risk capital adequacy framework was implemented. All licensed institutions were required to incorporate their market risk positions into the risk-weighted capital ratio (RWCR). |
| | The regulatory treatment for new CAGAMAS debt securities was revised as a measure to further improve the efficient functioning of the domestic bond market. |
| 2005 | Stamp duty and real property gains tax on mergers and acquisitions of companies listed on the KLSE exempted. |
| | Further relaxations to the foreign exchange administration policies were announced. |
| | The Credit Counselling and Debt Management Agency (CCDMA) was set up to provide consumers with financial management and credit counselling as well as debt-management services. |
| | New guidelines were introduced to ensure that the electronic broking system offered by money brokers operated in a manner that promoted the overall integrity and stability of the financial system. |
| | BNM announced that fixed deposits placed by large corporations and non-residents would be carried on a negotiated basis regardless of the amount placed. |

*Sources:* BNM (1989), Emery (1991), Yusof *et al.* (1994), Dekle and Pradhan (1997), Williamson and Mahar (1998), Ariff and Khalid (2000), Athukorala (2001), Goh *et al.* (2003), Detragiache and Gupta (2004) and BNM (various issues) *Annual Report*.

## Appendix 2: Sources of data

| *Mnemonics* | *Definition* | *Sources* |
|---|---|---|
| BCP | Domestic credit to the private sector | IFS |
| CAL | Commercial banks average lending rate | M&B (1994), MSB |
| CLR | Commercial banks liquidity ratio | M&B (1994), MSB |
| CPI | Consumer price index | M&B (1994), MSB |
| CTR | Company tax rate | MOF |
| DIR | 12-month fixed deposit interest rate | M&B (1994), MSB |
| EPF | Employee provident fund contributions | M&B (1994), MSB |
| FDI | Foreign direct investment | M&B (1994), MSB |
| GCF | Gross capital formation | M&B (1994), MSB, WDI |
| GDP | Gross domestic product | ER, WDI |
| GNP | Gross national product | M&B (1994), MSB |
| GNS | Gross national saving | M&B (1994), MSB |
| GPRI | Gross private fixed capital formation | M&B (1994), MSB |
| GPUB | Gross public fixed capital formation | M&B (1994), MSB |
| LF | Labour force | WDI |
| M2 | Broad money supply M2 | M&B (1994), MSB |
| MAD | Maximum deposit rate | AR, M&B (1994) |
| MAL | Maximum lending rate | AR, M&B (1994) |
| MID | Minimum deposit rate | AR, M&B (1994) |
| MIL | Minimum lending rate | AR, M&B (1994) |
| OAG | Old age dependency | WDI |
| PIR | Policy intervention rate | AR |
| PSL | Priority sector (*bumiputra* community) target rate | AR |
| PSR | Maximum lending rate for priority sectors | AR, M&B (1994) |
| PUC | Public consumption | M&B (1994), MSB |
| PUS | Public saving | AR, ER |
| SRR | Commercial banks statutory reserve requirements | AR, M&B (1994) |
| YAG | Young age dependency | WDI |

*Notes:* AR = Annual Reports of BNM, ER = Economic Reports of the Ministry of Finance Malaysia, IFS = International Financial Statistics (2005) of the International Monetary Fund, MOF = Ministry of Finance Malaysia, MSB = Monthly Statistical Bulletin of BNM, M&B = *Money and Banking in Malaysia* (1989, 1994) of BNM, and WDI = World Development Indicators (2005) of the World Bank.

## Appendix 3: Results of the unit root tests

Three unit root tests are used to assess the order of integration of the variables. The Augmented Dickey–Fuller (ADF) and Phillips–Perron (PP) test the null of a unit root against the alternative of stationarity, while the Kwiatkowiski–Phillips–Schmidt–Shin (KPSS) tests the null of stationarity against the alternative of a unit root. As shown in the table below, the testing results are mixed. Nevertheless, it is clear that none of the variables appears to be integrated at an order higher than one, allowing legitimate use of the ARDL bounds procedure.

*Table A* Unit root tests

| | *ADF* | | *PP* | | *KPSS* | | *Conclusion* |
|---|---|---|---|---|---|---|---|
| | *level* | *1st diff.* | *level* | *1st diff.* | *level* | *1st diff.* | |
| $BC_t$ | −6.835*** | −5.517*** | −6.824*** | −19.357*** | 0.485** | 0.271 | *I*(0)/*I*(1) |
| $\ln BCY_t$ | −1.123 | −7.252*** | −0.985 | −7.246*** | 0.207** | 0.334 | *I*(1) |
| $COC_t$ | −4.050*** | −6.176*** | −4.015*** | −12.803*** | 0.504** | 0.268 | *I*(0)/*I*(1) |
| $\ln FD_t$ | −0.824 | −3.547** | −0.573 | −7.352*** | 0.199** | 0.334 | *I*(1) |
| $\ln FDI_t$ | −3.947** | −9.056*** | −4.091** | −9.340*** | 0.075 | 0.080 | *I*(0) |
| $\ln FL_t$ | −2.961 | −6.723*** | −2.963 | −8.188*** | 0.159** | 0.104 | *I*(1) |
| $\ln GDP_t$ | −3.404* | −5.647*** | −2.016 | −5.655*** | 0.076 | 0.120 | *I*(0)/*I*(1) |
| $\ln LF_t$ | −1.669 | −4.621*** | −0.973 | −4.652*** | 0.133* | 0.204 | *I*(1) |
| $\ln M2Y_t$ | −2.832 | −7.269*** | −2.832 | −7.900*** | 0.151** | 0.155 | *I*(1) |
| $OAG_t$ | −0.944 | −2.235* | −0.255 | −4.551*** | 0.139* | 0.323 | *I*(1) |
| $\ln PDI_t$ | −2.237 | −5.642*** | −1.819 | −5.526*** | 0.155** | 0.146 | *I*(1) |
| $\ln PEN_t$ | −1.167 | −4.801*** | −1.304 | −4.886*** | 0.082 | 0.195 | *I*(0)/*I*(1) |
| $\ln PGDP_t$ | −2.167 | −5.657*** | −2.058 | −5.665*** | 0.088 | 0.103 | *I*(0)/*I*(1) |
| $\ln PPI_t$ | −2.736 | −6.776*** | −3.001 | −6.776*** | 0.118 | 0.151 | *I*(0)/*I*(1) |
| $\ln PRI_t$ | −1.991 | −5.027*** | −1.544 | −4.950*** | 0.131* | 0.181 | *I*(1) |
| $\ln PRK_t$ | −1.717 | −4.032*** | −0.032 | −3.980*** | 0.106 | 0.332 | *I*(0)/*I*(1) |
| $\ln PUB_t$ | −2.556 | −8.114*** | −4.364*** | −8.114*** | 0.102 | 0.267 | *I*(0)/*I*(1) |
| $\ln PUK_t$ | −1.874 | −4.474*** | −1.961 | −4.450*** | 0.085 | 0.155 | *I*(0)/*I*(1) |
| $\ln PUS_t$ | −3.831** | −5.488*** | −3.717** | −9.100*** | 0.140* | 0.147 | *I*(0)/*I*(1) |
| $\ln PRS_t$ | −03833 | −7.611*** | −3.033 | −7.907*** | 0.153** | 0.094 | *I*(1) |
| $RI_t$ | −4.391*** | −4.621*** | −4.362*** | −17.263*** | 0.068 | 0.064 | *I*(0) |
| $UNC_t$ | −0.418 | −2.538* | 0.160 | −6.699*** | 0.165** | 0.388 | *I*(1) |
| $\ln VPRS_t$ | −3.101 | −7.588*** | −3.101 | −8.084*** | 0.160** | 0.113 | *I*(1) |
| $YAG_t$ | −2.587 | −2.716* | −2.269 | −2.716* | 0.137* | 0.134 | *I*(1) |
| $\ln (S/Y)_t$ | −4.156** | −7.235*** | −4.121** | −10.119*** | 0.085 | 0.109 | *I*(0) |
| $\ln (I/Y)_t$ | −1.407 | −5.771*** | −1.662 | −5.771*** | 0.165** | 0.283 | *I*(1) |

*Notes:* *, ** and *** indicate 10%, 5% and 1% level of significance, respectively. For ADF, AIC is used to select the lag length and the maximum number of lags is set to be five. For PP and KPSS, Barlett–Kernel is used as the spectral estimation method. The bandwidth is selected using the Newey–West method.

## Appendix 4: Cointegration tests and lag length selection

*Table B.1* Financial deepening equation

| | *Model A* (*Dep.* = $\Delta lnBCY_t$) | | *Model B* (*Dep.* = $\Delta lnM2Y_t$) | |
|---|---|---|---|---|
| | $p = 1$ | $p = 2$ | $p = 1$ | $p = 2$ |
| *Cointegration tests* | | | | |
| *F*-statistic | 4.731** | 1.803 | 4.178* | 2.181 |
| *t*-statistic | –3.698* | –2.368 | –4.061** | –2.163 |
| *Lag length selection criteria* | | | | |
| *AIC* | –1.306 | –1.119 | –3.178 | –3.103 |
| *SBC* | –0.773 | –0.415 | –2.646 | –2.399 |

*Table B.2* Private saving equation

| | *Model A* *(Dep. = $\Delta lnPRS_t$)* | | *Model B* *(Dep. = $\Delta lnVPRS_t$)* | |
|---|---|---|---|---|
| | *p = 1* | *p = 2* | *p = 1* | *p = 2* |
| *Cointegration tests* | | | | |
| *F*-statistic | 4.410*** | 0.950 | 4.374*** | 0.844 |
| *t*-statistic | –4.622** | –0.561 | –5.074*** | –0.672 |
| *Lag length selection criteria* | | | | |
| *AIC* | –2.048 | –1.798 | –1.453 | –1.175 |
| *SBC* | –1.065 | –0.474 | –0.511 | 0.148 |

*Table B.3* Private investment equation

| | *Model A* ($Dep. = \Delta lnPRI_t$) | | *Model B* ($Dep. = \Delta lnPDI_t$) | | *Model C* ($Dep. = \Delta lnPDI_t$) | |
|---|---|---|---|---|---|---|
| | $p = 1$ | $p = 2$ | $p = 1$ | $p = 2$ | $p = 1$ | $p = 2$ |
| *Cointegration tests* | | | | | | |
| *F*-statistic | 1.963 | 6.044*** | 4.435* | 5.948*** | 2.109 | 7.394*** |
| *t*-statistic | –2.919 | –5.408*** | –4.818* | –4.346*** | –3.546 | –5.152*** |
| *Lag length selection criteria* | | | | | | |
| *AIC* | –1.161 | –2.096 | –0.803 | –1.203 | –0.718 | –1.919 |
| *SBC* | –0.301 | –0.854 | 0.056 | –0.169 | 0.264 | –0.637 |

*Table B.4* Investment and saving rates equation

| | *p* = *1* | *p* = *2* |
|---|---|---|
| *Cointegration tests* | | |
| *F*-statistic | 5.486* | 6.425** |
| *t*-statistic | −3.285** | −3.573** |
| *Lag length selection criteria* | | |
| *AIC* | −1.457 | −1.519 |
| *SBC* | −1.092 | −1.028 |

*Table B.5* Aggregate output equation

| | *Model A* | | *Model B* | |
|---|---|---|---|---|
| | *p* = *1* | *p* = *2* | *p* = *1* | *p* = *2* |
| *Cointegration tests* | | | | |
| *F*-statistic | 5.194*** | 4.552** | 5.237*** | 4.269** |
| *t*-statistic | −4.214** | −1.918 | −4.191** | −2.386 |
| *Lag length selection criteria* | | | | |
| *AIC* | −4.368 | −4.553 | −4.480 | −4.533 |
| *SBC* | −3.719 | −3.693 | −3.831 | −3.672 |

*Notes: p* is the optimal lag length for the conditional ECM. $AIC = -2(ll/T) + 2(k/T)$ and $SBC = -2(ll/T) + (k/T)(\ln T)$, where *ll* is the maximized log-likelihood value of the model at lag *p*, *k* is the number of estimated coefficients, and *T* is the sample size. *, ** and *** indicate 10%, 5% and 1% level of significance, respectively. The test statistics of the bounds tests are compared with the critical values reported in Pesaran *et al.* (2001), and the null hypothesis is that there is no long-run relationship.

## Appendix 5: Critical values for the ARDL bounds tests

*Table C.1* Critical value bounds for the F-test (unrestricted intercept and no trend)

| *k* | *1%* | | *5%* | | *10%* | |
|---|---|---|---|---|---|---|
| | *I(0)* | *I(1)* | *I(0)* | *I(1)* | *I(0)* | *I(1)* |
| 1 | 11.79 | 11.79 | 8.21 | 8.21 | 6.58 | 6.58 |
| 2 | 6.84 | 7.84 | 4.94 | 5.73 | 4.04 | 4.78 |
| 3 | 5.15 | 6.36 | 3.79 | 4.85 | 3.17 | 4.14 |
| 4 | 4.29 | 5.61 | 3.23 | 4.35 | 2.72 | 3.77 |
| 5 | 3.74 | 5.06 | 2.86 | 4.01 | 2.45 | 3.52 |
| 6 | 3.41 | 4.68 | 2.62 | 3.79 | 2.26 | 3.35 |
| 7 | 3.15 | 4.43 | 2.45 | 3.61 | 2.12 | 3.23 |
| 8 | 2.96 | 4.26 | 2.32 | 3.50 | 2.03 | 3.13 |

*Table C.2* Critical value bounds for the t-test (unrestricted intercept and no trend)

| *k* | *1%* | | *5%* | | *10%* | |
|---|---|---|---|---|---|---|
| | *I(0)* | *I(1)* | *I(0)* | *I(1)* | *I(0)* | *I(1)* |
| 1 | −3.43 | −3.43 | −2.86 | −2.86 | −2.57 | −2.57 |
| 2 | −3.43 | −3.82 | −2.86 | −3.22 | −2.57 | −2.91 |
| 3 | −3.43 | −4.10 | −2.86 | −3.53 | −2.57 | −3.21 |
| 4 | −3.43 | −4.37 | −2.86 | −3.78 | −2.57 | −3.46 |
| 5 | −3.43 | −4.60 | −2.86 | −3.99 | −2.57 | −3.66 |
| 6 | −3.43 | −4.79 | −2.86 | −4.19 | −2.57 | −3.86 |
| 7 | −3.43 | −4.99 | −2.86 | −4.38 | −2.57 | −4.04 |
| 8 | −3.43 | −5.19 | −2.86 | −4.57 | −2.57 | −4.23 |

*Notes:* $k$ = number of variables. If the test statistics exceed their respective upper critical values, the null is rejected and it can be concluded a long-run relationship exists. If the test statistics fall below the lower critical values, the null hypothesis of no cointegration cannot be rejected. If the statistics fall within the band, the statistical inference would be inconclusive.
*Source:* Pesaran *et al.* (2001).

# Notes

## 1 Introduction

1 For instance, De Gregorio and Guidotti (1995) argue that 'financial development' and 'financial intermediation' are often used interchangeably. This is a common source of confusion. Financial development is a broad term which includes all aspects of the development in the financial system whereas 'financial intermediation' only refers to services provided by banks.

## 2 Finance and development: a survey of literature

1 See Leland and Pyle (1977), Stiglitz and Weiss (1981), Diamond (1984) and Boyd and Prescott (1986).
2 See Williamson (1986) and Bernanke and Gertler (1989, 1990).
3 See Diamond (1984), Boyd and Prescott (1986), Williamson (1986) and King and Levine (1993b).
4 See Townsend (1979), Greenwood and Jovanovic (1990) and King and Levine (1993b).
5 In Gurley and Shaw's (1955) model, financial capacity (defined as borrowers' ability to absorb debt without reducing current consumption) is the key determinant of aggregate demand. Financial intermediaries extend households' financial capacity by facilitating lending and borrowing activities.
6 Both McKinnon (1973) and Shaw (1973) argue that financial repression policies are largely accountable for the poor economic performance of developing countries in the 1960s, where low saving, low investment and credit rationing were prevalent. Investment suffered both in terms of quantity and quality as funds were allocated at the discretion of policy makers instead of following the marginal productivity of each investment project. Financial liberalization, in terms of removal of all financial repression policies (e.g. interest rate ceiling, directed credit programs, and high reserve requirements) is therefore advocated.
7 To a lesser extent, the McKinnon–Shaw thesis is also riposted by the Keynesian or post-Keynesian school of thought, which postulates that high interest rates tend to reduce savings through discouraging investment. What matters for growth is not savings, but the incentives to invest, which is governed by the availability of bank credit (see, e.g., Davidson, 1986).
8 See, e.g., Greenwood and Jovanovic (1990), Bencivenga and Smith (1991, 1993), Saint-Paul (1992), King and Levine (1993b), Pagano (1993), Bencivenga *et al.* (1995), Greenwood and Smith (1997) and Blackburn and Hung (1998) for detailed expositions.
9 See Allen and Gale (1999, 2000), Beck and Levine (2002), Ergungor (2004) and

Levine (2005) for comprehensive discussions on the relative merits for each type of financial system.

10 See also Levine and Zervos (1998) and Blackburn *et al.* (2005).

11 Outside money refers to money held outside the monetary base, e.g. gold or cash. In contrast, inside money refers to any debt that is used as money.

12 See Demetriades and Hussein (1996), Arestis and Demetriades (1997), Demetriades and Andrianova (2004) and Kirkpatrick (2005).

13 For an insightful analysis on informal markets in developing countries, see Jagannathan (1987). Fry (1995) provides an excellent survey of studies on informal finance in Asia.

14 A possible way to improve on it is to consider imposing some theory models on VAR. However, econometric methodological philosophy is not considered here. Interested readers can refer to McKibbin *et al.* (1998) and Kapetanios *et al.* (2005) for interesting attempts to impose some theory models on VARs.

## 3 The Malaysian economy and its financial system

1 Malaysia is a plural society with the population made up of different ethnic groups. The major ethnic groups are the *bumiputras*, which comprises Malays and other indigenous people (61.4 per cent), ethnic Chinese (23.7 per cent), Indians (7.1 per cent) and others (7.8 per cent) (Department of Statistics, 2005).

2 Before 1997, there were many speculative bubbles and overheating in the Malaysian securities and real estate markets due partly to the ease of borrowing. As the crisis broke in Thailand, market confidence collapsed. Massive capital outflows exerted severe downward pressure on asset prices. These capital outflows accelerated in July when the Thai Baht was devalued. This was followed by a sharp depreciation in the ringgit, and a significant reduction in both domestic and external demand. Equity values and real estate values plunged, resulting in a significant erosion of individual financial wealth. During this period, investment projects launched by highly leveraged firms failed, non-performing loans increased significantly, and much uncertainty surrounded the economy.

3 For more debates on the causes of the Asian financial crisis, see Corsetti (1998), Corsetti, Pesenti and Roubini (1998a, b), Radelet and Sachs (1998), Stiglitz (1999a, b) and Krugman (2001).

4 The First Malaysia Plan (1966–1970) was the first economic plan for the whole of Malaysia, aimed at improving the living standards of all citizens.

5 Kohsaka (1996) provides a good review of the changing patterns of capital flows in the Asian-Pacific region. His study investigates the role of Japan as a major capital supplier as well as a financial intermediary in the Asian-Pacific region. The importance of FDI for Malaysia has been highlighted in this study, which shows that Malaysia depends on FDI for a crucial part of its net capital inflows and has an integrated capital market with Japan.

6 BNM introduced a new interest rate framework in 2004. Under the new framework, the Overnight Policy Rate (OPR) will be an indicator of the monetary policy stance as well as a target rate for the day-to-day liquidity operations of BNM.

7 As discussed previously in Chapter 2, the structuralist view proposes that the emergence of more financial institutions and a greater variety of financial products and services will encourage financial intermediating activities and hence stimulate economic growth.

8 A new framework for investment banks was announced in 2005. Under this new framework, discount houses and merchant banks will no longer be in the Malaysian financial system.

9 One of the key features of Islamic banking is the prohibition of paying or receiving interest, which is the backbone of conventional banking. Islamic banking

operates under the principle of profit and loss sharing. Capital is not costless but rewarded based on profits obtained from other permissible banking business (Kader and Hashim, 2005).

10 Bank-based or market-based systems may have different impacts on economic growth. A bank-based financial system tends to promote long-term economic growth as banks tend to offer longer-term loans to entrepreneurs. In contrast, a market-based financial system is more likely to have short-term effects as firms are primarily concerned with immediate performance.

11 The types of investment incentives given include pioneer status, investment tax allowance, abatement of adjusted income, abatement of adjustment income for exports, export allowance, and double deductions for certain types of expenses. For more details, see Yong (1988) and Boadway, Chua and Flatters (1995).

12 See Blonigen (2005) for a review.

13 For more discussion on FDI in Malaysia, see Ariff (1991).

14 An econometric analysis of the savings and investment relationship is provided in Chapter 8.

## 4 Data, variable construction and estimation methodology

1 Apart from the bumiputra community, directed credit programmes also include minimum lending to other priority sectors, including agriculture, manufacturing, small and medium-sized enterprises, and individuals for housing loans. Only the *bumiputra* sector, which is the largest beneficiary sector, is considered in the analysis since its data is available on a systematic basis and can be quantified.

2 Principal component analysis has often been used to reduce a large set of correlated variables into a smaller set of uncorrelated variables, known as principal components (see Stock and Watson, 2002a, b).

3 For example, see Edwards (1996), Horioka (1997), Masson *et al.* (1998), Loayza *et al.* (2000) and Athukorala and Tsai (2003).

4 Other commonly used measures include credit to the private sector in real terms and the ratio of private credit to GDP. The use of these measures is inappropriate in this case as they are highly correlated with other variables considered in the private investment model, notably output and public investment, with correlation coefficients higher than 0.95.

5 For a survey of other cointegration techniques such as the nonlinear least squares estimator of Stock (1987), the canonical correlations of Bossaerts (1988), the full information maximum likelihood (FIML) estimator for cointegrated system of Phillips (1988, 1991) and Phillips and Hansen (1990), the common trend approach of Stock and Watson (1988), and the three-stage FIML procedure of Engle and Yoo (1991), see Muscatelli and Hurn (1992, 1995) and Gonzalo (1994).

6 A variable is said to follow an I(2) process when it needs to be differenced twice to attain stationarity. Evidence of an I(2) variable can be established when the null hypothesis that the first-difference of a variable has a unit root is not rejected.

7 Inder (1993) shows that while endogeneity bias can be expected in an ARDL framework, it does not have a great influence on the estimated cointegrating relationships. He also demonstrates that the effects of endogeneity bias are far less severe compared with those of omitted lagged variables bias. Hence, Inder (1993) proposes the use an unrestricted ECM to deal with the problems of omitted lagged variables bias, and suggests using instruments to adjust for endogeneity bias, if this is a concern.

8 Pesaran and Shin (1998) have also highlighted that the error term may be correlated with current differenced terms. Thus, the specification needs to be augmented with a sufficient number of lagged differenced terms in order to make valid inference.

9 This involves running a simple OLS on the levels of the variables, which is the first step of the Engle and Granger (1987) two-step procedure.
10 See Hendry and Richard (1982), Gilbert (1986), Ericsson *et al.* (1990), Charemza and Deadman (1992), Hendry (1995) and Campos *et al.* (2005) for more detailed expositions on the general-to-specific modeling technique.

## 5 Financial deepening and its determinants

1 See Chapter 3 for more details.
2 For in-depth case studies on financial liberalization in developing countries, see Cheng (1986), Park (1994), Yusof *et al.* (1994), Sen and Vaidya (1999) and Ariff and Khalid (2000).
3 See e.g. Dekle and Pradhan (1997), Fry (1997) and Demirguc-Kunt and Detragiache (1998).
4 More research is required to provide some insight into this conjecture. To this end, Ang (2007b) has attempted to examine how each type of financial sector policy influences financial deepening in Malaysia. The results indicate that interest rate controls and capital liquidity requirements positively affect the level of financial development. However, higher statutory reserve requirements and the presence of directed credit programmes appear to be harmful for the development of the Malaysian financial system.

## 6 The patterns and determinants of private saving

1 The approaches adopted by these two studies are identical, although they differ in terms of empirical implementation. Munnell (1976) uses a dummy variable to indicate whether an individual expects to receive social security benefits upon retirement whereas Feldstein (1974) employs actual data on the level of social security benefits entitled by retired workers to capture the effects of social security.
2 The Ricardian equivalence proposition was first proposed by David Ricardo and later popularized by Robert Barro using the theory of rational expectation.
3 In the savings literature, the most commonly used saving variable is the private saving rate (ratio of private saving to nominal GDP). However, it is important to note that when saving is measured in ratio as $\ln(GNS_t / GDP_t) = \ln(GNS_t) - \ln(GDP_t)$, a restriction of one is imposed on the coefficient for $\ln(GDP_t)$. Such a restriction is a testable hypothesis. If it is not valid statistically, measurement errors will be introduced into the dependent variable. Hence, the focus here is on analysing real private saving rather than the rate of saving.
4 To measure financial development, the standard practice is to use bank credit to private sector as a ratio of GDP, as discussed previously in Chapter 4. Since the income variable used in the analysis of saving behaviour is private income, financial development is defined as bank credit to the private sector as a ratio of private income in the specification of the saving function. Using an alternative measure of M2/private income, similar estimation results are obtained.
5 The major phase of interest rates reforms took place in 1978. For more details, see Chapter 3.
6 The high collinearity observed between age dependency and the financial deepening indicators may have reduced statistical significance of the demographic variables. This does not affect the short-run results when all variables are expressed in first-differences.

## 7 The determinants of private investment

1 This is not a novel approach. Several key studies on investment analysis have also adopted this approach. See Sundararajan and Thakur (1980), Tun Wai and Wong (1982), Blejer and Khan (1984) and Athukorala and Sen (2002).
2 See, e.g., Guncavdi *et al.* (1998) and Athukorala and Sen (2002).
3 Irreversible investment expenditures are sunk costs which cannot be recovered or used in a different activity. For more discussion, see Hartman (1972), Pindyck (1991) and Dixit and Pindyck (1994).
4 It would be more appropriate to formulate the dynamic optimization problem in a continuous time manner. However, a discrete time model has been used for simplicity. Nevertheless, this simplification does not affect the qualitative aspects of the analysis.
5 Alternative measures of cost of capital such as relative price of capital and real interest rates have also been considered in the estimation. However, they were also found to be insignificant in explaining the determination of private investment. Hence, the results are robust to the use of different measures of cost of capital.
6 In the extreme case, a severe shortage of credit, dubbed 'credit crunch', can retard growth in the non-tradable sector and result in slow economic recovery as in the case of Mexico during the crisis period 1995–98 (see Krueger and Tornell, 1999).

## 8 The saving and investment nexus

1 The no Ponzi game condition rules out the possibility for the government to issue bonds and roll it over forever. By imposing such a scheme, the present value of the government's purchases cannot exceed the present value of revenues.
2 Using a slightly different approach, this model has also been derived by Otto (1992) and Ghosh (1995).
3 Assuming that saving and investment are random walk processes, the alternative approach proposed by Levy (2000) suggests that if and $I$, ~ $I(1)$, then saving and investment will be cointegrated with cointegrating vector [1 −1].
4 The magnitudes of the long-run coefficients are found to be 0.31–037 for Norway (Jansen and Schulze, 1996) and 0.20–0.93 for the US (De Vita and Abbott, 2002).

## 9 Financial intermediation and economic growth

1 See Chapter 3 for more details.
2 In view of the possibility that the results may be sensitive to the sample period covered, the pre-crisis period (1960–96) has also been considered in the estimation. While the results show some variations in the magnitudes of the coefficients obtained, the finding that public capital stock exerts an undesirable effect on aggregate output remains unaltered. Hence, it appears that the results are not significantly affected by the crisis episode. This is consistent with the finding that the Asian financial crisis dummy is insignificant.
3 As a check for robustness, the output equation has also been controlled for human capital and trade openness. However, the results show that these variables are statistically insignificant at the conventional level. Hence, the finding that financial deepening enhances growth through the productivity channel seems highly plausible.

# References


Agenor, P.-R. and Montiel, P. J. (1999). 'Introduction and Overview', in P.-R. Agenor and P. J. Montiel (eds.), *Development Macroeconomics*, Princeton: Princeton University Press.

Agosin, M. R. and Machado, R. (2005). 'Foreign Investment in Developing Countries: Does It Crowd in Domestic Investment?' *Oxford Development Studies*, 33: 149–62.

Agrawal, P. (2001). 'The Relation between Savings and Growth: Cointegration and Causality Evidence from Asia', *Applied Economics*, 33: 499–513.

—— (2004). 'Interest Rates and Investment in East Asia: An Empirical Evaluation of Various Financial Liberalisation Hypotheses', *Journal of Development Studies*, 40: 142–73.

Ahmed, S. (1998). 'Comment on "The Legal Environment, Banks, and Long-Run Economic Growth"', *Journal of Money, Credit, and Banking*, 30: 614–20.

Allen, F. and Gale, D. (1999). 'Diversity of Opinion and Financing of New Technologies', *Journal of Financial Intermediation*, 8: 68–89.

—— (2000) *Comparing Financial Systems*, Cambridge and London: MIT Press.

Allen, F., Qian, J. and Qian, M. (2005). 'Law, Finance, and Economic Growth in China', *Journal of Financial Economics*, 77: 57–116.

Ando, A. and Modigliani, F. (1963). 'The "Life-Cycle" Hypothesis of Saving: Aggregate Implications and Tests', *American Economic Review*, 53: 55–84.

Ang, J. B. (2007a). 'Financial Deepening and Economic Development in Malaysia' *Economic Papers*, 26(3): 249–60.

—— (2007b). 'Are Financial Sector Policies Effective in Deepening the Malaysian Financial System?' *Monash University, Department of Economics Discussion Paper Series 02–07*.

—— (2008a). 'Financial Development and the FDI–Growth Nexus: The Malaysian Experience', *Applied Economics*, forthcoming.

—— (2008b). 'What Are the Mechanisms Linking Financial Development and Economic Growth in Malaysia?', *Economic Modelling*, 38(1): 38–53.

—— (2008c). 'A Survey of Recent Developments in the Literature of Finance and Growth', *Journal of Economic Surveys*, 22(3): 536–76.

Ang, J. B. and McKibbin, W. J. (2007). 'Financial Liberalization, Financial Sector Development and Growth: Evidence from Malaysia', *Journal of Development Economics*, forthcoming.

Arestis, P. and Demetriades, P. O. (1996). 'On Financial Repression and Economic Development: The Case of Cyprus', in P. Arestis (ed.), *Essays in honour of Paul*

*Davidson, Volume 2: Employment, Economic Growth and the Tyranny of the Market*. Cheltenham: Edward Elgar.

—— (1997). 'Financial Development and Economic Growth: Assessing the Evidence', *Economic Journal*, 107: 783–99.

—— (1999). 'Financial Liberalization: The Experience of Developing Countries', *Eastern Economic Journal*, 25: 441–57.

Arestis, P., Demetriades, P. O. and Luintel, K. B. (2001). 'Financial Development and Economic Growth: The Role of Stock Markets', *Journal of Money, Credit, and Banking*, 33: 16–41.

Arestis, P., Demetriades, P. O., Fattouh, B. and Mouratidis, K. (2002). 'The Impact of Financial Liberalization Policies on Financial Development: Evidence from Developing Economies', *International Journal of Finance and Economics*, 7: 109–21.

Ariff, M. (1991) *The Malaysian Economy: Pacific Connections*, Singapore: Oxford University Press.

Ariff, M. and Khalid, A. M. (2000) *Liberalization, Growth and the Asian Financial Crisis: Lessons for Developing and Transitional Economies in Asia*, Cheltenham: Edward Elgar.

Aschauer, D. A. (1989a). 'Does Public Capital Crowd Out Private Capital?' *Journal of Monetary Economics*, 24: 171–88.

—— (1989b). 'Is Public Expenditure Productive?' *Journal of Monetary Economics*, 23: 177–200.

Athukorala, P.-C. (2001) *Crisis and Recovery in Malaysia: The Role of Capital Controls*, Cheltenham: Edward Elgar.

Athukorala, P.-C. and Menon, J. (1995). 'Developing with Foreign Investment: Malaysia.' *Australian Economic Review*, 109: 9–22.

Athukorala, P.-C. and Sen, K. (2002) *Saving, Investment, and Growth in India*, Oxford and New York: Oxford University Press.

Athukorala, P.-C. and Tsai, P.-L. (2003). 'Determinants of Household Saving in Taiwan: Growth, Demography and Public Policy', *Journal of Development Studies*, 39: 65–88.

Atje, R. and Jovanovic, B. (1993). 'Stock Markets and Development', *European Economic Review*, 37: 632–40.

Aziz, Z. A. (1984). 'Financial Institutions and Markets in Malaysia', in M. T. Skully (ed.), *Financial Institutions and Markets in Southeast Asia : A study of Brunei, Indonesia, Malaysia, Philippines, Singapore and Thailand*, London: Macmillan.

Bahmani-Oskooee, M. and Chakrabarti, A. (2005). 'Openness, Size, and the Saving–Investment Relationship', *Economic System*, 29: 283–93.

Baltagi, B. H. and Pinnoi, N. (1995). 'Public Capital Stock and State Productivity Growth: Further Evidence from An Error Components Model', *Empirical Economics*, 20: 351–59.

Bandiera, O., Caprio, G., Jr, Honohan, P. and Schiantarelli, F. (2000). 'Does Financial Reform Raise or Reduce Saving?' *Review of Economics and Statistics*, 82: 239–63.

Banerjee, A., Dolado, J. J., Hendry, D. F. and Smith, G. W. (1986). 'Exploring Equilibrium Relationships in Econometrics through Static Models: Some Monte Carlo Evidence', *Oxford Bulletin of Economics and Statistics*, 48: 253–77.

Banerjee, A., Dolado, J. and Mestre, R. (1998). 'Error-correction Mechanism Tests for Cointegration in a Single-equation Framework', *Journal of Time Series Analysis*, 19: 267–83.

Barro, R. J. (1974). 'Are Government Bonds Net Wealth?' *Journal of Political Economy*, 82: 1095–17.

—— (1978) *The Impact of Social Security on Private Saving*, Washington, D.C.: American Enterprise Institute.

—— (1991). 'Economic Growth in a Cross Section of Countries', *Quarterly Journal of Economics*, 106: 407–43.

Barro, R. J. and MacDonald, G. M. (1979). 'Social Security and Consumer Spending in an International Cross Section', *Journal of Public Economics*, 11: 275–89.

Bascom, W. O. (1994) *The Economics of Financial Reform in Developing Countries*, London: Macmillan.

Baxter, M. and Crucini, M. J. (1993). 'Explaining Saving–Investment Correlations', *American Economic Review*, 83: 416–36.

Bayoumi, T. (1990). 'Saving–Investment Correlations', *International Monetary Fund Staff Papers*, 37: 360–87.

Beck, T. and Levine, R. (2002). 'Industry Growth and Capital Allocation: Does Having a Market- or Bank-Based System Matter?' *Journal of Financial Economics*, 64: 147–80.

—— (2004). 'Stock Markets, Banks, and Growth: Panel Evidence', *Journal of Banking and Finance*, 28: 423–42.

Beck, T., Levine, R. and Loayza, N. (2000). 'Finance and the Sources of Growth', *Journal of Financial Economics*, 58: 261–300.

Bell, C. and Rousseau, P. L. (2001). 'Post-Independence India: A Case of Finance-Led Industrialization?' *Journal of Development Economics*, 65: 153–75.

Bencivenga, V. R. and Smith, B. D. (1991). 'Financial Intermediation and Endogenous Growth', *Review of Economic Studies*, 58: 195–209.

—— (1993). 'Some Consequences of Credit Rationing in an Endogenous Growth Model', *Journal of Economic Dynamics and Control*, 17: 97–122.

Bencivenga, V. R., Smith, B. D. and Starr, R. M. (1995). 'Transactions Costs, Technological Choice, and Endogenous Growth', *Journal of Economic Theory*, 67: 153–77.

Benhabib, J. and Spiegel, M. M. (2000). 'The Role of Financial Development in Growth and Investment', *Journal of Economic Growth*, 5: 341–60.

Bernanke, B. and Gertler, M. (1989). 'Agency Costs, Net Worth, and Business Fluctuations', *American Economic Review*, 79: 14–31.

—— (1990). 'Financial Fragility and Economic Performance', *Quarterly Journal of Economics*, 105: 87–114.

Bertrand, M., Schoar, A. S. and Thesmar, D. (2004). 'Banking Deregulation and Industry Structure: Evidence from the French Banking Reforms of 1985', *CEPR Discussion Papers*: No. 4488.

Bewley, R. (1979). 'The Direct Estimation of the Equilibrium Response in a Linear Dynamic Model.' *Economics Letters*, 3: 357–61.

Bhalla, S. and Kharas, H. (1992). 'Growth and Equity in Malaysia: Policies and Consequences', in H. Y. Teh and K. L. Goh (eds.), *Malaysia's Economic Vision: Issues and Challenges*, Kuala Lumpur: Pelanduk Publications.

Bischoff, C. W. (1967). 'The Effects of Alternative Lag Distributions', in G. Fromm (ed.), *Tax Incentives and Capital Spending*, Washington, D.C.: The Brookings Institutions.

—— (1970). 'A Model of Nonresidential Construction in the United States', *American Economic Review*, 60: 10–17.

—— (1971). 'Business Investment in the 1970s: A Comparison of Models', *Brookings Papers on Economic Activity*, 0: 13–63.

Blackburn, K. and Hung, V. T. Y. (1998). 'A Theory of Growth, Financial Development and Trade', *Economica*, 65: 107–24.

Blackburn, K., Bose, N. and Capasso, S. (2005). 'Financial Development, Financing Choice and Economic Growth', *Review of Development Economics*, 9: 135–49.

Blejer, M. I. and Khan, M. S. (1984). 'Government Policy and Private Investment in Developing Countries', *International Monetary Fund Staff Papers*, 31: 379–403.

Blonigen, B. A. (2005). 'A Review of the Empirical Literature on FDI Determinants', *National Bureau of Economic Research No. 11299*.

BNM *Bank Negara Malaysia Annual Report*, Kuala Lumpur: Bank Negara Malaysia.

—— *Monthly Statistical Bulletin*, Kuala Lumpur: Bank Negara Malaysia.

—— *Quarterly Bulletin*, Kuala Lumpur: Bank Negara Malaysia.

—— (1989) *Money and Banking in Malaysia*, Kuala Lumpur: Bank Negara Malaysia.

—— (1994) *Money and Banking in Malaysia*, Kuala Lumpur: Bank Negara Malaysia.

—— (1999) *The Central Bank and the Financial System in Malaysia: A Decade of Change 1989–1999*, Kuala Lumpur: Bank Negara Malaysia.

—— (2004) *Bank Negara Malaysia Annual Report 2004*, Kuala Lumpur: Bank Negara Malaysia.

Boadway, R. W., Chua, D. and Flatters, F. (1995). 'Investment Incentives and the Corporate Tax System in Malaysia', in A. Shah (ed.), *Fiscal Incentives for Investment and Innovation*, Oxford: Oxford University Press.

Bonser-Neal, C. and Dewenter, K. L. (1999). 'Does Financial Market Development Stimulate Savings? Evidence from Emerging Stock Markets', *Contemporary Economic Policy*, 17: 370–80.

Bossaerts, P. (1988). 'Common Nonstationary Components of Asset Prices', *Journal of Economic Dynamics and Control*, 12: 347–64.

Bosworth, B. P. and Collins, S. M. (1999). 'Capital Flows to Developing Economies: Implications for Saving and Investment', *Brookings Papers on Economic Activity*, 1999: 143–69.

Boyd, J. H. and Prescott, E. C. (1986). 'Financial Intermediary-Coalitions', *Journal of Economic Theory*, 38: 211–32.

Boyd, J. H. and Smith, B. D. (1998). 'The Evolution of Debt and Equity Markets in Economic Development', *Economic Theory*, 12: 519–60.

Buffie, E. F. (1984). 'Financial Repression, the New Structuralists, and Stabilization Policy in Semi-Industrialized Economies', *Journal of Development Economics*, 14: 305–22.

Cagan, P. (1956). 'The Monetary Dynamics of Hyperinflations', in M. Friedman (ed.), *Quantity Theory of Money*, Chicago: University of Chicago Press.

—— (1965) *The Effect of Pension Plans on Aggregate Savings*, New York: National Bureau of Economic Research.

Calderon, C. and Liu, L. (2003). 'The Direction of Causality between Financial Development and Economic Growth', *Journal of Development Economics*, 72: 321–34.

Callen, T. S., Hall, S. G. and Henry, S. G. B. (1990). 'Manufacturing Stocks: Expectations, Risks and Co-integration', *Economic Journal*, 100: 756–72.

Campbell, J. Y. (1987). 'Does Saving Anticipate Declining Labour Income? An Alternative Test of the Permanent Income Hypothesis', *Econometrica*, 55: 1062–88.

Campbell, J. Y. and Shiller, R. J. (1987). 'Cointegration and Test of Present Value Models', *Journal of Political Economy*, 95: 1062–88.

Campos, J., Ericsson, N. R. and Hendry, D. F. (2005). 'General-to-Specific Modeling: An Overview and Selected Bibliography', *Board of Governors of the Federal Reserve System, International Finance Discussion Papers*.

Caporale, G. M., Howells, P. and Soliman, A. M. (2005). 'Endogenous Growth Models and Stock Market Development: Evidence from Four Countries', *Review of Development Economics*, 9: 166–76.

Cardia, E. (1991). 'The Dynamics of Savings and Investment in Response to Monetary, Fiscal and Productivity Shocks.' *Journal of Monetary Economics*, 28: 411–34.

Cetorelli, N. and Gambera, M. (2001). 'Banking Market Structure, Financial Dependence and Growth: International Evidence from Industry Data', *Journal of Finance*, 56: 617–48.

Chandavarkar, A. (1992). 'Of Finance and Development: Neglected and Unsettled Questions', *World Development*, 20: 133–42.

Charemza, W. W. and Deadman, D. F. (1992) *New Directions in Econometric Practice: General to Specific Modelling, Cointegration and Vector Autoregression*, Aldershot: Edward Elgar.

Chee, H. L. (1990) *Health and health Care in Malaysia – Present Trends and Implications for the Future*, Kuala Lumpur: Institute of Advanced Studies, University of Malaya.

Cheng, H.-S. (1986) *Financial policy and reform in Pacific Basin countries*, Lexington: Lexington Books.

Chibber, A. and Shafik, N. (1992). 'Does Devaluation Hurt Private Investment? The Indonesian Case', in A. Chibber, M. Dailami and N. Shafik (eds.), *Reviving Private Investment in Developing Countries*, Amsterdam: Elsevier Science Publishers.

Chirinko, R. S. (1993). 'Business Fixed Investment Spending: Modeling Strategies, Empirical Results, and Policy Implications', *Journal of Economic Literature*, 31: 1875–911.

Choe, C. and Moosa, I. A. (1999). 'Financial System and Economic Growth: The Korean Experience', *World Development*, 27: 1069–82.

Christopoulos, D. K. and Tsionas, E. G. (2004). 'Financial Development and Economic Growth: Evidence from Panel Unit Root and Cointegration Tests', *Journal of Development Economics*, 73: 55–74.

Claessens, S., Djankov, S. and Lang, L. H. P. (1999). 'Corporate Ownership and Valuation: Evidence from East Asia', in A. Harwood, R. Litan and M. Pomerleano (eds.), *Financial Markets and Development: The Crisis in Emerging Markets*, Washington D.C.: Brookings Institution Press.

Coakley, J., Kulasi, F. and Smith, R. (1996). 'Current Account Solvency and the Feldstein–Horioka Puzzle.' *Economic Journal*, 106: 620–27.

Cole, D. C. (1988). 'Financial Development in Asia', *Asia-Pacific Economic Literature*, 2: 26–47.

Collins, S. M. and Bosworth, B. P. (1996). 'Economic Growth in East Asia: Accumulation versus Assimilation', *Brookings Papers on Economic Activity*, 27(2): 135–204.

Corden, M. (1996) *Pragmatic Orthodox: Macroeconomic Policies in Seven East Asian Economies*, San Francisco: International Centre for Economic Growth.

Cornelli, F., Portes, R. and Schaffer, M. (1996). 'Banking and the Financial System in CEEs', in A. Kohsaka and K. Ohno (eds.), *Structural Adjustment and Economic Reform: East Asia, Latin America, and Central and Eastern Europe*, Tokyo: Institute of Developing Economies.

Corsetti, G. (1998). 'Interpreting the Asian Financial Crisis: Open Issues in Theory and Policy', *Asian Development Review*, 16: 18–63.

Corsetti, G., Pesenti, P. and Roubini, N. (1998a). 'What Caused the Asian Currency and Financial Crisis? Part I: A Macroeconomic Overview', *NBER Working Papers No: 6833*.

—— (1998b). 'What Caused the Asian Currency and Financial Crisis? Part II: The Policy Debate', *NBER Working Papers No: 6834*.

Crouch, H. (1996) *Government and Society in Malaysia*, Sydney: Allen and Unwin.

Cukierman, A. (1992) *Central Bank Strategy, Credibility, and Independence: Theory and Evidence* Cambridge, Massachusetts: MIT Press.

Cukierman, A., Webb, S. B. and Neyapti, B. (1992). 'Measuring the Independence of Central Banks and Its Effect on Policy Outcomes', *World Bank Economic Review*, 6: 353–98.

Davidson, P. (1986). 'Finance, Funding, Saving and Investment', *Journal of Post-Keynesian Economics*, 9: 101–10.

Dayal-Ghulati, A. and Thinmann, C. (1997). 'Saving in Southeast Asia and Latin America Compared: Searching for Policy Lessons', *IMF Working Papers No. 97/110*.

Deaton, A. S. (2005). 'Franco Modigliani and the Life Cycle Theory of Consumption', *Research Program in Development Studies and Center for Health and Well-being, Princeton University*.

De Gregorio, J. and Guidotti, P. E. (1995). 'Financial Development and Economic Growth', *World Development*, 23: 433–48.

Dekle, R. and Pradhan, M. (1997). 'Financial Liberalization and Money Demand in ASEAN Countries: Implications for Monetary Policy', *IMF Working Papers No: 97/36*.

Demetriades, P. O. and Andrianova, S. (2004). 'Finance and Growth: What We Know and What We Need to Know', in C. A. E. Goodhart (ed.), *Financial Development and Growth: Explaining the Links*, Basingstoke: Palgrave Macmillan.

Demetriades, P. O. and Hussein, K. A. (1996). 'Does Financial Development Cause Economic Growth? Time-Series Evidence from Sixteen Countries', *Journal of Development Economics*, 51: 387–411.

Demetriades, P. O. and Luintel, K. B. (1996). 'Financial Development, Economic Growth and Banker Sector Controls: Evidence from India', *Economic Journal*, 106: 359–74.

—— (1997). 'The Direct Costs of Financial Repression: Evidence from India', *Review of Economics and Statistics*, 79: 311–20.

—— (2001). 'Financial Restraints in the South Korean Miracle', *Journal of Development Economics*, 64: 459–79.

Demirguc-Kunt, A. and Detragiache, E. (1998a). 'The Determinants of Banking Crises in Developing and Developed Countries', *International Monetary Fund Staff Papers*, 45: 81–109.

—— (1998b). 'Financial Liberalization and Financial Fragility', *International Monetary Fund Working Papers No: 98/83*.

Demirguc-Kunt, A. and Maksimovic, V. (1998). 'Law, Finance, and Firm Growth', *Journal of Finance*, 53: 2107–37.

—— (2002). 'Funding Growth in Bank-Based and Market-Based Financial Systems: Evidence from Firm-Level Data', *Journal of Financial Economics*, 65: 337–63.

Detragiache, E. and Gupta, P. (2004). 'Foreign Banks in Emerging Market Crises: Evidence from Malaysia', *IMP Working Paper*, 04/129.

De Vita, G. and Abbott, A. (2002). 'Are Saving and Investment Cointegrated? An ARDL Bounds Testing Approach', *Economics Letters*, 77: 293–99.

Diamond, D. W. (1984). 'Financial Intermediation and Delegated Monitoring', *Review of Economic Studies*, 51: 393–414.

Diamond, D. W. and Dybvig, P. H. (1983). 'Bank Runs, Deposit Insurance, and Liquidity', *Journal of Political Economy*, 91: 401–19.

Diaz-Alejandro, C. F. (1985). 'Good-bye Financial Repression, Hello Financial Crash.' *Journal of Development Economics*, 19: 1–24.

Dickey, D. A. and Fuller, W. (1979). 'Distribution of the Estimators for Autoregressive Time Series with a Unit Root', *Journal of the American Statistical Association*, 74: 427–31.

Diebold, F. (2004) *Elements of Forecasting*, Ohio: Thompson Learning.

Dixit, A. K. and Pindyck, R. S. (1994) *Investment under Uncertainty*, Princeton: Princeton University Press.

Dooley, M. P., Frankel, J. and Mathieson, D. J. (1987). 'International Capital Mobility: What Do Saving–Investment Correlations Tell Us?' *International Monetary Fund Staff Papers*, 34: 503–30.

DOS *Yearbook of Statistics Malaysia*, Kuala Lumpur: Department of Statistics Malaysia.

—— (1965) *National Accounts of the States of Malaya, 1955–1963*, Kuala Lumpur: Department of Statistics.

—— (2005) *Yearbook of Statistics Malaysia*, Kuala Lumpur: Department of Statistics Malaysia.

Drake, P. J. (1969a) *Financial Development in Malaya and Singapore*, Canberra: Australian University Press.

—— (1969b). 'The New-Issue Boom in Malaya and Singapore, 1961–64', *Economic Development and Cultural Change*, 18: 73–91.

Driffill, J. (2003). 'Growth and Finance', *Manchester School*, 71: 363–80.

Edwards, S. (1996). 'Why Are Latin America's Savings Rates So Low? An International Comparative Analysis', *Journal of Development Economics*, 51: 5–44.

Emery, R. F. (1991) *The Money Markets of Developing East Asia*, New York: Praeger Publishers.

Enders, W. (2004) *Applied Econometric Time Series*, Hoboken: John Wiley & Sons.

Engle, R. F. and Granger, C. W. J. (1987). 'Co-integration and Error Correction: Representation, Estimation, and Testing', *Econometrica*, 55: 251–76.

Engle, R. F. and Yoo, B. S. (1991). 'Cointegrated Economic Time Series: An Overview with New Results', in R. F. Engle and C. W. J. Granger (eds.), *Long-run Economic Relationships: Readings in Cointegration*, Oxford: Oxford University Press.

Ergungor, O. E. (2004). 'Market- vs. Bank-Based Financial Systems: Do Rights and Regulations Really Matter?' *Journal of Banking and Finance*, 28: 2869–87.

Ericsson, N. R., Campos, J. and Tran, H.-A. (1990). 'PC-GIVE and David Hendry's Econometric Methodology', *Revista de Econometrica*, 10: 7–117.

Ericsson, N. R., Irons, J. S. and Tryon, R. W. (2001). 'Output and Inflation in the Long Run', *Journal of Applied Econometrics*, 16: 241–53.

Evans, O. (1983). 'Social Security and Household Saving in the United States: A Re-examination', *International Monetary Fund Staff Papers*, 30: 601–18.

Fatai, K., Oxley, L. and Scrimgeour, F. G. (2003). 'Modeling and Forecasting the Demand for Electricity in New Zealand: A Comparison of Alternative Approaches', *Energy Journal*, 24: 75–102.

Feldstein, M. (1974). 'Social Security, Induced Retirement, and Aggregate Capital Accumulation', *Journal of Political Economy*, 82: 905–26.

—— (1980). 'International Differences in Social Security and Saving', *Journal of Public Economics*, 14: 225–44.

—— (1983). 'Domestic Saving and International Capital Movements in the Long Run and the Short Run.' *European Economic Review*, 21: 129–51.

Feldstein, M. and Bacchetta, P. (1989). 'National Saving and International Capital Flows', *National Bureau of Economic Research No. 3164*.

Feldstein, M. and Horioka, C. (1980). 'Domestic Saving and International Capital Flows', *Economic Journal*, 90: 314–29.

Feldstein, M. and Pellechio, A. (1979). 'Social Security and Household Wealth Accumulation: New Microeconometric Evidence', *Review of Economics and Statistics*, 61: 361–68.

Fisman, R. and Love, I. (2003). 'Trade Credit, Financial Intermediary Development, and Industry Growth', *Journal of Finance*, 58: 353–74.

Frankel, J. A. and MacArthur, A. T. (1988). 'Political Vs. Currency Premia in International Real Interest Rate Differentials', *European Economic Review*, 32: 1083–114.

Friedman, M. (1957) *A Theory of the Consumption Function*, Princeton: Princeton University Press.

Fry, M. J. (1988) *Money, Interest, and Banking in Economic Development*, Johns Hopkins Studies in Development series Baltimore and London: Johns Hopkins University Press.

—— (1991). 'Domestic Resource Mobilization in Developing Asia: Four Policy Issues', *Asian Development Review*, 9: 15–39.

—— (1995). 'Financial Development in Asia: Some Analytical Issues', *Asian-Pacific Economic Literature*, 9: 40–57.

—— (1997). 'In Favor of Financial Liberalization', *Economic Journal*, 107: 754–70.

Gan, W.-B. and Soon, L.-Y. (2000). 'Input versus Productivity Driven Growth: Implications for the Malaysian Economy', in L. Soon and S. Nagaraj (eds.), *The seventh Malaysia plan: Productivity for sustainable development*, Kuala Lumpur: University of Malaya Press.

Ganesh-Kumar, A., Sen, K. and Vaidya, R. R. (2001). 'Outward Orientation, Investment and Finance Constraints: A Study of Indian Firms', *Journal of Development Studies*, 37: 133–49.

—— (2003) *International Competitiveness, Investment and Finance*, London: Routledge.

Garretsen, H., Lensink, R. and Sterken, E. (2004). 'Growth, Financial Development, Societal Norms and Legal Institutions', *Journal of International Financial Markets, Institutions and Money*, 14: 165–83.

Ghani, E. and Suri, V. (1999). 'Productivity Growth, Capital Accumulation and the Banking Sector: Some Lessons from Malaysia', *World Bank Policy Research Working Paper 2252*.

Ghosh, A. R. (1995). 'International Capital Mobility Amongst the Major Industralised Countries: Too Little or Too Much?' *Economic Journal*, 105: 107–28.

Gilbert, C. L. (1986). 'Professor Hendry's Econometric Methodology', *Oxford Bulletin of Economics and Statistics*, 48: 283–307.

Gillam, A. (1982). 'An Introduction to Employee Benefits in Malaysia', *Benefits International*, 11: 11–15.

Goh, S. K., Alias, M. H. and Olekalns, N. (2003). 'New Evidence on Financial Openness in Malaysia', *Journal of Asian Economics*, 14: 311–25.

Goldsmith, R. W. (1969) *Financial Structure and Development*, New Haven: Yale University Press.

Gomez, E. T. (1990) *Politics in Business: UMNO's Corporate Investments*, Kuala Lumpur: Forum.

Gonzalo, J. (1994). 'Five Alternative Methods of Estimating Long-Run Equilibrium Relationships', *Journal of Econometrics*, 60: 203–33.

Granger, C. W. J. and Newbold, P. (1974). 'Spurious Regressions in Econometrics', *Journal of Econometrics*, 2: 111–20.

Greene, J. and Villanueva, D. (1991). 'Private Investment in Developing Countries: An Empirical Analysis', *International Monetary Fund Staff Papers*, 38: 33–58.

Greenwood, J. and Jovanovic, B. (1990). 'Financial Development, Growth, and the Distribution of Income', *Journal of Political Economy*, 98: 1076–107.

Greenwood, J. and Smith, B. D. (1997). 'Financial Markets in Development, and the Development of Financial Markets', *Journal of Economic Dynamics and Control*, 21: 145–81.

Guncavdi, O., Bleaney, M. F. and McKay, A. (1998). 'Financial Liberalisation and Private Investment: Evidence from Turkey', *Journal of Development Economics*, 57: 443–55.

Gupta, K. L. (1984) *Finance and Economic Growth in Developing Countries*, London: Croom Helm.

—— (1987). 'Aggregate Savings, Financial Intermediation, and Interest Rate', *Review of Economics and Statistics*, 69: 303–11.

Gurley, J. G. and Shaw, E. S. (1955). 'Financial Aspects of Economic Development', *American Economic Review*, 45: 515–38.

—— (1960) *Money in A Theory of Finance*, Washington: Brookings Institution.

Haggard, S. (2004). 'Political and Institutional Lessons from the Asian Financial Crisis', in A. Kohsaka (ed.), *New Development Strategies: Beyond the Washington Consensus*, London: Palgrave Macmillan.

Hall, R. E. and Jorgenson, D. W. (1969). 'Tax Policy and Investment Behavior: Reply and Further Results', *American Economic Review*, 59: 388–401.

Hartman, R. (1972). 'The Effects of Price and Cost Uncertainty on Investment', *Journal of Economic Theory*, 5: 258–66.

Hasan, P. (1980). 'Growth, Structural Change, and Social Progress', in K. Young, W. C. F. Bussink and P. Hasan (eds.), *Malaysia: growth and equity in a multiracial society*, Baltimore: Johns Hopkins University Press.

Hellmann, T. F., Murdock, K. C. and Stiglitz, J. E. (2000). 'Liberalization, Moral Hazard in Banking, and Prudential Regulation: Are Capital Requirements Enough?' *American Economic Review*, 90: 147–65.

Hendry, D. and Juselius, K. (2000). 'Explaining Cointegration Analysis: Part 1', *Energy Journal*, 21: 1–42.

Hendry, D. F. (1983). 'Econometric Modelling: The "Consumption Function" in Retrospect', *Scottish Journal of Political Economy*, 30: 193–220.

—— (1995) *Dynamic Econometrics*, New York and Oxford: Oxford University Press.

Hendry, D. F. and Richard, J.-F. (1982). 'On the Formulation of Empirical Models in Dynamic Econometrics', *Journal of Econometrics*, 20: 3–33.

Hendry, D. F. and von Ungern-Sternberg, T. (1981). 'Liquidity and Inflation Effects on Consumers' Expenditure', in A. S. Deaton (ed.), *Essays in the Theory and Measurement of Consumer Behavior (In Honour of Sir Richard Stone)*, Cambridge: Cambridge University Press.

Hendry, D. F., Pagan, A. R. and Sargan, J. D. (1984). 'Dynamic Specification', in Z. Griliches and M. D. Intriligator (eds.), *Handbook of Econometrics*, Vol. II. Amsterdam: North-Holland.

Hicks, J. R. (1969) *A Theory of Economic History*, Oxford: Oxford University Press.

Hill, H. (2005). 'Malaysia Economic Development in Comparative Southeast Asian Perspective', *Conference Paper for 'Malaysia and Sino-Malaysian relations', Institute of Malaysian Studies, Centre for Southeast Asian Studies, Xiamen University, China.*

Ho, T.-W. (2003). 'The Savings–Retention Coefficient and Country-Size: The Feldstein– Horioka Puzzle Reconsidered', *Journal of Macroeconomics*, 25: 387–96.

Hoffmann, M. (2004). 'International Capital Mobility in the Long Run and the Short Run: Can We Still Learn from Saving–Investment Data?' *Journal of International Money and Finance*, 23: 113–31.

Holtz-Eakin, D. (1994). 'Public Sector Capital and the Productivity Puzzle', *Review of Economics and Statistics*, 76: 12–21.

Hoover, K. D. and Perez, S. J. (1999). 'Data Mining Reconsidered: Encompassing and the General-to-Specific Approach to Specification Search', *Econometrics Journal*, 2: 167–91.

—— (2004). 'Truth and Robustness in Cross-Country Growth Regressions', *Oxford Bulletin of Economics and Statistics*, 66: 765–98.

Horioka, C. Y. (1997). 'A Cointegration Analysis of the Impact of the Age Structure of the Population on the Household Saving Rate in Japan', *Review of Economics and Statistics*, 79: 511–16.

Huff, W. G. (2003). 'Currency Boards and Chinese Banks in Malaya and the Philippines before World War II', *Australian Economic History Review*, 43: 125–39.

Hussein, A. A. (1994). 'Financial System', in K. S. Jomo (ed.), *Malaysia's Economy in the Nineties*, Petaling Jaya: Pelanduk Publications.

Hussein, K. A. (1998). 'International Capital Mobility in OECD Countries: The Feldstein–Horioka "Puzzle" Revisited.' *Economics Letters*, 59: 237–42.

Hussein, K. A. and Thirlwall, A. P. (1999). 'Explaining Differences in the Domestic Savings Ratio across Countries: A Panel Data Study', *Journal of Development Studies*, 36: 31–52.

IMF (2005) *International Financial Statistics 2005 (CD ROM)*, Washington: IMF and World Bank.

Inder, B. (1993). 'Estimating Long-Run Relationships in Economics: A Comparison of Different Approaches', *Journal of Econometrics*, 57: 53–68.

Jaffee, D. M. and Russell, T. (1976). 'Imperfect Information, Uncertainty, and Credit Rationing', *Quarterly Journal of Economics*, 90: 651–66.

Jagannathan, V. N. (1987) *Informal Markets in Developing Countries*, New York: Oxford University Press.

Jansen, J. W. and Schulze, G. G. (1996). 'Theory-Based Measurement of the Saving–Investment Correlation with an Application to Norway', *Economic Inquiry*, 34: 116–32.

Jansen, K. (1995). 'The Macroeconomic Effects of Direct Foreign Investment: The Case of Thailand', *World Development*, 23: 193–210.

Jappelli, T. (2005). 'The Life-Cycle Hypothesis, Fiscal Policy and Social Security', *Working Papers from Centre for Studies in Economics and Finance (CSEF), University of Salerno, Italy*.

Johansen, S. (1991). 'Estimation and Hypothesis of Testing of Cointegrating Vectors in Gaussian Vector Autoregressive Models', *Econometrica*, 59: 1551–80.

—— (1995) *Likelihood-Based Inference in Cointegrated Vector Autoregressive Models*, Oxford: Oxford University Press.

Jorgenson, D. W. (1963). 'Capital Theory and Investment Behavior', *American Economic Review Papers and Proceedings*, 53: 247–59.

—— (1967). 'The Theory of Investment Behavior', in R. Ferber (ed.), *Determinants Investment Behavior: A Conference of the Universities National Bureau Committee for Economic Research*, New York: National Bureau of Economic Research.

—— (1971). 'Econometric Studies of Investment Behavior: A Survey', *Journal of Economic Literature*, 9: 1111–47.

Jung, W. S. (1986). 'Financial Development and Economic Growth: International Evidence', *Economic Development and Cultural Change*, 34: 333–46.

Kader, R. A. and Hashim, H. (2005). 'Islamic Banking in Malaysia: Am Evaluation of Performance', *Economic Kaleidoscope: Current Issues and Perspectives*, Kuala Lumpur: University of Malaya Press.

Kapetanios, G., Pagan, A. R. and Scott, A. (2005). 'Making a Match: Combining Theory and Evidence in Policy-oriented Macroeconomic Modeling', *CAMA Working Paper Series, The Australian National University*.

Kapur, B. K. (1976). 'Alternative Stabilization Policies for Less-developed Economies', *Journal of Political Economy*, 84: 777–95.

Kasuga, H. (2004). 'Saving–Investment Correlations in Developing Countries', *Economics Letters*, 83: 371–76.

Kenny, C. and Williams, D. (2001). 'What Do We Know about Economic Growth? Or, Why Don't We Know Very Much?' *World Development*, 29: 1–22.

Keynes, J. M. (1936) *The General Theory of Employment, Interest and Money*, London: Macmillan.

Khan, M. H. (2002). 'When Is Economic Growth Pro-Poor? Experiences in Malaysia and Pakistan', *IMF Working Papers No: 02/85*.

Kim, D. D.-K. and Seo, J.-S. (2003). 'Does FDI Inflow Crowd Out Domestic Investment in Korea?' *Journal of Economic Studies*, 30: 605–22.

King, R. G. and Levine, R. (1993a). 'Finance and Growth: Schumpeter Might Be Right', *Quarterly Journal of Economics*, 108: 717–37.

—— (1993b). 'Finance, Entrepreneurship, and Growth: Theory and Evidence', *Journal of Monetary Economics*, 32: 513–42.

Kirkpatrick, C. (2005). 'Finance and Development: Overview and Introduction', *Journal of Development Studies*, 41: 631–35.

Kohsaka, A. (1996). 'Interdependence through Capital Flows in Pacific Asia and the Role of Japan', in T. Ito and A. O. Krueger (eds.), *Financial Deregulation and Integration in East Asia*, Chicago: University of Chicago Press.

—— (2004). 'A Fundamental Scope for Regional Financial Cooperation in East Asia', *Journal of Asian Economics*, 15: 911–37.

Kraay, A. (2000). 'Household Saving in China', *World Bank Economic Review*, 14: 545–70.

Krueger, A. and Tornell, A. (1999). 'The Role of Bank Restructuring in Recovering from Crises: Mexico 1995–98', *NBER Working Paper No. 7042*.

Krugman, P. (2001). 'What Happened to Asia?' in G. Irwin and D. Vines (eds.), *Financial Market Integration and International Capital Flows*, Cheltenham: Edward Elgar.

Kwiatkowski, D., Phillips, P. C. B., Schmidt, P. and Shin, Y. (1992). 'Testing the Null Hypothesis of Stationarity against the Alternative of a Unit Root: How Sure Are We That Economic Time Series Have a Unit Root?' *Journal of Econometrics*, 54: 159–78.

Lau, S. T. and McInish, T. H. (2002). 'Cross-listing and Home Market Trading Volume: The Case of Malaysia and Singapore', *Journal of Financial Research*, 25: 477–84.

Lee, H. L. (1971) *Household Saving in West Malaysia and the Problem of Financing Economic Development*, Kuala Lumpur: Khee Meng Press.

—— (1981) *Public Policy, Commercial Banks and Other Deposit Institutions in Malaysia: A Study in Resource Mobilization in Malaysia*, Kuala Lumpur: UMCP Publication.

Lee, M.-L. and Chao, S.-W. (1988). 'Effects of Social Security on Personal Saving', *Economics Letters*, 28: 365–68.

Lee, S.-Y. (1986) *The Monetary and Banking Development of Singapore and Malaysia*, Singapore: Singapore University Press.

Leland, H. E. and Pyle, D. H. (1977). 'Informational Asymmetries, Financial Structure, and Financial Intermediation', *Journal of Finance*, 32: 371–87.

Lesnoy, S. D. and Leimer, D. R. (1985). 'Social Security and Private Saving: Theory and Historical Evidence', *Social Security Bulletin*, 48: 14–30.

Levine, R. (1997). 'Financial Development and Economic Growth: Views and Agenda', *Journal of Economic Literature*, 35: 688–726.

—— (1999). 'Law, Finance, and Economic Growth', *Journal of Financial Intermediation*, 8: 8–35.

—— (2002). 'Bank-Based or Market-Based Financial Systems: Which Is Better?' *Journal of Financial Intermediation*, 11: 398–428.

—— (2005). 'Finance and Growth: Theory and Evidence', in P. Aghion and S. Durlauf (eds.), *Handbook of economic growth*, Netherlands: Elsevier Science.

Levine, R. and Zervos, S. (1998). 'Stock Markets, Banks, and Economic Growth', *American Economic Review*, 88: 537–58.

Levine, R., Loayza, N. and Beck, T. (2000). 'Financial Intermediation and Growth: Causality and Causes', *Journal of Monetary Economics*, 46: 31–77.

Levy, D. (2000). 'Investment–Saving Comovement and Capital Mobility: Evidence from Century Long U.S. Time Series', *Review of Economic Dynamics*, 3: 100–136.

Lim, D. (1975). 'The Economic, Political and Social Background to Development Planning in Malaysia', in D. Lim (ed.), *Readings on Malaysian economic development*, Kuala Lumpur: Oxford University Press.

Lin, S.-Y. and Chung, T. F. (1995). 'Money Markets in Malaysia', in D. C. Cole, H. S. Scott and P. A. Wellons (eds.), *Asian Money Markets*, New York: Oxford University Press.

Lipsey, R. E. (2000). 'Interpreting Developed Countries' Foreign Direct Investment', *NBER Working Paper No. 7810*.

—— (2004). 'Home- and Host-Country Effects of Foreign Direct Investment', in R. E. Baldwin and L. A. Winters (eds.), *Challenges to Globalization: Analyzing the Economics*, Chicago: University of Chicago Press.

Liu, L.-Y. and Woo, W.-T. (1994). 'Saving Behavior Under Imperfect Financial

Markets and the Current Account Consequences', *Economic Journal*, 104: 512–27.

Loayza, N., Schmidt-Hebbel, K. and Serven, L. (2000). 'What Drives Private Saving across the World?' *Review of Economics and Statistics*, 82: 165–81.

Lucas, R. E., Jr (1988). 'On the Mechanics of Economic Development', *Journal of Monetary Economics*, 22: 3–42.

Lucas, R. E. B. and Verry, D. W. (1996). 'Growth and Income Distribution in Malaysia', *International Labour Review*, 135: 553–75.

Luintel, K. B. and Khan, M. (1999). 'A Quantitative Reassessment of the Finance–Growth Nexus: Evidence from a Multivariate VAR', *Journal of Development Economics*, 60: 381–405.

McKibbin, W. J., Pagan, A. R. and Robertson, J. C. (1998). 'Some Experiments in Constructing a Hybrid Model for Macroeconomic Analysis', *Carnegie–Rochester Conference Series on Public Policy*, 49: 113–42.

MacKinnon, J. G. (1996). 'Numerical Distribution Functions for Unit Root and Cointegration Tests', *Journal of Applied Econometrics*, 11: 601–18.

McKinnon, R. I. (1973) *Money and Capital in Economic Development*, Washington, D.C.: Brookings Institution.

McKinnon, R. I. and Pill, H. (1997). 'Credible Economic Liberalizations and Overborrowing', *American Economic Review*, 87: 189–93.

Masson, P. R., Bayoumi, T. and Samiei, H. (1998). 'International Evidence on the Determinants of Private Saving', *World Bank Economic Review*, 12: 483–501.

Mathieson, D. J. (1980). 'Financial Reform and Stabilization Policy in a Developing Economy', *Journal of Development Economics*, 7: 359–95.

Mehmet, O. (1988) *Development in Malaysia: Poverty, Wealth and Trusteeship*, London: Croom Helm.

Merican, M. (1992). 'The Employees' Provident Fund and Its Investment Policies', in H. Y. Teh and K. L. Goh (eds.), *Malaysia's Economic Vision*, Kuala Lumpur: Pelanduk Publications.

Merton, R. C. and Bodie, Z. (2004). 'The Design of Financial Systems: Towards a Synthesis of Function and Structure', *Journal of Investment Management*, 3: 1–23.

Modigliani, F. (1966). 'The Life Cycle Hypothesis of Saving, the Demand for Wealth and the Supply of Capital', *Social Research*, 33: 160–217.

—— (1970). 'The Life Cycle Hypothesis of Saving and Intercountry Differences in the Saving Ratio', in W. A. Eltis, M. F. Scott and J. N. Wolfe (eds.), *Induction, growth and trade: Essays in honour of Sir Roy Harrod*, Oxford: Oxford University Press.

—— (1986). 'Life Cycle, Individual Thrift, and the Wealth of Nations', *American Economic Review*, 76: 297–313.

—— (1993). 'Recent Declines in the Savings Rate: A Life Cycle Perspective', in M. Baldassari, L. Paganetto and E. S. Phelps (eds.), *World Saving, Prosperity and Growth*, London: Macmillan.

Modigliani, F. and Brumberg, R. H. (1954). 'Utility Analysis and the Consumption Function: An Interpretation of Cross-section Data', in K. K. Kurihara (ed.), *Post-Keynesian Economics*, New Brunswick, N.J.: Rutgers University Press.

Modigliani, F. and Sterling, A. (1983). 'Determinants of Private Saving with Special Reference to the Role of Social Security – Cross Country Tests', in F. Modigliani and R. Hemming (eds.), *The Determinants of National Saving and Wealth*, London: Macmillan Press.

MOF *Economic Report*, Kuala Lumpur: Ministry of Finance Malaysia.

Molho, L. E. (1986). 'Interest Rates, Saving, and Investment in Developing Countries: A Re-examination of the McKinnon–Shaw Hypotheses', *International Monetary Fund Staff Papers*, 33: 90–116.

Morck, R. and Steiler, L. (2005). 'The Global History of Corporate Governance – An Introduction', in R. Morck and L. Steiler (eds.), *The history of corporate governance around the world: Family business groups to professional managers*, Chicago: University of Chicago Press.

Moreno, R. (1997). 'Saving–Investment Dynamics and Capital Mobility in the US and Japan', *Journal of International Money and Finance*, 16: 837–63.

Munnell, A. H. (1976). 'Private Pensions and Savings: New Evidence', *Journal of Political Economy*, 84: 1013–32.

Muscatelli, V. and Hurn, S. (1992). 'Cointegration and Dynamic Time Series Models', *Journal of Economic Surveys*, 6: 1–43.

—— (1995). 'Cointegration and Dynamic Time Series Models', in L. Oxley, D. A. R. George and C. J. Roberts (eds.), *Surveys in Econometrics* Oxford: Blackwell Publishers.

Narayanan, S. (2004). 'Malaysia', in A. Kohsaka (ed.), *Fiscal Deficits in the Pacific Region*, London: Routledge.

Nazrin, R. (2000) *Essays on Economic Growth in Malaysia in the Twentieth Century*, Harvard University PhD Dissertation.

Ndikumana, L. (2000). 'Financial Determinants of Domestic Investment in Sub-Saharan Africa: Evidence from Panel Data', *World Development*, 28: 381–400.

Neusser, K. and Kugler, M. (1998). 'Manufacturing Growth and Financial Development: Evidence from OECD Countries', *Review of Economics and Statistics*, 80: 638–46.

Newlyn, W. T. (1977). 'The Financial Constraint', in W. T. Newlyn (ed.), *The Financing of Economic Development*, Oxford: Oxford University Press.

Nickell, S. J. (1978) *Investment Decisions of Firms*, Cambridge: Cambridge University Press.

—— (1985). 'Error Correction, Partial Adjustment and All That: An Expository Note', *Oxford Bulletin of Economics and Statistics*, 47: 119–29.

Noorzoy, M. S. (1979). 'Flows of Direct Investment and Their Effects on Investment in Canada', *Economics Letters*, 2: 257–61.

Obstfeld, M. (1986). 'Capital Mobility in the World Economy: Theory and Measurement', *Carnegie–Rochester Conference Series on Public Policy*, 24: 55–103.

Ogaki, M., Ostry, J. D. and Reinhart, C. M. (1996). 'Saving Behavior in Low- and Middle-Income Developing Countries: A Comparison', *International Monetary Fund Staff Papers*, 43: 38–71.

Othman, A. (1987). 'Challenges and Prospects of Financing Malaysian Development Through the 1980s', in F. Shahadan and N. A. H. Idris (eds.), *Financing for Development: With Special Reference to ASEAN* Singapore: Oxford University Press.

Otto, G. (1992). 'Testing a Present-Value Model of the Current Account: Evidence from US and Canadian Time Series', *Journal of International Money and Finance*, 11: 414–30.

Owen, P. D. and Solis-Fallas, O. (1989). 'Unorganized Money Markets and "Unproductive" Assets in the New Structuralist Critique of Financial Liberalization', *Journal of Development Economics*, 31: 341–55.

Ozcan, K., Gunay, A. and Ertac, S. (2003). 'Determinants of Private Savings Behaviour in Turkey', *Applied Economics*, 35: 1405–16.

Ozler, S. and Rodrik, D. (1992). 'External Shocks, Politics and Private Investment: Some Theory and Empirical Evidence', *Journal of Development Economics*, 39: 141–62.

Pagan, A. R. (1987). 'Three Econometric Methodologies: A Critical Appraisal', *Journal of Economic Surveys*, 1: 3–24.

Pagan, A. R. and Wickens, M. R. (1989). 'A Survey of Some Recent Econometric Methods', *Economic Journal*, 99: 962–1025.

Pagano, M. (1993). 'Financial Markets and Growth: An Overview', *European Economic Review*, 37: 613–22.

Park, J. Y. and Phillips, P. C. B. (1988). 'Statistical Inference in Regressions with Integrated Processes: Part 1', *Econometric Theory* 4: 468–97.

Park, Y. (1994). 'Korea: Development and Structural Change of the Financial System', in H. T. Patrick and Y. Park (eds.), *The financial development of Japan, Korea, and Taiwan: Growth, repression, and liberalization*, New York: Oxford University Press.

Patrick, H. T. (1966). 'Financial Development and Economic Growth in Underdeveloped Countries', *Economic Development and Cultural Change*, 14: 174–89.

Payne, J. E. (2005). 'Savings–Investment Dynamics in Mexico', *Journal of Policy Modeling*, 27: 525–34.

Pechman, J. A., Aaron, H. J. and Taussig, M. K. (1968) *Social Security: Perspectives for Reform*, Washington: Brookings Institution

Pelagidis, T. and Mastroyiannis, T. (2003). 'The Saving–Investment Correlation in Greece, 1960–1997: Implications for Capital Mobility', *Journal of Policy Modeling*, 25: 609–16.

Penati, A. and Dooley, M. (1984). 'Current Account Imbalances and Capital Formation in Industrial Countries, 1949–81', *International Monetary Fund Staff Papers*, 31: 1–24.

Pesaran, M. H. and Shin, Y. (1998). 'An Autoregressive Distributed-Lag Modelling Approach to Cointegration Analysis', in S. Strom (ed.), *Econometrics and Economic Theory in the Twentieth Century: The Ragnar Frisch Centennial Symposium*, Cambridge: Cambridge University Press.

Pesaran, M. H. and Smith, R. (1995). 'Estimating Long-Run Relationships from Dynamic Heterogeneous Panels', *Journal of Econometrics*, 68: 79–113.

Pesaran, M. H., Shin, Y. and Smith, R. J. (2001). 'Bounds Testing Approaches to the Analysis of Level Relationships', *Journal of Applied Econometrics*, 16: 289–326.

Phillips, P. C. B. (1988a). 'Reflections on Econometric Methodology', *Economic Record*, 64: 344–59.

—— (1988b). 'Spectral Regression for Cointegrated Time Series', *Cowles Foundation Discussion Papers No: 872*.

—— (1991). 'Optimal Inference in Cointegrated Systems', *Econometrica*, 59: 283–306.

Phillips, P. C. B. and Hansen, B. (1990). 'Statistical Inference in Instrumental Variables Regression with I(1) Processes', *Review of Economic Studies*, 57: 99–125.

Phillips, P. C. B. and Perron, P. (1988). 'Testing for a Unit Root in Time Series Regression', *Biometrika*, 75: 335–46.

Pindyck, R. S. (1991). 'Irreversibility, Uncertainty, and Investment', *Journal of Economic Literature*, 29: 1110–48.

Queisser, M. (1999). 'The Role of Pension Funds in the Stabilisation of the Domestic Financial Sector', in D. H. Brooks and M. Queisser (eds.), *Financial Liberalisation in Asia: Analysis and Prospects* Paris: Development Centre of the Organisation for Economic Co-operation and Development.

Radelet, S. and Sachs, J. (1998). 'The Onset of the East Asian Financial Crisis', *NBER Working Papers No: 6680*.

Rajan, R. G. and Zingales, L. (1998). 'Financial Dependence and Growth', *American Economic Review*, 88: 559–86.

Ram, R. (1999). 'Financial Development and Economic Growth: Additional Evidence', *Journal of Development Studies*, 35: 164–74.

Rao, S. K. (1977). 'Constraints on Credit Expansion in Three South Asian Countries', in W. T. Newlyn (ed.), *The financing of economic development*, Oxford: Oxford University Press.

Rebelo, S. (1991). 'Long-Run Policy Analysis and Long-Run Growth', *Journal of Political Economy*, 99: 500–521.

Rioja, F. and Valev, N. (2004a). 'Does One Size Fit All? A Reexamination of the Finance and Growth Relationship', *Journal of Development Economics*, 74: 429–47.

—— (2004b). 'Finance and the Sources of Growth at Various Stages of Economic Development', *Economic Inquiry*, 42: 127–40.

Robinson, J. (1952) *The Rate of Interest and Other Essays*, London: Macmillan.

Rousseau, P. L. and Vuthipadadorn, D. (2005). 'Finance, Investment, and Growth: Time Series Evidence from 10 Asian Economies', *Journal of Macroeconomics*, 27: 87–106.

Rousseau, P. L. and Wachtel, P. (2000). 'Equity Market and Growth, Cross Country Evidence on Timing and Outcomes 1980–95', *Journal of Banking and Finance*, 24: 1933–57.

Sachs, J. D. (1981). 'The Current Account and Macroeconomic Adjustment in the 1970s', *Brookings Discussion Papers in International Economics*, 1981: 201–68.

Saint-Paul, G. (1992). 'Technological Choice, Financial Markets and Economic Development', *European Economic Review*, 36: 763–81.

Sarel, M. (1997). 'Growth and Productivity in ASEAN Countries', *IMF Working Papers No. 97/97*.

Schmidt-Hebbel, K. and Muller, T. (1992). 'Private Investment Under Macroeconomic Adjustment in Morocco', in A. Chibber, M. Dailami and N. Shafik (eds.), *Reviving Private Investment in Developing Countries*, Amsterdam: Elsevier Science Publishers.

Schumpeter, J. A. (1911) *The Theory of Economic Development*, Oxford: Oxford University Press.

Searle, P. (1999) *The Riddle of Malaysian Capitalism: Rent-Seekers or Real Capitalists?*, Honolulu: Allen & Unwin

Sen, K. and Vaidya, R. (1999) *The Process of Financial Liberalization in India*, Oxford: Oxford University Press.

Shafik, N. (1992). 'Modeling Private Investment in Egypt', *Journal of Development Economics*, 39: 263–77.

Shaw, E. S. (1973) *Financial Deepening in Economic Development*, New York: Oxford University Press.

Sheffrin, S. M. and Woo, W.-T. (1990). 'Present Value Tests of an Intertemporal Model of the Current Account', *Journal of International Economics*, 29: 237–53.

Shome, P. and Saito, K. (1980). 'Creating Capital Through Social Security Institutions: The Asian Experience', *Domestic Finance Studies (World Bank)* No. 61.

Sims, C. A. (1974). 'Output and Labour Input in Manufacturing', *Brookings Papers in Economic Activity*, 3: 695–735.

Snodgrass, D. R. (1980) *Inequality and Economic Development in Malaysia* Kuala Lumpur: Oxford University Press.

Solow, R. M. (1956). 'A Contribution to the Theory of Economic Growth', *Quarterly Journal of Economics*, 70: 65–94.

—— (2001). 'Applying Growth Theory across Countries', *World Bank Economic Review*, 15: 283–88.

Stiglitz, J. E. (1994). 'The Role of the State in Financial Markets', in M. Bruno and B. Pleskovic (eds.), *Proceedings of the World Bank Annual Conference on Development Economics, 1993: Supplement to The World Bank Economic Review and The World Bank Research Observer*, Washington, D.C.: World Bank.

—— (1999a). 'The East Asian Crisis: Lessons for Today and for Tomorrow: Introduction', *Economic Notes*, 28: 249–54.

—— (1999b). 'Reforming the Global Economic Architecture: Lessons from the Recent Crises', *Journal of Finance*, 54: 1508–21.

Stiglitz, J. E. and Weiss, A. (1981). 'Credit Rationing in Markets with Imperfect Information', *American Economic Review*, 71: 393–410.

Stock, J. H. (1987). 'Asymptotic Properties of Least Squares Estimators of Co-integrating Vectors', *Econometrica*, 55: 1035–56.

Stock, J. H. and Watson, M. W. (1988). 'Testing for Common Trends', *Journal of the American Statistical Association*, 83: 1097–07.

—— (2002a). 'Forecasting Using Principal Components from a Large Number of Predictors', *Journal of the American Statistical Association*, 97: 1167–79.

—— (2002b). 'Macroeconomic Forecasting Using Diffusion Indexes', *Journal of Business and Economic Statistics*, 20: 147–62.

Sun, H. (1998). 'Macroeconomic Impact of Direct Foreign Investment in China: 1979–96', *World Economy*, 21: 675–94.

Sundararajan, V. and Thakur, S. (1980). 'Public Investment, Crowding Out, and Growth: A Dynamic Model Applied to India and Korea', *International Monetary Fund Staff Papers*, 27: 814–55.

Swan, T. W. (1956). 'Economic Growth and Capital Accumulation', *Economic Record*, 32: 334–61.

Tanzi, V. and Davoodi, H. (1997). 'Corruption, Public Investment, and Growth', *IMF Working Papers No. 97/139*.

Taylor, A. M. (1998). 'Argentina and the World Capital Market: Saving, Investment, and International Capital Mobility in the Twentieth Century', *Journal of Development Economics*, 57: 147–84.

Taylor, L. (1983) *Structuralist Macroeconomics: Applicable Models for the Third World*, New York: Basic Books.

Thangavelu, S. M. and Ang, J. B. (2004). 'Financial Development and Economic Growth in Australia: An Empirical Analysis', *Empirical Economics*, 29: 247–60.

Thiel, M. (2001). 'Finance and Economic Growth: A Review of Theory and the Available Evidence', *European Commission Economic Paper*: No. 158.

Tobin, J. and Brainard, W. C. (1963). 'Financial Intermediaries and the Effectiveness of Monetary Control', *American Economic Review*, 53: 383–400.

Townsend, R. M. (1979). 'Optimal Contracts and Competitive Markets with Costly State Verification', *Journal of Economic Theory*, 21: 265–93.

Tracy, M. B. (1995). 'Income Programs for the Elderly in Malaysia: A Policy Process Analysis', in J. Dixon and R. P. Scheurell (eds.), *Social Security Programs: A Cross-cultural Comparative Perspective* Westport: Greenwood Press.

Tun Wai, U. and Wong, C. (1982). 'Determinants of Private Investment in Developing Countries', *Journal of Development Studies*, 19: 19–36.

UNCTAD (2004) *World Investment Report 2004*, New York: United Nations.

Van Loo, F. (1977). 'The Effect of Foreign Direct Investment on Investment in Canada', *Review of Economics and Statistics*, 59: 474–81.

van Wijnbergen, S. (1982). 'Stagflationary Effects of Monetary Stabilization Policies: A Quantitative Analysis of South Korea', *Journal of Development Economics*, 10: 133–69.

—— (1983). 'Interest Rate Management in LDCs', *Journal of Monetary Economics*, 12: 433–52.

Villanueva, D. and Mirakhor, A. (1990). 'Strategies for Financial Reforms: Interest Rate Policies, Stabilisation and Bank Supervision in Developing Countries', *International Monetary Fund Staff Papers*, 37: 509–36.

Voridis, H. (1993). 'Ceilings on Interest Rates and Investment: The Example of Greece', *Review of Economics and Statistics*, 75: 276–83.

Vos, R. (1988). 'Saving, Investment and Foreign Capital Flows: Have Capital Markets Become More Integrated?' *Journal of Development Studies*, 24: 310–34.

Wachtel, P. (2003). 'How Much Do We Really Know about Growth and Finance?' *Federal Reserve Bank of Atlanta Economic Review*, 88: 33–47.

Warman, F. and Thirlwall, A. P. (1994). 'Interest Rates, Saving, Investment and Growth in Mexico 1960–90: Tests of the Financial Liberalisation Hypothesis', *Journal of Development Studies*, 30: 629–49.

WDI (2005) *World Development Indicators 2005 (CD ROM)*, Philadelphia: World Bank.

Wicksell, K. J. G. (1935) *Lectures on Political Economy, Volume 2*, London: Routledge and Kegan Paul.

Williamson, J. and Mahar, M. (1998). 'A Survey of Financial Liberalization', *Essays in International Finance No. 211, Department of Economics, Princeton University, Princeton.*

Williamson, S. D. (1986). 'Costly Monitoring, Financial Intermediation, and Equilibrium Credit Rationing', *Journal of Monetary Economics*, 18: 159–79.

Wong, D. Y. (1990). 'What Do Saving–Investment Relationships Tell Us about Capital Mobility?' *Journal of International Money and Finance*, 9: 60–74.

Wurgler, J. (2000). 'Financial Markets and the Allocation of Capital', *Journal of Financial Economics*, 58: 187–214.

Xu, Z. (2000). 'Financial Development, Investment, and Economic Growth', *Economic Inquiry*, 38: 331–44.

Yaakop, R. B. (1988) *Financial Intermediation and Economic Growth: The Case of Malaysia, 1960–1985*, The University of Wisconsin-Milwaukee, PhD Dissertation.

Yong, P. C. (1988) *A Guide to Investments and Taxation in Malaysia*, Kuala Lumpur: Longman.

Young, A. (1995). 'The Tyranny of Numbers: Confronting the Statistical Realities of the East Asian Growth Experience', *Quarterly Journal of Economics*, 110: 641–80.

Yusof, Z. A. (1992). 'Financial Services: The Role and Tasks Ahead', in H. Y. Teh and K. L. Goh (eds.), *Malaysia's Economic Vision: Issues and Challenges*, Kuala Lumpur: Pelanduk Publications.

Yusof, Z. A., Hussin, A. A., Alowi, I., Lim, C.-S. and Singh, S. (1994). 'Financial Reform in Malaysia', in G. Caprio, I. Atiyas and J. A. Hanson (eds.), *Financial Reforms: Theory and Experience*, Cambridge: Cambridge University Press.

# Index

Routledge

www.ingramcontent.com/pod-product-compliance
Lightning Source LLC
LaVergne TN
LVHW011129300926
849160LV00008B/569
*9780415596152*